Quality Assurance in Vietnamese Higher Education

Cuong Huu Nguyen · Mahsood Shah
Editors

Quality Assurance in Vietnamese Higher Education

Policy and Practice in the 21st Century

Editors
Cuong Huu Nguyen
University of Education
Vietnam National University
Hanoi, Vietnam

Mahsood Shah
Swinburne University of Technology
Sydney, Australia

ISBN 978-3-030-26858-9   ISBN 978-3-030-26859-6 (eBook)
https://doi.org/10.1007/978-3-030-26859-6

© The Editor(s) (if applicable) and The Author(s) 2019
This work is subject to copyright. All rights are solely and exclusively licensed by the Publisher, whether the whole or part of the material is concerned, specifically the rights of translation, reprinting, reuse of illustrations, recitation, broadcasting, reproduction on microfilms or in any other physical way, and transmission or information storage and retrieval, electronic adaptation, computer software, or by similar or dissimilar methodology now known or hereafter developed.
The use of general descriptive names, registered names, trademarks, service marks, etc. in this publication does not imply, even in the absence of a specific statement, that such names are exempt from the relevant protective laws and regulations and therefore free for general use.
The publisher, the authors and the editors are safe to assume that the advice and information in this book are believed to be true and accurate at the date of publication. Neither the publisher nor the authors or the editors give a warranty, expressed or implied, with respect to the material contained herein or for any errors or omissions that may have been made. The publisher remains neutral with regard to jurisdictional claims in published maps and institutional affiliations.

Cover image: © Marina Lohrbach_shutterstock.com

This Palgrave Macmillan imprint is published by the registered company Springer Nature Switzerland AG
The registered company address is: Gewerbestrasse 11, 6330 Cham, Switzerland

Contents

1   Development of the Higher Education Sector in Vietnam   1
Kim Anh Thi Le, Martin Hayden and Thuy Thi Nhan

2   Internationalisation of Higher Education in Vietnam   25
Thuy Thi Nhan and Kim Anh Thi Le

3   History of Quality Assurance in Vietnamese Higher Education   59
Huong Thi Pham and Cuong Huu Nguyen

4   Quality Assurance and Accreditation as a Mechanism for Accountability   81
Do Thi Ngoc Quyen

5   Fifteen Years of Accreditation in Vietnam   97
Nhi Thi Tran and Phuong Anh Thi Vu

6	**Drivers of Vietnamese Higher Education Quality Assurance** *Nhung Tuyet Thi Pham, Thanh Quy Nguyen and Cuong Huu Nguyen*	121
7	**Stakeholders' Engagement in Quality Assurance in Vietnam** *Huong Thi Pham*	137
8	**Access and Equity in Vietnamese Higher Education** *Thi Tuyet Tran*	163
9	**Institutional and Programme Accreditation** *Hien Thu Thi Ta, Huong Thu Thi Nguyen and Tuan Van Pham*	183
10	**Digital Innovation and Impact on Quality Assurance** *Tuan Van Pham, Hien Thu Thi Ta and Huong Thu Thi Nguyen*	213
11	**Building National Capacity for Quality Assurance** *Cuong Huu Nguyen*	241
12	**The Future of Quality Assurance in Vietnamese Higher Education** *Cuong Huu Nguyen and Kim Dzung Nguyen*	261
	Index	287

Editors and Contributors

About the Editors

Cuong Huu Nguyen has been working as a specialist of quality assurance and accreditation for Vietnam Education Quality Management Agency, Ministry of Education and Training for over ten years. He is also an adjunct lecturer and researcher of the VNU University of Education. He earned his Master of Assessment and Evaluation from the University of Melbourne and his Ph.D. in Education from the University of New South Wales, Australia. His research interests include assessment, quality assurance, accreditation, higher education policy, leadership, management, and human resource development in education. He has published dozen of papers in scholarly journals and refereed conference proceedings, and over 50 English practice test workbooks. He is also a reviewer for several international journals. Dr. Nguyen's background is in policy-making in evaluation, quality assurance, and accreditation for Vietnam's higher education.

Mahsood Shah is the Professor and inaugural Dean of Swinburne University of Technology, Sydney Campus. In this new role, Mahsood provides overall leadership and management of the campus. Mahsood is responsible for the growth of the campus, management of campus facilities and resources, staffing, monitoring quality, and standard, improving quality of student experience and other academic outcome measures. Prior to joining the Swinburne University of Technology, Mahsood led learning and teaching at faculty level at a number of Australian universities. Mahsood is an active researcher. His areas of research include quality in higher education, measurement and enhancement of student experience, student retention and attrition, student engagement in quality assurance, international higher education, widening participation, and private higher education.

Contributors

Martin Hayden is a Professor at Southern Cross University, Australia. He is the former Head of School of Education, Southern Cross University, Australia. Previously, he has extensive working experiences at the Melbourne University and La Trobe University, Australia. He is a leading scholar in higher education governance. His main interests are in higher education governance, institutional autonomy, higher education policy studies, and organizational and disciplinary cultures. He is also well-known as an international expert to the Ministry of Education of Lao, Cambodia, Vietnam, Malaysia, and other ASEAN countries, and visiting professor at various universities in ASEAN region.

Huong Thi Pham holds a Ph.D. in quality assurance and accreditation from Victoria University of Wellington, New Zealand, and is a Fulbright visiting scholar at a regional accrediting agency, SACSCOC in the USA. She is currently a Director of Research Center for Education Evaluation and Accreditation and International Relations, Institute of Education Research, Ho Chi Minh City University of Education, Vietnam. She is also a recognized assessor for higher education accreditation and has been a member of external evaluation teams. Her areas of interest include internal and external quality assurance, quality culture in higher education, program development and evaluation, internationalization in education, higher education management and governance, and competence-based assessment. She has published several academic papers discussing quality assurance and accreditation in Vietnam.

Kim Anh Thi Le was a lecturer at Hanoi National University of Education. At present, she works for the Enhancing Teacher Education Program (Ministry of Education and Training of Vietnam). Her main interest focuses on the issues of higher education governance, the development of academic culture at universities. Her recent research focuses are on teacher education: the institutional quality assurance, measurement and evaluation in pre-service teacher education, and continuous professional development for school teachers and principals. She has extensive teaching experiences at Hanoi University of Education in teaching Vietnamese. She earned Ph.D. at Southern Cross University, Australia, in higher education governance. Her master at the Melbourne University, Australia, was in educational measurement, and evaluation.

Huong Thu Thi Nguyen is the Secretary of Accreditation Council of the Center of Educational Accreditation—Vietnam National University, Hanoi. She completed her Ph.D. in Linguistics and Educational Assessment and Measurement in Russia in 2011 and took the courses of Quality Assurance and Curriculum Design in Higher Education in the USA in 2007, Philippine in 2010, Australia in 2014. Her research focuses on university governance, stratification and ranking in higher education, quality assurance and accreditation systems, and educational assessment and evaluation in Vietnam and other countries in the world. She participated in national research projects on the innovation for university administration, stratification for Vietnam universities, educational assessment, and evaluation; published 22 papers in the local and 2 papers international magazines; and was an advisor for 21 master and 3 Ph.D. students.

Kim Dzung Nguyen works at Institute for Educational Research as an Acting Vice-Director General. She is considered as a specialist in the field of Educational Evaluation and Accreditation. Dr. Nguyen has won many prizes of the universities in Russia, Australia, and the USA. She is also a member of the Asia-Pacific Quality Network (APQN) which belongs to the International Network for Quality Assurance Agencies in Higher Education (INQAAHE) and Ho Chi Minh City Association of Education and Psychology. Her studies focus mainly on program design and development, solutions on enhancing higher education quality, constructing the system of quality assurance in Vietnam, evaluating the effectiveness of training at the gifted high schools, institutional and program accreditation, etc. In addition, she is the author of over 40 papers published in the prestige specialized international and national journals. She also lectures for many postgraduate courses on educational management, educational evaluation and accreditation, curriculum development, research methods in education, teaching methods in higher education. She is also a national consultant of World Bank on project to enhance the capacity of teacher training universities in Vietnam, higher education projects, a visiting Fulbright scholar at the Higher Learning Commission in Chicago with a research on a possibility to establish independent accreditation agencies in Vietnam.

Thanh Quy Nguyen is a Professor in Sociology at VNU University of Education. He has rich experience in education quality assurance in general and in accreditation as one of its mechanism in particular. He used to be the Director of VNU Institute for Education Quality Assurance and has to lead the first legally established in Vietnam accreditation agency. He has a number of publications in educational research, especially in educational measurement and assessment. As a practitioner, he has been a Chair for more than 30 external reviews panels for assessing and granting accreditation to Vietnamese universities and colleges.

Thuy Thi Nhan is currently a doctoral student at Melbourne Graduate School of Education, the University of Melbourne, Australia. Her research focuses on educational alignment between assessments and standards of competencies. Her other research interests include transnational academic mobility, educational measurement, and language-related policies in higher education settings. Before undertaking her doctoral studies, Thuy earned her Master of TESOL from the University of Melbourne, Australia, and had a career background in English language education and administration at Da Nang Architecture University, Vietnam. She also had experience with language education and academic support for international students in Australia.

Nhung Tuyet Thi Pham is a faculty at Hue University-College of Foreign Languages. She received Ph.D. in Curriculum and Instruction and Master in Higher Education from Texas Tech University, USA. She is currently doing a postdoc in the USA. For her three-year postdoc, she provides leadership for strategic planning in relationship to assessment and institutional effectiveness for accreditation purposes, oversees the assessment of student learning outcomes for 150 academic programs and general education program, provides annual professional development of institutional and program assessment for program coordinators of 150 academic programs, oversees university's assessment management system (AMS), and prepares university assessment reporting to internal and external stakeholders. She is also a recognized peer reviewer for Higher Learning Commission in 2018 and engages in reviewing the accreditation report for other US universities. She has published several academic papers discussing assessment and accreditation issues in the USA and Vietnam.

Do Thi Ngoc Quyen holds a master degree in educational effectiveness, awarded by the University of Groningen, and a Ph.D. in higher education studies, conferred by the University of Melbourne. She currently works as a researcher and an independent consultant for international organizations, including the World Bank and USAID, local authorities and organizations, and universities. She was previously Director of Quality Assurance, University of Economics and Business, Manager of Quality Assurance, Institute of Quality Assurance, Vietnam National University, Hanoi, and has extensive working experience in different local educational contexts and settings. Her areas of expertise cover quality assurance and improvement (specifically benchmarking, accreditation, and rankings), university governance, performance indicators in higher education, model borrowing, testing, and educational productivity models.

Hien Thu Thi Ta is the Vice-Director of the Center of Educational Accreditation—Vietnam National University, Hanoi, and the Deputy Head of Department of Education Quality Assurance and Accreditation, Faculty of Management Quality, VNU University of Education (VNU-UED). She received her Ph.D. in Educational Assessment and Measurement at VNU Institute for Education Quality Assurance in 2016. She took the 5 courses in terms of knowledge and skills in conducting national surveys for monitoring student achievement by Melbourne University, IIEP, UNESCO, ACER, and World Bank processing in 2007–2008 and the course of Quality Assurance and Curriculum Design in Higher Education in Australia in 2014. Her research focused on quality assurance and accreditation systems and policies, educational assessment and measurement in Vietnam and other countries in Asia-Pacific Region. She participated in national research projects of HEP 2 and the innovation for higher education administration and published dozens of papers in local and international scholarly journals. She is also an advisor for a master student.

Phuong Anh Thi Vu is currently Director of Educational Quality Assurance of Nguyen Hoang Education Group (NHG), a position she took up in October 2018. In her current position, she is responsible for supervising and supporting NHG's member schools and universities in their quality efforts. Before working for NHG, Dr. Vu had worked full time in various positions as lecturer, researcher, academic leader, as well as administrator. Her previous positions include Dean of Foreign Languages; Director of Educational Assessment and Quality Assurance; and Director of International Relations and Research Affairs in different public and private universities in Ho Chi Minh City. She earned a bachelor's degree in English from Ho Chi Minh University (1983), a Postgraduate Diploma in TESOL from the University of Canberra (1991, Australia), and a Ph.D. in Education from La Trobe University (1998, Australia). Besides teaching and research, Dr. Vu is also a columnist who writes on education topics for Tia Sang, a non-specialist journal published by the Ministry of Science and Technology. Her main research interests are in quality management in higher education, student assessment, English language testing and assessment, and educational policy studies.

Nhi Thi Tran is currently a Ph.D. student at the University of Newcastle, Australia. She has a background in teacher training and higher education institution management. She received her bachelor's degree in teaching English as a foreign language from Thai Nguyen University, Vietnam, and her master's degree in linguistics from Vietnam National University—Hanoi. Prior to her doctoral degree research program in Australia, she was the Deputy Head of Thai Nguyen University School of Foreign Languages where she worked as a high school English teacher trainer and supervised academic, research, and international cooperative issues. She led innovative programs in quality improvement at her school. She has published journal articles, conference papers, and textbooks in English language teaching and teacher professional development. She has developed projects on learning environment improvement, teacher professional development, and international cooperation in higher education. Her current research focuses on quality assurance in higher education.

Thi Tuyet Tran (June Tran) received her Ph.D. in education from La Trobe University, Australia. She is a mobile lecturer and researcher. She has worked in three countries, Australia, Vietnam, and Germany, and has developed an interest in interdisciplinary research. Her interests range from labor economics, human resource management, to various areas in management and education research such as graduate employability, work-integrated learning, university-industry collaboration, language education, and cultural study. She is currently based herself at RMIT University and working toward a research project investigating workplace integration of professional skilled migrants in the Australian labor market.

Tuan Van Pham is the Director of Department of Educational Testing and Quality Assurance; Secretary, University Council; AUN-QA Assessor; National Quality Assessor, Danang University of Technology (DUT), University of Danang. He received Dr. technology degree in Electrical Engineering from Graz University of Technology (2007). He was granted with a postdoctoral scholarship at TUGraz (2007–2008) and promoted to Associate Professor at UD-DUT since 2012, then was assigned to Principal Lecturer since 2016. He was designated to

Vice-Chair of ETE Department from 2010 to 2014, Deputy Director of Center of Excellence, UD-DUT since 2011, and then Director of Educational Testing & Quality Assurance Department since 2014. He became the Campus Liaison of ASEA-UNINET at DUT since 2007, the Project Leader of Capstone Project DUT 2014–2016, the DUT Project Manager of HEEAP in 2010–2018, VULII in 2012–2016, BUILD-IT in 2016–2020 and the UD-DUT Project Leader for CDIO in 2016–2019.

List of Figures

Fig. 1.1	Publication trends by ASEAN countries over the two recent decades (*Source* Compiled from Scopus database [2018])	11
Fig. 2.1	Approximate numbers of Vietnamese students in selected host countries	31
Fig. 2.2	ASEAN countries and the national frameworks for internationalising higher education (adapted from British Council [2012, 2017, 2018])	36
Fig. 2.3	Research output by Southeast Asian countries 2001–2010 (T. V. Nguyen & Pham, 2011, p. 11)	45
Fig. 3.1	AUN-QA model for programme (3rd version) (AUN, 2016, p. 9)	72
Fig. 3.2	AUN-QA framework for institutional level (2nd version) (AUN, 2016, p. 10)	73
Fig. 4.1	Developments of accreditation in Vietnamese higher education (Compiled by author)	87
Fig. 4.2	AUN-QA framework for institutional level (AUN-QA, 2016)	87
Fig. 7.1	Qualitative classes of stakeholders (Mitchel et al., 1997, p. 872)	139

Fig. 7.2	Stakeholder typology (Mitchel et al., 1997, p. 874)	140
Fig. 7.3	Student engagement in QA processes in Scotland (University of Glasgow Academic Quality Framework as cited in Matei and Iwinska [2016])	148
Fig. 9.1	Criteria that 20% or more of the 117 accredited universities throughout the country had failed to fulfill (*Note* Criterion = Cr (TC))	202
Fig. 9.2	Comparison of the percentage (%) of underachieved criteria (*Note* Criterion = Cr)	205
Fig. 12.1	Elements of quality culture (*Source* Adapted from Loukkola & Zhang, 2010)	275
Fig. 12.2	A proposed new model for Vietnam's higher education quality assurance	281

List of Tables

Table 2.1	Student mobility	29
Table 2.2	Top 10 countries of outbound mobile tertiary students	29
Table 2.3	Forms of cross-border educational programmes and providers in Vietnam	33
Table 2.4	Decision-making power in Vietnamese higher education	39
Table 7.1	Results found by Leisyte and Westerheijden (2014, p. 89)	147
Table 7.2	Results found on employers as stakeholders in QA in Europe by Leisyte and Westerheijden (2014, p. 92)	150
Table 8.1	Number of HEIs and the students (MoET, 2012, 2015, 2018)	167
Table 8.2	Number of HEIs and the students in non-public sector (MoET, 2015, 2018)	168
Table 8.3	Proportion of population aged 15 and older by highest certificate levels (General Statistics Office, 2016)	169
Table 8.4	Reasons for stopping education/training before completing (ILO, 2016)	171
Table 8.5	Children highest education certificate levels by father's qualifications (ILO, 2016)	174
Table 9.1	The number of institutions and programmes externally assessed and accredited by MoET standards	198

Table 9.2	Educational institutions evaluated and accredited by overseas agencies (VQA, 2018a)	200
Table 9.3	Number of programmes accredited by overseas agencies (VQA, 2018b)	201
Table 9.4	The consolidated quality accreditation results of 8 programmes under the set of quality assessment standards	205

Quality Assurance of Higher Education in Vietnam: An Overview

Introduction

Vietnam, a transitional economy in the Asia—Pacific region, has a population of over 96 million people (as of April 2019). The literacy rate of people ages 15 and above is 95.8% (VGP News, 2019). The Vietnamese general education system is divided into three levels: primary education (grades 1–5), lower secondary education (grades 6–9), and upper secondary education (grades 10–12). Higher education in Vietnam consists of universities and academies which are classified into three categories: public-, private-, and foreign-related. In the academic year 2017–2018, Vietnam has 236 higher education institutions with over 5000 programmes (MoET, 2018; Nguyen, 2018). In 2003, quality assurance through mandatory accreditation mechanism for both institutions and programmes was officially introduced into Vietnam's higher education. Several studies observed and discussed certain aspects of Vietnam's accreditation (e.g. Do, Pham, & Nguyen, 2017; Nguyen, 2018; Nguyen, Evers, & Marshall, 2017; Pham, 2018, 2019a). However, it seems that there has not been any research systematically and critically investigating the development of Vietnam's higher education quality assurance and accreditation system since its establishment in 2003.

This book contains 12 chapters which provide an overview and critical analysis of Vietnamese higher education quality assurance under the centralised management of the government after 15 years of development. By implementing quality assurance and accreditation, the Vietnamese government expected to control and improve the quality of the higher education system (Do et al. 2017; Nguyen & Ta, 2018; Nguyen, Ta, & Nguyen, 2017). This book, therefore, investigates and analyses policies and practices related to the establishment and development of the national quality assurance organisation, accrediting agencies, and internal quality assurance units at universities; the implementation of institutional and programme accreditation; drivers of quality assurance; stakeholders engaged in quality assurance; digital innovation and its impact on quality assurance; and the future of quality assurance in Vietnam higher education.

This book serves the following purposes:

- Providing an overview of Vietnam's higher education quality assurance and accreditation mechanisms, an emerging quality assurance system in the Asia-Pacific region
- Discussing the higher education quality assurance and accreditation model in Vietnam in comparison with other countries in the Asia-Pacific region and across the world
- Exploring drivers of quality assurance and stakeholders engaged in quality assurance in Vietnam
- Analysing the achievements and challenges of higher education accreditation in Vietnam 15 years post-implementation

Overview of the Chapters

The book begins with Chapter 1 by Le, Hayden, and Nhan (2019). The first chapter provides an overview of Vietnam higher education. Vietnam's higher education sector, which has expanded dramatically over the past 20 years, has now reached a point where it is ready to become more research-oriented and better networked internationally. The sector has been expected to make fundamental contribution to Vietnam's industrialisation, modernisation, and integration. There are, however, aspects of the sector that remain desperately in need of further reform. This chapter provides a contemporary review of the state of the higher education sector in Vietnam from the perspective that the sector needs to become more research-focused and more internationally engaged. The first section begins with an overview of the history of Vietnamese higher education since the first university was established one thousand years ago. This section also sketches the components of and access to tertiary training at Vietnamese higher education as well as the legal frameworks that guide higher education entities and activities. This section further discusses the growth of the sector and major reforms, especially in the past two decades. It argues that while major transformations have been witnessed, the system has not grown adequately regarding both quality and quantity up to the demand of the country's fast-growing economy and population. The second section of the chapter identifies specific challenges for the sector terms of governance, funding, staffing, curriculum, research and research training, graduate employability, and quality assurance. Specifically, this section identifies the highly centralised and hierarchical governance of higher education to hold accountable for a number of issues. Staffing, for example, is among many areas heavily affected by the state control mechanism and funding pressures, which often results in an inadequate structure of qualified and competent academics, a common situation shared by Vietnamese institutions. Research activities are also poorly practised and generally assumed to be limited to research institutes and research universities. While Vietnam has taken measures to encourage the national research capacity via a number of incentives as well as penalties for institutions, scarce achievements have been recorded. Employing a case study of Vietnam National University, Hanoi, a leading research university in Vietnam that has been granted with the highest level of autonomy, this section casts light on the existing imprints of state governance and the negotiation of the university itself to maintain its self-reliance and quality of training and research. Centralisation in governance has also been blamed for slow changes in curriculums and assessments of students' performance. Both the government and institutions seek to switch from a passive learning culture to a curriculum where critical, independent, and creative learning takes place. However, a missing coherent and systemic support from policy-making bodies and an institutional inadequate capacity are hindering the whole process. After all, the country is still witnessing an oversupply of university graduates with poor employability skills that can hardly meet labour market needs. The transformation as well as existing issues in Vietnam's higher education sector generally reflects the contemporary landscape of East Asian higher education. Discussions of policies, strategies, and practices adopted by Vietnam's neighbouring countries are included in this section, especially the massification and diversification of many Asian higher education systems to meet the demand of globalised economies for university-trained labour force. Similar to many other Southeast Asian countries, including even middle-income economies like Singapore or Malaysia, that are undergoing a difficult phase of skills shortages for the labour force, Vietnam has an abundant supply of labour yet suffers from continuous and serious deficiencies of qualified and skilled employees. This section explores how outdated curricula, the frequent mismatch between theory and practice, and the societal preference for tertiary qualifications over vocational education contribute to an increasing unemployment figures among Vietnamese graduates with a bachelor or master degree. Critical thinking, communication skills, English language proficiency, and a training for a wide range of occupations and industries are argued to be among the essential industry requirements that Vietnamese students need to be urgently equipped with. To conclude, the chapter presents a glimpse of what the future of the higher education sector might entail. It argues that unless there are actions taken to improve the teaching and research capacity of both tertiary education and vocational training, develop international partnerships, and enhance graduates' employability assets, significant constraints on national economic growth, future production structures, and long-term socio-economic development are unavoidable.

The book continues with Chapter 2 titled Internationalisation of Higher Education in Vietnam by Nhan and Le (2019). Recognising the importance of internationalising its higher education, Vietnam has introduced different strategies and developed its legal system to cater for a growing need of international standards in educational services. Many Vietnamese institutions have also expressed a renewed interest in entering the world-class education arena and have therefore become more active in seeking and forming cross-border teaching and research partnerships. This chapter provides an overview of the internationalisation process in higher education in Vietnam, starting with overall statistics of inbound and outbound students to and from Vietnam and the diverse representations of transnational collaboration between Vietnamese and foreign partners. Government strategies, including recognising credentials, facilitating student and academic mobility, sending students to study overseas, and funding key universities and training universities, are also discussed to provide readers with some background information. Comparisons with major importers or providers of educational services in East Asia, including China, Singapore, South Korea, Malaysia, or Singapore, reveal both similarities and differences between Vietnam and these neighbouring countries in terms of policies, strategies, and practices at both governmental and institutional levels towards the task of internationalising higher education. More specifically, transnational higher education activities in Vietnam have so far served to supplement the domestic higher education provision as in the situation of Hong Kong rather than a strategy for world-class university building as in the case of Singapore, South Korea, and Japan. A discussion on regional educational hubs is also included to highlight the scale of internationalisation beyond the matter of individual institutions in such active receiving destinations as Singapore or India. RMIT University Vietnam, the Vietnamese branch of the Australian research institution The Royal Melbourne Institute of Technology, is among the scarce examples of a foreign-owned campus operating in the country. RMIT Vietnam is used as a case study to explore the apparent motivation to satisfy local demands for foreign qualifications rather than a strategic action plan for world-class research and development. Following this, the chapter discusses how internationalising higher education is socially and economically benefiting key stakeholders. It then critically reflects on how institutions are implementing their transnational programmes in terms of partner selection, curriculum adoption, staffing, and quality management. It argues that a centralised mechanism from the government is still an obstacle for institutions to efficiently manage partnerships with foreign providers. This is a challenge that is also witnessed in highly centralised educational systems like China. Loopholes in the legal system have also created opportunities for many for-profit partnerships to grow in Vietnam, a situation which is also common in India. A number of institutions also risk sacrificing long-term benefits and reputations by being lenient in selecting foreign providers and by 'importing' the whole Western-curriculum and pedagogy package into a still dominantly Confucian context of teaching and learning. To conclude, the chapter emphasises the need for an independent quality assurance body at governmental level, institutional autonomy, and quality assurance capacity among institutions themselves to make the most out of cross-border education practices.

Chapter 3 by Pham and Nguyen (2019) outlines the history of quality assurance in Vietnam higher education. Vietnam is one of the countries which do not have a tradition of higher education evaluation and accreditation until as late as 2003 with the establishment of the General Department of Educational Testing and Accreditation (GDETA) (renamed as Vietnam Education Quality Management Agency, VQA since 25 May 2017), a department of the Ministry of Education and Training (MOET). The department laid the first foundation for Vietnam's national quality assurance system in higher education. Since then, various approaches and attempts have been made to develop quality assurance systems in Vietnam, including the introduction of development strategies to 2020 for higher education by the MOET, the establishment of policies and strategies for educational development and the identification of approaches and mechanisms in management via monitoring, inspection, and accreditation of educational quality, the development of a system to evaluate and control the quality of higher education and teaching and training based on a standard set of criteria, three-year pilot projects with international supports, the organisation of many national workshops and conferences on quality assurance, and the current new sets of standards for both programmatic and institutional accreditation. This chapter will tell a story of quality assurance in Vietnam education after nearly fifteen years of development into three major sub-sections: historical developments, past and present developments, and future implication. By highlighting the key stages and achievements in the development of the quality assurance system including internal and external quality assurance arrangements as well as comparing the developments of quality assurance in Vietnam with other countries in the same region including Cambodia, Indonesia, Malaysia, and Thailand, the chapter will open up an academic discussion on the future development of quality assurance in general and accreditation in particular in the country.

Chapter 4 by Do (2019) highlights the quality assurance and accreditation mechanisms. The national quality assurance and accreditation of Vietnam's higher education, the General Department of Education Testing and Accreditation (now called Vietnam Education Quality Management Agency), a unit belonging to the Ministry of Education and Training, was established in 2003. However, it was until 2005 when accreditation was piloted in Vietnamese higher education, a quality assurance system has been gradually formed with accreditation as a key pillar. Therefore, the development of the quality assurance system is closely associated with the extent to which accreditation penetrates into and spreads across higher education institutions. This chapter provides a panorama of the national quality assurance arrangements in Vietnamese higher education and a closer look particularly at its accreditation system. Bringing in an analysis of the roles of different actors in the system, including the government and the Ministry of Education and Training, universities and colleges, and other external stakeholders, the chapter also sheds light on the dynamics of the driving forces in the quality assurance system and on how these players have influenced the development of this sub-system. Since the introduction of accreditation, the national quality assurance system has been driven by a top-down approach adopted by the government through a variety of centralised mechanisms and regulations with a focus on compliance rather than on continuous improvement. Only until recently have top universities played a greater part in leading quality assurance activities in the system. Internal quality assurance and external quality assurance activities are having mutual impact, yet effectiveness is an open question still. In addition to the Vietnamese quality assurance contexts and arrangements, a snapshot of common quality assurance practices in similar regional systems in the ASEAN is also provided in the chapter, which is expected to bring in an international comparative perspective in the issue. This partly shows how quality assurance movements have reflected in national higher education developments.

Chapter 5 presents an overview of the 15 years history of accreditation in Vietnam and discusses the challenges that Vietnam's accreditation as a system will face in the coming decades. Tran and Vu (2019) begin this chapter with an account of the establishment of the accreditation system in Vietnam, starting from the day when the concept was completely alien in the prior to the year 2003 to an eager embrace of accreditation as a panacea to help solve all quality problems in education, which generated all the exciting though a bit chaotic activities during the next five years (2003–2007). Disappointment then followed, resulting in a 'stagnation period' of 2008–2014, which allowed time for reflection and building of the 'human infrastructure' for accreditation activities. Finally, the revival of interest and activities since 2015 provides the background for a discussion of the achievements and setbacks of the 'accreditation movement' in Vietnam in the past 15 years. The role of international actors, such as the World Bank or Asian Development Bank, and regional networks and projects, such as the Asia-Pacific Quality Network (APQN) and the ASEAN University Network-Quality Assurance (AUN-QA), is also discussed. In particular, the development of a quality assurance network with AUN-QA, and Vietnam's active involvement in it, helps explain the move from the stagnation period of 2008–2014 to the current revival period and points to the international nature of the accreditation whose impact cannot be forgotten. Furthermore, the development of Vietnam's higher education accreditation after 15 years of implementation is benchmarked with that of several countries in the Asia-Pacific region that started their quality assurance and accreditation system at the same time as Vietnam. In place of a conclusion, the chapter ends with an analysis of the challenges facing accreditation in Vietnam in the future, especially in the context of increasing privatisation, regional integration as well as international competition.

Chapter 6 by Pham, Nguyen, and Nguyen (2019) reviews global developments in quality assurance, especially quality assurance approaches in Western higher education systems, including the long-established US model of quality accreditation, quality audit as practised in the UK and Australia, or benchmarking, and university ranking, among others. It also discusses the developments of quality assurance in Asia and ASEAN region and their influence of international and regional quality assurance bodies such as the International Network for Quality Assurance Agencies in Higher Education (INQAAHE), the Asia-Pacific Quality Network (APQN), or the ASEAN University Network-Quality Assurance (AUN-QA) on the quality assurance system in Vietnam. It looks at how Western quality assurance policies have been borrowed in and shaped the development of quality assurance in Vietnam's higher education, as described in the previous chapters. In particular, the chapter discusses the challenges when Western policies are borrowed into the system. It is argued that successful implementation of quality assurance policies depend on how systemic and institutional challenges are addressed. These include at the systemic level, the regulatory and oversight role played by the Ministry of Education and Training (MOET); the intentionality of the quality assurance policies; and the integrity and competence of truly independent quality assurance agencies. Successful borrowing of Western quality assurance policies at the institutional level, on the other hand, requires strong commitment of institutional leaders; institutional governance autonomy; effective and transparent internal quality assurance structures and regulations; and engagement of all stakeholders, especially staff and students. It is also argued that while accreditation may be a necessary starting point, a combination of different quality assurance measures is required to ensure effective and sustainable enhancement of the quality of higher education in Vietnam.

Chapter 7, which is written by Pham (2019b), focuses on stakeholders' engagement in quality assurance. Stakeholder engagement has become a norm in higher education governance in many countries. A number of recent studies have focused on stakeholder identification, their expectations, and engagement to higher education, particularly in the area of quality assurance. Various stakeholder groups may have diverse expectations and experiences which are expected to contribute to a more effective and comprehensive quality assurance system.

On the other hand, it has been argued that the diversity of expectations could be one of the key challenges to any attempts to assure and improve quality. A lack of agreement about the objectives of quality assurance can inhibit effective implementation of the system. The main purpose of this chapter is to discuss the extent to which different particular stakeholders have engaged in quality assurance processes in Vietnam. The chapter will focus on the different levels of involvement among government, universities (university leaders, students, and academic staff), representatives of the professional bodies, and employers. Best practices of stakeholders' engagement in quality assurance in some regions and countries (e.g. Malaysia and Thailand in ASEAN, New Zealand and Australia in Asia-Pacific region, and some other countries in Europe, as well as in the USA) will be discussed in comparison with the current state of affairs of stakeholders' engagement in quality assurance in Vietnam. Any possible challenges to build a common understanding among stakeholders will also be discussed. The chapter will end up with recommendations to the Vietnamese government and higher education institutions on how both can develop and can deepen this engagement and open up an academic discussion on the future development of this engagement in the country.

Chapter 8 written by Tran (2019) discusses the assess and equity in Vietnam higher education. Quality and equity are both long-standing and continuous policy strands on higher education agendas worldwide; nonetheless, they are usually separate strands that use different spheres for implementation. This chapter, however, forwards a strong argument that strong equity policies need to be reflected in the frameworks and processes used by quality assurance schemes. This is especially important for Asian Confucian Heritage countries like Vietnam and China whose higher education systems have been expanded rapidly but educational inequality has remained strong. The disadvantages groups such as female youth, minority groups, and youth from rural, remote, and mountainous areas are still under-represented in total higher education enrolment. This is partly due to the cultural thinking in a Masculinity dominated society and partly due to the increasing expensive expenses for higher education that not all low social background families can afford. Higher education is considered a way to help young people from the disadvantaged groups to integrate into the mainstream society and to contribute to the economic competitiveness of the country, but it does not offer immediate and short-term benefits. In order to promote inclusive higher education, related policies and support mechanisms to these young people in participating in higher education need to be in place. It is also suggested that the above-mentioned equity concern should be permeated in the quality models and processes by the government, who, in the case of Vietnam, has remained the dominant stakeholder of higher education and the initiator of the quality assurance system. If this is to be done, quality assurance does not only have the primary function of ensuring standards, but also become a means to monitor and contribute to the implementation of equity policies.

Chapter 9 Ta, Nguyen, and Pham (2019) presents the current state of the institutional and programme accreditation implementation in Vietnam. First, this chapter illustrates the legal corridor system for higher education accreditation and the organisational structure of the accreditation system, clarifying the state management, roles and responsibilities of the Ministry of Education and Training and line ministries, and roles of accrediting agencies in Vietnam's higher education quality assurance and accreditation. The second section in this chapter presents the objectives of higher education accreditation in Vietnam, as well as several other sets of institutional and programme accreditation standards. It also discusses changes in accreditation processes and standards that the Ministry of Education and Training, as the central regulating body, has promulgated and instructed universities to implement. The third section depicts the current processes and procedures of the institutional and programme accreditation based on the Vietnamese qualification framework. Additionally, this section analyses the standards and criteria for institutional and programme accreditation in comparison with those used by several regional and international accrediting agencies. Next, the status of implementation of accreditation activities in Vietnam's higher education at both institutional and programme level is highlighted, followed by an evaluation of the advantages, disadvantages, and challenges of the accreditation processes. In addition, best practices of implementation of institutional and programme accreditation at several Vietnamese universities will be highlighted. Finally, the lessons learned from the implementation of institutional and programme accreditation are discussed, for use in understanding accreditation results, higher education quality improvement, and innovation of university administration and governance. These lessons could also be used to plan the restructuring of Vietnam's higher education system and serve as regional and international benchmarks.

In Chapter 10, Pham, Ta, and Nguyen (2019) discuss issues with digital innovation in science and technology that affect quality assurance of higher education in a global context and in Vietnam. The first section presents potential approaches in Vietnamese higher education to meet workforce needs in the 4th Industrial Revolution, the application of IT strength in higher education administration and autonomy, management of teaching, learning and research, and comprehensive reform approaches to higher education for providing future workforces with skill sets that meet the demands of Industry 4.0. The second section discusses developing trends in Asian higher education and introduces models of advanced universities in Asia and their application in Vietnam. These models include national qualification framework, changes in the mode of education, development of open education, integration of education development, innovation in educational administration, and application of information technology in Asian education. The third section addresses the rise of international higher education providers in Vietnam. This section focuses on types of overseas higher education providers, the international education market in Vietnam, cross-border higher education, the university-business model, joint venture and domestic investment, cooperation activities for training and scientific research, and competition in higher education in Vietnam. Fourth, the chapter outlines Vietnam's development perspectives on the trend of autonomy in higher education, Vietnam's views and approaches of investment in higher education economic sectors, issues of privatisation in education, and advantages, barriers, and integration opportunities. Additionally, the impact of innovation within higher education sector will be emphasised. Specifically, several cases and stories of best practices in this regard will be highlighted. Finally, this chapter outlines the implications of digital innovation on quality assurance, describes quality accreditation of higher education as an impact of Industry 4.0, and discusses data analysis and assessment for the purpose of quality improvement of higher education. It proposes the application of digital framework on internal and external quality assurance mechanisms during the integration of this digital age to meet educational reform requirements.

Chapter 11 by Nguyen (2019) discusses primary strategies and the involvement of key stakeholders in the building capacity of quality assurance for Vietnam's entire higher education system. Challenges are identified and recommendations are proposed. First, this chapter reviews general national policies in human resource development, particularly in capacity building for higher education quality assurance staff and practitioners in Vietnam. The second section presents the main capacity building strategies implemented in Vietnam's higher education quality assurance system, including training, workshops, study visits, leadership in quality assurance, and the culture of improvement. Examples of organisations and institutions good at capacity building in quality assurance are also highlighted in this section. The third section discusses the involvement of key local stakeholders in quality assurance capacity building, including Vietnamese higher education institutions, research institutes, national projects, other government ministries, and organisations. The fourth section focuses on support from international partners, particularly from organisations such as the World Bank, and UNESCO, from international and regional quality assurance networks such as the International Network for Quality Assurance Agencies in Higher Education (INQAAHE), the Asia-Pacific Network (APQN), and the ASEAN Quality Assurance Network (AQAN), and support from several countries, including Australia, Germany, The Netherlands, and the USA. Next, this chapter discusses several challenges facing capacity building in Vietnam's quality assurance, for example, the incompleteness of the national quality assurance framework, the inadequacy of quality assurance specialists, and the lack of formal professional development policies for quality assurance staff at all levels of the quality assurance system. Finally, this chapter draws lessons learned and suggests recommendations to improve quality assurance capacity building policies and practices at the macro-level (national quality assurance organisation), meso-level (accrediting agencies), and micro-level (higher education institutions).

Chapter 12 by Nguyen and Nguyen (2019) outlines the future of quality assurance in Vietnam higher education. It begins with a discussion of regional and global developments and innovations in quality assurance (with a focus on Malaysia, the Philippines, the USA, and several European countries) and opportunities for Vietnam. Second, this chapters suggests that professional accreditation be implemented to accredit specific programmes, for example engineering, medicine, and health, as the current programme accreditation process uses the same standards and criteria to evaluate all programmes. Third, this chapter argues for the diversity of national quality assurance arrangements and instruments. Quality assurance in Vietnam should not just seek accreditation in higher education, but also other methods for quality assurance and quality enhancement, including benchmarking, peer review, and ranking. Fourth, distance education or online learning programmes have emerged as an area of great concern in Vietnam. Ways to assure quality in this training method will be discussed in this section. Next, capacity building and professional development are significant at all levels of the accreditation system. This section focuses on building and implementing professional competency frameworks for internal quality assurance staff and external quality assurance practitioners. Moreover, this chapter highlights the need to build and promote a quality culture inside Vietnamese higher education institutions. In addition, international partnership is part of Vietnam's quality assurance development. Promoting collaboration and cooperation between local and international quality assurance agencies and networks should be a priority in Vietnam's future quality assurance agenda. Finally, as higher education quality assurance in Vietnam is currently centralised, implementing full independence and autonomy of the national quality assurance organisation and accrediting agencies is vitally important to the sustainable development of the Vietnam quality assurance system.

Concluding Remarks

Quality assurance has been implemented in many higher education systems across the world during the past few decades for the purposes of quality control, quality improvement, and accountability. In the context of Vietnam, although quality assurance and accreditation have been implemented for 15 years, there is a lack of research investigating the achievements, challenges, and future directions of this accreditation system. In a broader context, there is a lack of literature discussing the establishment and development of higher education quality assurance and accreditation mechanisms in developing countries in the Asia-Pacific region. By focusing the discussion and analysis on Vietnam's higher education quality assurance and accreditation system, this book is expected to fill these gaps. Additionally, this book discusses issues such as higher education internationalisation, quality and equity in higher education, impact of Industry 4.0 on quality assurance, and capacity building in quality assurance, which are common concerns in higher education systems worldwide.

Cuong Huu Nguyen
Mahsood Shah

References

Do, Q. T. N. (2019). Quality assurance and accreditation as a mechanism for accountability. In C. H. Nguyen & M. Shah (Eds.), *Quality assurance in Vietnamese higher education: Policy and practice in the 21st century*. London: Palgrave Macmillan.

Do, Q. T. N., Pham, H. T., & Nguyen, K. D. (2017). Quality assurance in Vietnamese higher education: A top-down approach and compliance-driven QA. In M. Shah & Q. T. N. Do (Eds.), *The rise of quality assurance in Asian higher education* (pp. 51–66). Cambridge: Chandos Publishing.

Le, K. A. T., Hayden, M., & Nhan, T. T. (2019). Development of the higher education sector in Vietnam. In C. H. Nguyen & M. Shah (Eds.), *Quality assurance in Vietnamese higher education: Policy and practice in the 21st century*. London: Palgrave Macmillan.

Ministry of Education and Training (MOET). (2018). *Education and training Viet Nam 2018*. Hanoi: MOET.

Nguyen, C. H. (2019). Building national capacity for quality assurance. In C. H. Nguyen & M. Shah (Eds.), *Quality assurance in Vietnamese higher education: Policy and practice in the 21st century*. London: Palgrave Macmillan.

Nguyen, C. H., & Nguyen, K. D. (2019). The future of quality assurance in Vietnamese higher education. In C. H. Nguyen & M. Shah (Eds.), *Quality assurance in Vietnamese higher education: Policy and practice in the 21st century*. London: Palgrave Macmillan.

Nguyen, H. C. (2018). How to fulfil Vietnam's higher education accreditation strategic plan 2017–2020? *International Journal of Educational Organization and Leadership*, *24*(3/4), 17–25. https://doi.org/10.18848/2329-1656/CGP/v24i03/17-25.

Nguyen, H. C., Evers, C., & Marshall, S. (2017). Accreditation of Viet Nam's higher education: Achievements and challenges after a dozen years of development. *Quality Assurance in Education*, *25*(4), 475–488. https://doi.org/10.1108/QAE-11-2016-0075.

Nguyen, H. C. & Ta, T. T. H. (2018). Exploring impact of accreditation on higher education in developing countries: A Vietnamese view. *Tertiary Education and Management*, *24*(2), 154–167. https://doi.org/10.1080/13583883.2017.1406001.

Nguyen, H. C., Ta, T. T. H., & Nguyen, T. T. H. (2017). Achievements and lessons learned from Vietnam's higher education quality assurance system after a decade of establishment. *International Journal of Higher Education*, *6*(2), 153–161. https://doi.org/10.5430/ijhe.v6n2p153.

Nhan, T. T., & Le, K. A. T. (2019). Internationalisation of higher education in Vietnam. In C. H. Nguyen & M. Shah (Eds.), *Quality assurance in Vietnamese higher education: Policy and practice in the 21st century*. London: Palgrave Macmillan.

Pham, H. T. (2018). Impacts of higher education quality accreditation: A case study in Vietnam. *Quality in Higher Education*, *24*(2), 168–185. https://doi.org/10.1080/13538322.2018.1491787.

Pham, H. T. (2019a). Limited legitimacy among academics of centrally driven approaches to internal quality assurance in Vietnam. *Journal of Higher Education Policy and Management*, *41*(2), 172–185. https://doi.org/10.1080/1360080X.2019.1565298.

Pham, H. T. (2019b). Stakeholders' engagement in quality assurance in Vietnam. In C. H. Nguyen & M. Shah (Eds.), *Quality assurance in Vietnamese higher education: Policy and practice in the 21st century*. London: Palgrave Macmillan.

Pham, H. T., & Nguyen, C. H. (2019). History of quality assurance in Vietnamese higher education. In C. H. Nguyen & M. Shah (Eds.), *Quality assurance in Vietnamese higher education: Policy and practice in the 21st century*. London: Palgrave Macmillan.

Pham, N. T., Nguyen, T. Q.,& Nguyen, C. H. (2019). Drivers of Vietnamese higher education quality assurance. In C. H. Nguyen & M. Shah (Eds.), *Quality assurance in Vietnamese higher education: Policy and practice in the 21st century*. London: Palgrave Macmillan.

Pham, T. V., Ta, H. T. T., & Nguyen, H. T. T. (2019). Digital innovation and impact on quality assurance. In C. H. Nguyen & M. Shah (Eds.), *Quality assurance in Vietnamese higher education: Policy and practice in the 21st century*. London: Palgrave Macmillan.

Ta, H. T. T., Nguyen, H. T. T., &Pham, T. V. (2019). Institutional and programme accreditation. In C. H. Nguyen & M. Shah (Eds.), *Quality assurance in Vietnamese higher education: Policy and practice in the 21st century*. London: Palgrave Macmillan.

Tran, N. T., & Vu, P. A. T. (2019). Fifteen years of accreditation in Vietnam. In C. H. Nguyen & M. Shah (Eds.), *Quality assurance in Vietnamese higher education: Policy and practice in the 21st century*. London: Palgrave Macmillan.

Tran, T. T. (2019). Access and equity in Vietnamese higher education. In C. H. Nguyen & M. Shah (Eds.), *Quality assurance in Vietnamese higher education: Policy and practice in the 21st century*. London: Palgrave Macmillan.

VGP News. (2019). *Infographics: Key population facts and figures of 2019 national census*. http://news.chinhphu.vn/Home/Infographics-Key-population-facts-and-figures-of-2019-National-Census/20197/37043.vgp.

1

Development of the Higher Education Sector in Vietnam

Kim Anh Thi Le, Martin Hayden and Thuy Thi Nhan

Introduction

Vietnam has showed a remarkable development over the past two decades. It began with the transformation in the economy in late 1980 when the country departed from the socialist model of State centralisation to a socialist market economy. Because of sustaining a high economic growth rate over the past two decades, Vietnam has succeeded in gaining membership in the group of 'low middle income' economies according to World Bank classification. With continuing high economic growth rates in recent years and strong determinations in economic reforms, Vietnam is expected to

---

K. A. T. Le (✉)
Hanoi National University of Education, Hanoi, Vietnam
e-mail: anhltk.etep@moet.gov.vn

M. Hayden
School of Education, Southern Cross University, Lismore, NSW, Australia

T. T. Nhan
Melbourne Graduate School of Education, The University of Melbourne, Melbourne, VIC, Australia

achieve the status of 'high income' on the World Bank classification by 2035 (World Bank, 2016).

The higher education system has grown up double in size for the recent two decades. The enrolment rate was 10.6% in 1999 and was almost three times in 2013 (UNESCO, 2017). Since 2011, the growth rate has dropped because of a slowdown in the natural birth rate but remains high in recent years. In 2017, there were 446 universities and colleges all over Vietnam (Ministry of Education and Training [MOET], 2017a) with enrolments reaching a figure of 2.24 million (MOET, 2017a). The quality improvements of the sector have been reported in numerous aspects. The composition student enrolment is improved: the rate of enrolments in postgraduate education has increased steadily, and the one at colleges has decreased gradually to 14% as of 2017. The quality of academic staff members has shown significant improvements. The rate of Ph.D. holders among academic staff flatted at 10% until 2014 (MOET, 2012, 2015) and recently has improved and reached 22.7% in 2017 (MOET, 2018). Quality assurance has been implemented at both institutional and programme levels (Nguyen, Evers, & Marshall, 2017; Nguyen & Ta, 2018). Almost all universities have completed institutional self-assessment reports, and 113 higher education institutions (HEIs) have been accredited by National Accreditation Standards as of 2018 (Nguyen, Nguyen, & Banh, 2018). Significant improvements have also been reported in the quality of undergraduate training programmes. Nearly 70 high quality and collaborative with overseas universities undergraduate programmes, which have been offered since the early 2010s, at present, produced high-quality graduates (MOET, 2015, 2016a, 2017b, 2018). Continuing investments over the recent twenty years have also contributed to significant improvements in the quality of physical infrastructure. The quality of research and research education also has been facilitated by new regulations on Ph.D. graduation and awarding professoriate titles in effect since 2016 and mechanisms that encourage publication productivity by academic staff members. The number of articles published by university academics has been reported to double between 2012 and 2017 with 6400 publications produced (Scimago, 2018).

Reforming the higher education sector in Vietnam demands strong determinations and intensive reforms but at the same has always been a desperately difficult task. Vietnam aspires to have a higher education system that can produce a highly productive and globally competitive labour force in its contribution to the country's industrialisation and building, yet many aspects still remain in need of urgent and consistent improvements.

Individual academic staff members are being seen as the primary actors in the development of the organisation—the university and its departments (see, e.g., Clark, 1987). Therefore, this chapter focuses more closely on the issues that are challenging individual works by academic staff members at public universities. The chapter starts with a brief on the development of the sector over the past two decades. The challenges that constrain the development of academic culture at the system's organisational and departmental levels are then identified and discussed. The chapter concludes with some recommendations that might be taken into account by the sector in its future reforming efforts to forge the academic culture in Vietnamese universities.

This chapter is built on a rich source of international and local literature which concerns the development of the higher education sector in Vietnam. More recent works include Le and Hayden (2017), Le (2017), Nguyen (2016), Dao (2015), Dao and Hayden (2015), Harman, Hayden, and Pham (2010), Pham and Briller (2015), Pham and Hayden (2015), Tran et al. (2014), and Hayden and Pham (2015).

Recent Reforms

Early significant reforms in the higher education sector were initiated in the 1990s. A landmark Prime Ministerial decree (Decree No. 90/NĐ-TTg) issued in 1993 pronounced a strong determination and promulgated a process for departure from Soviet Union's influence on higher education sector. Until this date, HEIs were small, confined to teaching functions only and provided educational programmes in narrowly specialised areas. Immediately, in 1994, two national universities in Hanoi and Ho Chi Minh City and three regional universities in Thai Nguyen, Hue and Da Nang were established by mean of merging smaller monodisciplinary institutions. Education programmes in multidisciplinary areas were offered and followed an American model of qualification frameworks with four-year programmes for universities and three-year programmes for colleges.

A number of changes are of importance to note. This was for the first time that graduates were no longer provided with employment guarantee; students were not given scholarship; tuition fees were first introduced for all students, except those attending teacher education institutions and some HEIs were under army and security force authorities. It is also for the first time that research began to be seen as the responsibility of the university rather than the sole duty of research institutes. Another importance was that the private sector of universities and colleges was permitted to be established. Universities began to be not only own and run by the State but by various local communities. These developments have been critical in enabling the system to become ready to meet the tenfold growth in regard to the number of enrolments in the coming three decades.

The next significant reform was the approval of 'Higher Education Reforming Agenda—HERA' by the government in 2005 (Resolution No. 14/2005/NQ-CP dated November 2, 2005, Government, 2005) which targets various objectives by 2020. An important goal of HERA was the abandonment of line management control by various government ministries and provincial instrumentalities on the university management. HERA insisted universities to have their own governing boards. Another goal set in HERA is that Vietnam will have a group of research-oriented universities which will enrol 20% of the student population. The other main goals set in HERA were that 35% of university lecturers will hold a Ph.D. degree; 40% of university revenues will be generated from research and research applications; the ratio of academic staff members to students will be reduced; and Vietnam inspires to have one university ranked among the top 200 universities in the world. The private sector was expected to grow up to the extent that 40% of students will enrol in a private university by 2020.

The aims set in HERA are ambitious as the main figures by 2018 are well behind the targets set, as reported earlier in the chapter; however, HERA is still an important policy document and initiative given the insistence that it has placed on the future directions for Vietnam's higher education sector.

The next reform of significant importance was the development and adoption of Higher Education Law (Law No. 8/2012/QH13 dated June 18, 2012, National Assembly, 2012). The operation of HEIs was previously regulated by separate circulars and decrees which were accommodated with ones of school education and vocational education in Education Law (2005). It is significant that Higher Education Law, for the first time, has brought together all incremental regularities, decrees and guidelines on the system under a single legal document. Higher Education Law (2012) prescribed the development of multi-tier higher education system, which consisted of research-oriented universities at the top tier, research-applied universities at the second tier and profession-oriented universities at the third tier.

The Higher Education Law (2012) and the Revised Higher Education Law (2018) continuously insisted on the development of the university autonomy. All HEIs are being placed under pressure to establish a university board (public universities) or university governing board (private universities) capable of taking responsibilities on behalf of the government instrumentalities, for example, for setting up its strategic decisions, developing regulations on institutional structure, issuing guidelines for educational programs, for staff recruitment, implementing staff development, and regulating institutional use of public funds, students' fees, and other incomes. Strong determinations and pressures on the forming of the university board and delegating it prescribed role and responsibility are perceived to be compatible with those at developed HEIs globally.

Another important reform was the government's approval of Resolution on 'Fundamental and Comprehensive Education Reform to meet the needs for country's industrialisation, modernisation in context of market economy with socialism direction and global integration (FCER)' (Resolution No. 29/2013/NQ-TW dated November 4, 2013, Communist Party Central Committee [CPCC], 2013). FCER has placed the fostering of institutional autonomy at the centre of HEIs reform activities. The specific objectives of the higher education reform set out in FCER (2013, p. 5) included producing highly qualified human resources, cultivating talents, fostering self-learning values and capacities, fostering the capacity for self-enriching and innovation of learners, perfecting the HEIs network, profession structure, and education levels in alignment with the planning of national human resources development, having some HEIs and education programmes achieve ASEAN and international levels, and diversifying HEIs meeting the needs in technological development, the country's development, defence, and international integration.

A recent study (Nghiem & VNU Research Team, 2018) on the evaluation of the 5-year implementation of FCER and the Higher Education Law identified both certain improvements and the issues that required further improvements. Regarding achievements, 23 universities have been operated as being fully autonomous and have been granted autonomy in many important areas, such as recruiting students, initiating education programmes and cooperation, setting tuition fees, raising liable income for academic staff members, and improving the quality of academic staff members. These autonomous universities also enjoy higher authority in making decisions in research development, research applications and selling research products. The study also described a number of critically important issues that require urgent reforms. A lack of a single point for higher education governance is identified as the most critical and continuing weakness of the system (also see, Dao & Hayden, 2015; Hayden & others, 2012; Le & Hayden, 2017). The current legal framework for institutional autonomy was seen as deficient, asynchronised and overlapping. There was a lack of authorities in decision-making in such critical areas as appointing university boards and rectors, in staff positions, staff salary and payment norms for research.

Vietnam Higher Education Contemporary Issues

A rich source of recent literature provided accounts and analysis on contemporary issues that the higher education sector in Vietnam urgently needs to tackle (see, e.g., Dao & Hayden, 2015; Harman et al., 2010; Pham & Briller, 2015; Tran et al., 2014). Comprehensive review of contemporary issues that the system faced was provided by Le and Hayden (2017). This chapter focuses more closely on the issues that are challenging individual works by academic staff members at public universities. Five issues are widely considered the most important and are being discussed here.

Governance

The issue of governance remains identified as the most problematic but has not been adequately tackled. A lack of a single point for governing HEIs in Vietnam is remarkably evident and has been documented in various works by Hayden, Dao, and Lam (2012), Dao and Hayden (2015), Le and Hayden (2017), and Nghiem and VNU Research Team (2018).

Under the Soviet model's influence and the State-centralised mechanism, HEIs in Vietnam are specialised and are being established and run by various ministries and local authorities to serve their specific needs. Universities in generally exercise a little autonomy in the management of their own matters. As discussed earlier, the 2012 Higher Education Law insisted a shift moving higher responsibilities and autonomy to universities. HEIs in Vietnam (according to Articles 28, 29, and 32 of the Higher Education Law) have been granted higher authority in decision-making in the several aspects as described above, yet the process of decision-making remains under the tight control of the relevant line management authorities.

The Government expressed its determination for abolishing line ministry management (HERA, 2005), but there is a meagre improvement in this regard reported. About four hundred of universities in Vietnam are being in charge by the governing line management instrumentalities and are being run by various ministries and government authorities, corporations and other entities. Currently, 53 HEIs are run under MOET authorities 90 by private entities, hundreds of them by provincial authorities, a few of them by either organisational unions or corporations and five of them by international ownership. These various instrumentalities control the flow of funds to universities. In the other critical areas, the lack of coordination is also present. University governing boards, for instance, do not have the authority to appoint rectors and confer academic staff members professoriate or academic titles. Decision-making power in these important matters remains firmly within the sole control of line management ministries.

While decisions to be made in relation to academic staff positions and remuneration schemes are decided by Ministry of Internal Affairs, decisions on matters related to the regulation of core curriculum frameworks and working conditions of staff members are set by MOET (Circular No. 47/2014/TT-BGDĐT dated November 31, 2014). In the meantime, the Office of the Prime Minister independently sets regulations on standards of awarding professoriate titles (Decision No. 20/2012/QĐ-TTg dated April 27, 2012, Prime Minister, 2012). Appointment of university rectors is of approval by line ministry authorities (National Assembly, 2012). In a number of recent investigations (Le, 2017; Nguyen, 2016), most academic staff members have expressed their concerns that they have less freedom in the matters related to their workload, which constrains their research capacity and motivation. Initial academics in particular have expressed their despair about the low monthly salary of only less than US$200, with which they could not afford their family's basic living needs and that they have a little room to decide the extent of their research and teaching job. Similarly, Dao and Hayden (2015, p. 323) stressed that 'in Vietnam, public universities and colleges are not generally able to make their own decisions, especially about matters that are fundamentally important to them as academic communities'. There is an urgent reform required for establishing a single point for governing and coordination of the system.

Higher Education Finance and Funding Mechanism

The Government of Vietnam has shown its strong and incremental commitments in its investment in education and particularly in higher education. Over the last twenty years, the expenditure on education and science and technology has steadily increased, representing a proportion of 20% of public expenditure (MOET, 2018). Spending on education reached VND 248,100 billion, a figure which has increased by VND 92,500 billion for the recent 5-year period from 2013 to 2017. Expenditure on science and technology has also increased steadily from a share of 0.87% of the country's GDP in 2013 and is expected to rise to 2% of GDP in

2020 (Ministry of Science and Technology [MOST], 2015). These figures are high compared to those of neighbouring ASEAN countries and compatible with OECD standards (World Bank, 2017).

As stipulated in the Higher Education Law (2012) and the Revised Higher Education Law (2018), Articles 64 & 65, universities generate their incomes from different sources, namely government funds, tuition fees, training and research-related activities, community services, loans, gifts and foreign investments. Public HEIs are granted high proportion of their income from State funds and State supports for both their training and research activities. For public universities, government funding has remained the first substantial income, which can represent up to 50% of their incomes. Tuition fees represent up to 40% of the income for public universities; public universities also receive government funding on scientific and technological research projects. There are a small number of public universities with strong capacity in research that have their some incomes generated from selling their research applications and from technological transfers.

A lack of a single point in regard to funding mechanism is evident (Le & Hayden, 2017; Nghiem & VNU Research Team, 2018; Pham, 2013). Ministry of Finance (MOF) grants annual funds to public universities through their line ministry and governmental instrumentalities for training expenses, physical buildings and infrastructure, and staff salaries and remuneration. This annual block grant permits universities to enjoy more autonomy in the management of their own budget, especially in making decisions on the specific category expenditure according to their own needs regulated by various 'framework norms' set by MOF. But complaints were expressed that institutional annual financial plans often have been approved late, normally by the end of the first quarter of the years; the financial surplus and undisbursed financial amount were not permitted to be carried out over to the next year. Therefore, the ineffectiveness and inefficiency of the use of this fund were widely reported.

Ministry of Science and Technology (MOST) channels its funds to the ministries, government and provincial entities responsible for certain universities. Recently, since 2007, MOST has also channelled its funds directly to HEIs and research institutes by the National Fund for Science and Technology Development (NAFOSTED) scheme. Among these various finding channels, only the funding mechanism deployed by NAFOSTED has been regarded as efficient and transparent and mirrored those of developed higher education funding schemes worldwide. However, NAFOSTED fund represents only about 5% of the government's research fund (MOST, 2015). Academic staff members have expressed their concerns and complaints about funding decisions to their research by various government authorities (Le, 2017; Pham, 2013).

Although improvement in physical infrastructure has been reported (MOET, 2015, 2018), a severe concern is that universities have been underfunded, particularly in three major related matters (Le, 2017; Nguyen, 2016). Firstly, in regard to physical conditions to research and teaching, a lack of essential equipment and laboratories required for teaching, even at undergraduate level, and for conducting research has repeatedly been reported. There is also insufficiency in allocating budget for equipment repairs and maintenance, in supplying consumable material and chemicals. Secondly, the library conditions have been inadequately improved. All participants across 4 leading research universities in Vietnam in an investigation conducted by Le (2017) claimed that updated books, reference books and periodic journals required for teaching, especially at postgraduate level, and research were not available. There were severely insufficient library spaces for individual learning across all the universities under investigation. Thirdly, in departments of humanities and social, and social applied studies, the minimum working conditions for individual's private work were not available: desks and computers with internet access were not provided for academic staff members. These poorly provided working conditions have been widely considered as severe obstacles preventing the quality of teaching, research and supervising students' works.

Research and Research Training

Vietnam's research performance, particularly by university academic staff members, for the two past decades, has been viewed as being a severe weakness. According to ASEAN standards, Vietnam has produced relatively poorly in the number of peer-reviewed papers per millions of population (Pham, 2010, p. 617; Scimago, 2018). Research poor performance is evident until recently. The factor that contributes to this poor performance is that until the present, academic staff members are not required to produce international publications. In 2017, while there were 16,514 Ph.D.-qualified university academic staff and 4687 associate and full professors, there were only 6393 peer-reviewed papers produced nationwide, meaning two-thirds of highly qualified staff do not publish at international standards. This issue appears to be more problematic in the field of humanities and social sciences. Over two decades, Scimago indicators (Scimago, 2018) show that only 471 of 42,330 peer-reviewed papers have been produced by scholars in humanities and art sciences and in 2017 only 51 papers in these fields were produced. All main research indicators of Vietnam have been for the two decades poor against ASEAN benchmarks. The gap between the research performance of Vietnam and that of its neighbouring countries has not been improved as seen in Fig. 1.1.

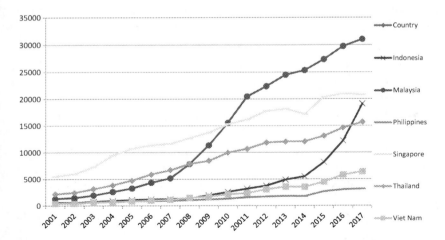

Fig. 1.1 Publication trends by ASEAN countries over the two recent decades (*Source* Compiled from Scopus database [2018])

The relative weakness of research performance in the disciplines of humanities and social sciences is of special note. Research funding agencies in Vietnam demonstrably favour research in science and technologies (MOST, 2015, p. 88). NAFOSTED, for example, gives weight to international publications, which tends to disadvantage researchers in the humanities and social sciences whose research topics are more likely to focus on matters of national or local interest. Further, the primary research outputs in the humanities and social sciences continue to be books and extended reports written in Vietnamese, which means that they do not achieve international impact. It is noteworthy that the nature of global academic competition has increased enormously in the humanities and social science disciplines, as has been shown by Gibbons et al. (1994, pp. 90–96), Delanty (2001, pp. 116–120), and Slaughter and Leslie (1997, pp. 23, 117, 118, 197, 211). In developed higher education systems, the need to mark out intellectual territory more speedily in these fields has led to the publication of journal articles overtaking the publication of books which simply become out-dated by the time they reach print. Vietnamese scholars engaged in the studies of humanities and social sciences are technologically disadvantaged in these terms. An additional consideration is that research methodology in the field of social sciences in Vietnam tends to be ideologically limited in scope, restricted mainly to a positivist paradigm, which is consistent with Marxist dialectical materialism (Bùi Ngọc Hoàn, 2014; *Thanh Nien Newspaper*, 2016a, 2016b). The lack of research skills in the humanities and social sciences in terms of the application of inductive logic and post-positivist research methodologies is deeply concerning (Le Thi Kim Anh, 2017).

In general, low enrolment levels in postgraduate education are widely seen to be a significant factor contributing to the low proportion of Ph.D.-qualified members of academic staff in Vietnamese universities. The quality of postgraduate training in Vietnam is a further source of concern. Various weaknesses in postgraduate education were identified, including an overall lack of university-based research, a lack of well-developed linkages between university research and industry, and an imbalance in postgraduate enrolments across the range of academic disciplines, with a higher level of enrolment in academic disciplines under social sciences and humanities and a lower level of enrolments in the natural sciences and technologies (Harman & Ngoc, 2010; Le, 2017).

Conditions of Academic Employment

To better understand the nature of academic life in Vietnam, it is important to consider the conditions of employment in the higher education system. As reported earlier in this chapter, academic employment in HEIs in Vietnam is regulated by a range of legislative and regulatory instruments, important among which are the Revised Higher Education Law of 2018, the Science and Technology Law of 2013, the Higher Education Law of 2012 and the Education Law of 2005. In addition, there are various ministerial decisions and circulars that apply to academic employment.

All HEIs in Vietnam are responsible for employing their own members of academic staff. The conditions applying to academic employment at public HEIs are, however, so tightly prescribed by the State. The Higher Education Law of 2012 and the Revised Higher Education Law 2018, Article 55 requires that academic staff members at public universities should teach, undertake research and participate in professional development. Teaching refers to the delivery of academic programmes at diploma, bachelor, master's and Ph.D. levels. Article 15 of the Law indicates that the teaching role also involves a commitment to self-improvement and to setting an example for students. Reflecting Confucian values, Article 15 of the Law commits the State to providing the 'necessary material and spiritual conditions for teachers to fulfil their roles and responsibilities, preserving and developing the tradition of respecting teachers and honouring the teaching profession'.

Professional development refers to attendance at courses intended to improve the capacity of academic staff members in three areas, namely political knowledge, knowledge in an academic specialisation and knowledge of pedagogy as prescribed by Article 55 of the Law. Acquiring enhanced political knowledge about Marxism-Leninism and the thoughts of Ho Chi Minh is particularly important in Vietnam for academic staff members seeking to achieve managerial and leadership positions. Relevant training programmes are routinely provided in the form of short courses conducted by Party authorities.

There are five academic appointment levels in Vietnam (Article 54): assistant lecturer, lecturer, senior lecturer, associate professor and professor. While individual HEIs may have additional requirements, the minimum requirement for appointment to any of these levels is the attainment of a master's degree qualification. A new member of academic staff typically starts as an assistant lecturer and is then promoted to higher levels based on years of experience acquired through the attainment of academic achievements in the form of higher degree qualifications or scholarly publications may also impact positively on promotion and appointment opportunities. Full-time research appointments at universities in Vietnam, though rare, are permitted, with appointment levels designated as assistant researcher, researcher, senior researcher and highly ranked researcher. The Science and Technology Law of 2013 prescribes that researchers who then engage in some teaching will be eligible for appointment as associate professors or professors.

As prescribed in Decision No. 20/2012/QD-TTg dated April 27, 2012 (Prime Minister, 2012), appointment to associate professor requires the attainment of a doctoral qualification and continuous experience of teaching for at least 3 to 5 years after the attainment of a Ph.D. qualification and successful team leadership experience in completing a significant research project that has been approved at either institutional or ministerial level. Experience with the supervision of Ph.D. candidates to completion and fluency in one of the five foreign languages, English, French, Chinese, Russian or German, are also the requirements for appointment to associate professor level.

A candidate for appointment as a professor must demonstrate relevant expertise and qualifications for the role. Professorial appointees must now have been an associate professor for at least three years, have supervised through to completion at least two Ph.D.s and have achieved the equivalent of at least six peer-reviewed publications in international journals. The importance attached to peer-reviewed research publications in the context of promotion decisions to associate professor and professor positions has dramatically increased over the past decade. Applicants for promotion to associate professor must now achieve at least 6 publication points, and applicants for promotion to professor must achieve 12, with points allocated thus: from 0.25 to 1.0 point for each national publication, and 2.0 points for each peer-reviewed international publication.

Recently in Circular No. 47/2014/TT-BGDĐT dated December 31, 2014, MOET (2014) has mandated that all appointment levels should have the same workload allocation of a little over 50% for teaching and 33% for research. This pattern of allocation is more or less in line with profiles for other national higher education systems, including Norway's (Kyvik, 2000) and Australia's (Harman, 2000; McInnis, 2000).

Salaries for academic staff members in public HEIs are based on seniority and regulated by the government. Salary increments are awarded every three years, depending upon successful completion of assigned tasks, as assessed by senior academic managers. The monthly salary for an assistant lecturer currently starts at 2 million VND (US$100) and increases over nine steps (at three-year intervals) to 6 million VND (US$300) at the top of the scale. For a professor, the starting salary is 8 million VND (US$400) per month, increasing in six steps (one step every three years) to 12 million VND (US$600) at the top of the scale. With additional responsibilities, senior academic staff members may achieve the highest possible income level of 15 million VND (US$750) per month. In general, these salary levels are insufficient to maintain a family, according to several sources (*Thanh Niên Newspaper*, 2016a; *Tiên Phong Newspaper*, 2016; *Tuổi Trẻ Newspaper*, 2015a, 2015b). Many academic staff members feel obliged, therefore, to earn a supplementary income. Those employed at public HEIs readily find opportunities for part-time and casual employment at private HEIs which function on a business model that involves a heavy reliance on the employment of part-time and casual teaching staff. Academics also take on extra work outside the academy, such as teaching in evening classes, in-service programs. These extra works are perceived as being time consuming and exhausting, which prevent performing the main universities activities of teaching and research, especially by young academics (Le, 2017).

Academic appointments at public HEIs are made on a full-time, continuing basis and continue until the compulsory age of retirement, which is 55 years of age for females and 60 years of age for males. Associate professors and professors may keep their titles beyond retirement and can only have their titles removed if they are judged by their rector to have been delinquent in some way. This situation differs from what happens in many higher education systems where maintaining a professorial title is only possible with an emeritus appointment beyond retirement.

Evolving of Academic Culture in Vietnamese Universities

One of the authors conducted an ethnography investigation on the development of academic culture at 4 leading research universities in Vietnam. Semi-structured interviews were carried out with 30 experienced in research and teaching academic members across departments of natural and natural applied sciences, humanities and social sciences, and social applied sciences education (Le, 2017). The investigation pointed out a keenly developing academic culture and a developing sense of academic identity at these institutions. Three types of academic identities were identified.

Cosmopolitan and outward-looking sense of identity, namely as 'cosmopolitan researcher', was most strongly evident in the natural and applied sciences, where participants in the investigation manifested a well-developed sense of allegiance to global disciplinary communities. These participants reported a depth of engagement with global knowledge networks. They worked strenuously to reinforce this engagement through their publishing activities. They strongly engaged in national and international networking collaborative works.

In the more individualistic research specialisms of the humanities and social sciences, local and inward-looking sense of identity, namely as 'local researcher', is more evident. The desire for an affinity with global disciplinary communities was also widely reported, but research outcomes in terms of international publications were comparatively far less in evidence. Publishing in the humanities remained for the most part locally focused and intermittent. The networking is strong nationally.

Academics working in the applied social sciences, particularly in teacher education, were the least globally engaged, reporting meagre links with international scholarly networks. This group was described as 'reluctant researcher'. Typically, in the field of teacher education, an understanding of the need to mark out intellectual territory through publishing research findings in peer-refereed journals was acknowledged, but it was an attainment that was also considered to be wholly out of reach in practical terms.

An important discovery was the identification of academic staff members able to be described as 'cosmopolitan researchers'. There were academic staff members, coming mainly but not exclusively from the natural and applied sciences, few of them were from humanities and social sciences, who were highly productive as international researchers. All these participants had obtained their Ph.Ds abroad, most had also completed postdoctoral research programs, some have working experiences as lecturers or researchers at foreign research-intensive universities. Though constrained by limited funding support, and tending to be 'inbred' to an extent because of their inclination to return to the same university at which they had completed their undergraduate studies, they fitted neatly with Clark's (1985, p. 38) description of faculty members at leading research universities in the United States: where academic life was centred on research, teaching commitments were light, and professors enjoyed the rituals of their disciplines as well as high standing within their disciplinary enclaves. The 'cosmopolitan researchers' were, in other words, members of an elite group with a refined sense of academic identity within their international 'club'. These were the kinds of scholars that the Government and individual 'research-oriented' universities will need to rely upon to provide Vietnam with a globally competitive higher education sector in the not-too-distant future.

The two other groups identified were the 'local researchers', that is academics who were active as researchers but who published mainly or entirely in Vietnam, and 'reluctant researchers', that is academics who preferred to focus on teaching and who were not inclined to engage in research. Humanities scholars were more likely to be 'local researchers', and the 'reluctant researchers' were mainly scholars from the social sciences (including teacher education). Of concern is the finding among teacher education academics. Two-thirds of the participants earned their Ph.D. qualification at foreign research universities, but they were appeared more evidently as 'reluctant researchers', as their main focus is being confined to teaching only, research was implemented as in order to fulfil their academic prescribed responsibility. These participants are almost not engaged in their peer networks. The severe concern among local research is their 'pure inbreeding status'.

Practical measures are required to nurture and support the development of a 'cosmopolitan researcher' culture in Vietnam's higher education sector. The discussion in the earlier part of this paper has drawn attention to aspects of the sector that, if left unattended, will delay the development of this culture. In general, there is a need for public universities in Vietnam to have more capacity to act independently in cultivating the immense talent that they attract in the form of academic staff members and students.

Concluding Remarks

This paper has discussed the issues that Vietnam's higher education sector has faced as it responds to the need to become more research-oriented and more globally competitive and that support fully individual works by their academic staff members. There are significant achievements of the sector that make the shift to internationally competitive and global academic networking, but vast areas of the sector identified remain engaged firmly with the values and practice of the past. Five aspects of the sector that now urgently require immediate actions: increasing academic salaries and addressing the regulatory environment regarding academic employment; providing more financial support for research and deploying NAFOSTED funding mechanism across all research funding schemes; improving physical conditions for academic works; revising policies that will promote the positive impacts from increased internationalisation; and improving the conditions of academic employment (see also, Le & Hayden, 2017).

The need to achieve international standards by Vietnam's higher education sector is of urgent importance. Given the high speed of change in higher education systems worldwide, Vietnam's higher education urges to take giant steps not only for its improvements but also for catching up with the global pace of the changes.

References

Bùi Ngọc Hoàn. (2014, January 10). Research in social sciences in Vietnam. *Tia Sáng*. Retrieved October 25, 2018 from http://tiasang.com.vn/-quan-ly-khoa-hoc/Nghien-cuu-khoa-hoc-xa-hoi-o-Viet-Nam.

Clark, B. R. (1985). Listening to the professoriate. *Change, 17*(5), 36–43.

Clark, B. R. (Ed.). (1987). *The academic profession: National, disciplinary and institutional settings*. Berkeley: University of California Press.

Communist Party Central Committee (CPCC). (2013). *Resolution No. 29-NQ/TW dated November 4, 2013 of the eighth Party Congress XI on fundamental and comprehensive reform of education and training, meeting the needs for industrialisation, modernisation in the context of market economy with socialist direction and international integration*. Retrieved October 25, 2018 from http://www.vnep.org.vn/Upload/Education%20and%20training.pdf.

Dân Trí Newspaper. (2016, February 2). New graduates in banking cannot find employment, but the banks lack human resources. Retrieved November 2, 2018 from http://dantri.com.vn/tin-tuyen-sinh/tan-cu-nhan-nganh-tai-chinh-ngan-hang-that-nghiep-nhung-ngan-hang-van-dang-khat-nhan-luc-20160202192339212.htm.

Dao, V. K. (2015). Key challenges in the reform of governance, quality assurance, and finance in Vietnamese higher education a case study. *Studies in Higher Education, 40*(5), 745–760.

Dao, V. K., & Hayden, M. (2015). Higher education governance reform in Vietnam. In K. M. Joshi & S. Paivandi (Eds.), *Global higher education: Issues in governance* (pp. 315–338). New Delhi: B.R. Publishing Corporation.

Delanty, G. (2001). *Challenging knowledge: The university in the knowledge society*. Buckingham: Open University Press.

Gibbons, M., Limoges, C., Nowotny, H., Schwartzman, S., Scott, P., & Trow, M. (1994). *The new production of knowledge: The dynamics of science and research in contemporary societies*. London: Sage.

Harman, G. (2000). Academic work and values in Australian higher education, 1977 to 1997. In M. Tight (Ed.), *Academic work and life: What it is to be an academic, and how this is changing* (pp. 73–116). Amsterdam: JAI Press.

Harman, G., & Ngoc, L. T. B. (2010). The research role of Vietnam's universities. In G. Harman, M. Hayden, & P. T. Nghi (Eds.), *Reforming higher education in Vietnam: Challenges and priorities* (pp. 87–102). Dordrecht: Springer.

Harman, G., Hayden, M., & Pham, T. N. (Eds.). (2010). *Reforming higher education in Vietnam: Challenges and priorities*. Dordrecht: Springer.

Hayden, M., & Pham, T. L. (2015). Higher education access and inclusion: Lessons from Vietnam. In R. T. Taranishi, L. B. Pazich, M. Knobel, & W. R. Allen (Eds.), *Mitigating inequality: Higher education research, policy, and practice in an era of massification and stratification* (pp. 19–33). London: Emerald Group.

Hayden, M., Dao, V. K, & Lam, Q. T. (2012). *Master plan for Vietnam's higher education system* (Unpublished Report). Lismore, Australia: Southern Cross University.

Kyvik, S. (2000). Academic work in Norwegian higher education. In M. Tight (Ed.), *Academic work and life: What it is to be an academic, and how this is changing* (pp. 33–72). Amsterdam: JAI Press.

Le, T. K. A. (2017). *Developing the academy in Vietnam: An investigation of the formation of academic identity by university lecturers in Vietnam* (PhD thesis). Southern Cross University, Lismore, Australia.

Le, T. K. A., & Hayden, M. (2017). The road ahead for the higher education sector in Vietnam. *Journal of International and Comparative Education, 6*(2), 77–89.

McInnis, C. (2000). Towards new balance or new divides? The changing work roles of academics in Australia. In M. Tight (Ed.), *Academic work and life: What it is to be an academic, and how this is changing* (pp. 117–146). Amsterdam: JAI Press.

Ministry of Education and Training (MOET). (2014). *Circular No. 47/2014/TT-BGDĐT dated November 31, 2014 on the regulations of the work norms by university lecturers.*

Ministry of Education and Training (MOET). (2015). *Report on the conference on annual work of academic year 2014–2015 and major tasks of academic year 2015–2016 of university and college sectors* (Unpublished Report).

Ministry of Education and Training (MOET). (2016a). *Report on the conference on annual work of academic year 2015–2016 and major tasks of academic year 2016–2017 of university and college sectors* (Unpublished Report).

Ministry of Education and Training (MOET). (2016b). *Statistic figures on higher education*. Retrieved October 25, 2018 from http://www.moet.gov.vn/thong-ke/Pages/thong-ko-giao-duc-dai-hoc.aspx?ItemID=4041.

Ministry of Education and Training (MOET). (2017a). *Report on the conference on annual work of academic year 2016–2017 and major tasks of academic year 2017–2018 of university and college sectors* (Unpublished Report).

Ministry of Education and Training (MOET). (2017b). *Circular No. 08/2017/TT- BGD ĐT dated April 4, 2017 'Regulations on recruitment of PhD students and implementation of PhD programs'.*

Ministry of Education and Training (MOET). (2018). *Report on the conference on annual work of academic year 2017–2018 and major tasks of academic year 2018–2019 of university and college sectors* (Unpublished Report).

Ministry of Science and Technology (MOST). (2015). *Ministry of Science and Technology of Vietnam 2014*. Hanoi: Science and Technical Publishing House.

National Assembly (NA). (2005). *Law No. 382005/QH11 dated June 14, 2005, Education Law*.

National Assembly (NA). (2012). *Law No. 08/2012/QH13 dated June 18, 2012, Higher Education Law*.

National Assembly (NA). (2018). *Law No. 34/2018/QH14 dated November 19, 2018, Revised Higher Education Law*.

Nghiem, X. H., & VNU Research Team. (2018, September 18). *Report on institutional autonomy at universities in Vietnam: Current trends and barriers*. Paper presented at the National Conference "An Evaluation of 05 year implementation of FCER", Vietnam National University, Hanoi, Vietnam.

Nguyen, H. C., Evers, C., & Marshall, S. (2017). Accreditation of Viet Nam's higher education: Achievements and challenges after a dozen years of development. *Quality Assurance in Education, 25*(4), 475–488.

Nguyen, H. C., & Ta, T. T. H. (2018). Exploring impact of accreditation on higher education in developing countries: A Vietnamese view. *Tertiary Education and Management, 24*(2), 154–167.

Nguyen, P. N., Nguyen, V. D., & Banh, T. L. (2018, September 18). *Report on institutional accreditation and quality assurance in Vietnam*. Paper presented at the National Conference "An Evaluation of 05 year implementation of FCER', in Vietnam National University, Hanoi, Vietnam.

Nguyen, T. L. H. (2016). Building human resources management capacity for university research: The case at four leading Vietnamese universities. *The International Journal of Higher Education Research, 71*(2), 231–251.

Pham, D. H. (2010). A comparative study of research capabilities of East Asian countries and implications for Vietnam. *Higher Education, 60*(6), 615–625.

Pham, T. L. (2013). Case study: The effectiveness of research and innovation management at policy and institutional levels in Vietnam. In A. Olsson & L. Meek (Eds.), *Effectiveness of research and innovation management at policy and institutional levels in Cambodia, Malaysia, Thailand and Vietnam* (pp. 140–162). Paris: OECD.

Pham, T. L., & Briller, V. (2015). Private higher education in Vietnam and recent policy development. *VNU Journal of Science, 31*(4), 58–66.

Pham, T. L., & Hayden, M. (2015). Vietnam's higher education in transition: The struggle to achieve potential. In B. Rajika & L. Alessia (Eds.), *Asia: The* next higher education superpower? (pp. 145–160). New York: The Institute of International Education.

Prime Minister. (2012). *Decision No. 20/2012/QĐ-TTg dated April 27, 2012 on standards for appointment and abolition of academic titles of associate and full professors.*

Scimago. (2018). *Country rankings.* Retrieved November 4, 2018 from http://www.scimagojr.com/countryrank.php.

Slaughter, S., & Leslie, L. L. (1997). *Academic capitalism: Politics, policies, and the entrepreneurial university.* Baltimore: Johns Hopkins University Press.

Thanh Niên Newspaper. (2016a, April 25). Không thể 'bình dân hóa' luận án tiến sĩ [Must not "simplify" PhD thesis]. Retrieved from http://thanhnien.vn/giao-duc/khong-the-binh-dan-hoa-luan-an-tien-si-695597.html.

Thanh Niên Newspaper. (2016b, April 27). Chuyện làm tiến sĩ ở Việt Nam [A story about doing PhD in Vietnam]. Retrieved from http://thanhnien.vn/toi-viet/chuyen-lam-tien-si-o-viet-nam-696148.html,

Thanh Niên Newspaper. (2016c, October 13). Salary of government's officers afford only 50% of basic living needs. Retrieved October 20, 2018 from http://thanhnien.vn/doi-song/luong-cong-chuc-chi-du-song-50-754532.html.

The Government of Vietnam (GoV). (1993). *Decree No. 90/1993/NĐ-CP dated November 24, 1993 of regulations on framework of the national education system and degrees' and certificates' system on education and training of the Socialist Republic of Vietnam.*

The Government of Vietnam (GoV). (2005). *Resolution No. 14/2005/NQ-CP dated November 2, 2005 of Higher Education Reforming Agenda—HERA'.*

Tiền Phong Newspaper. (2016, June 2). Salary of VND three million, many PhD researchers have quitted their job. Retrieved August 23, 2017 from http://www.tienphong.vn/xa-hoi/luong-3-trieu-nhieu-tien-si-bo-viec-1011246.tpo.

Tran, T. L., Marginson, S., Do, M. H., Do, T. N. Q., Le, T. T. T., Nguyen, T. N., ... Ho, T. H. T. (Eds.). (2014). *Higher education in Vietnam: Flexibility, mobility and practicality in the global knowledge economy.* Basingstoke: Palgrave Macmillan.

Tuổi Trẻ Newspaper. (2015a, January 25). Anxiety about the redundancy of human resources. Retrieved October 20, 2018 from http://tuyensinh.tuoitre.vn/tin/20150125/lo-lang-truoc-nhung-nganh-hot-sap-bao-hoa-lao-dong/703380.html.

Tuổi Trẻ Newspaper. (2015b, November 16). By what time will teachers be able to live on their salary? Retrieved October 20, 2018 from http://tuoitre.vn/

tin/giao-duc/20151116/bao-gio-giao-vien-song-duoc-bang-luong/1003564. html.
UNESCO. (2017). *Education: Tertiary graduates by level of education.* Retrieved August 23, 2017 from http://data.uis.unesco.org/index.aspx?queryname= 162.
World Bank. (2016). *New report lays out path for Vietnam to reach upper middle income status in 20 years.* Retrieved October 20, 2018 from http://www.worldbank.org/en/news/press-release/2016/02/23/new-report-lays-out-path-for-vietnam-to-reach-upper-middle-income-status-in-20-years.
World Bank. (2017). *World Bank open data.* Retrieved October 20, 2018 from http://data.worldbank.org.

2

Internationalisation of Higher Education in Vietnam

Thuy Thi Nhan and Kim Anh Thi Le

Introduction

While the internationalisation of the higher education sector has been practised at varying degrees within different historical and political timeframes in Vietnam, the country has truly exercised its engagement in internationalisation activities for the past few decades following the *Đổi Mới*. The literature on higher education internationalisation in Vietnam has significantly been enriched by local and international researchers who cover a wide range of aspects from government commitment and initiatives (Dang, 2011; Hayden & Lam, 2007; Hoang, Tran, & Pham, 2018; L. T. Tran & Marginson, 2018a; L. T. Tran et al., 2014; Welch, 2010), student and educational provision mobility (C. H. Nguyen, 2013, 2018), student experiences and institutional practices (Chalapati, Chalapati, &

T. T. Nhan (✉)
Melbourne Graduate School of Education, The University of Melbourne, Melbourne, VIC, Australia
e-mail: thuy.nhan@unimelb.edu.au

K. A. T. Le
Hanoi National University of Education, Hanoi, Vietnam

© The Author(s) 2019
C. H. Nguyen and M. Shah (eds.), *Quality Assurance in Vietnamese Higher Education*, https://doi.org/10.1007/978-3-030-26859-6_2

Weibl, 2015; A. T. Nguyen, 2009; D. P. Nguyen, Vickers, Ly, & Tran, 2016, 2018; Phan, 2017; L. T. Tran et al., 2014; Welch, 2012; Wilmoth, 2004; Ziguras & Pham, 2017), to issues of accountability and quality assurance (Q. T. N. Do, 2018; Ly, 2013; Nhan & Nguyen, 2018). It is generally agreed that with growing national interests, Vietnamese higher education is an emerging yet a proactive player in the regional and global landscape of higher education internationalisation. In the meantime, there still exist very pronounced areas of weaknesses that need to be redressed so that the level of concerted engagement in internationalising the sector can be elevated. This chapter reviews different dimensions in the internationalisation process of Vietnamese higher education, including a statistical overview of student, programme and provider mobility, the national policy framework and institutional practices.

Internationalisation of Vietnamese Higher Education: Key Drivers and a Statistical Overview

The drivers for countries' efforts in internationalising higher education are generally widely known and closely related to national policies and strategic planning. The higher education sector in Vietnam is driven towards internationalisation by a number of political, social, economic and academic factors (Pham, 2018a; L. T. Tran & Marginson, 2018a) and has expanded as a result of both the government's planned moves and the public's spontaneous demand. Following the downfall of the socialist states in the late 1980s, Vietnam has expanded its diplomatic and economic network to the world, especially by marking its key membership in the Association of Southeast Asian Nations (ASEAN) and the Asia Free Trade Area in 1995, the Asia Pacific Economic Cooperation in 1998, and more recently the World Trade Organization in 2007.

The wealth of benefits that are expected out of the internationalisation process are consistently recognised in the Vietnamese government's strategic planning and policies. Vietnam is among emerging economies that have grown strongly and thus is in great demand for a workforce of adequate size, structure and quality that can sustain and further advance its socio-economic development (British Council, 2012; Dang, 2011; Gribble, 2011; L. T. Tran & Marginson, 2018a; Trung & Swierczek, 2009; Ziguras & Pham, 2017). In the 2017 report released by the General Statistics Office of Vietnam (GSO), the country had over 800,400 underemployed and 1.1 million unemployed labourers. College, university graduates and postgraduates occupied the largest share of 53.8% among the unemployed population who had undertaken technical and qualification training of 3 months and over. A trend reported by the International Labour Office (2016) is that tertiary graduates in underdeveloped and developing countries have a greater likelihood to be unemployed than workers with lower educational levels due to the gap between the level of educational attainment and the availability of matching jobs and expectations. Not a small number of publications have documented persistent issues in terms of the labour force in Vietnam, especially drawing attention to the lack of graduate work-readiness and the mismatch between graduate attributes and industries' needs (e.g. Gribble, 2011; Hayden & Lam, 2010; Nankervis, Prikshat, & Cameron, 2018; L. T. Tran et al., 2014; Trung & Swierczek, 2009; World Bank, 2013). In addition to this, Vietnam's labour productivity is reported to be low in comparison with that of neighbouring countries (GSO, 2016a) and to lag far behind the productivity level of average workers in higher-income economies (International Labour Office, 2016). A focus on massifying the higher education sector without adequate attention to the quality aspects is argued to be the problem (L. T. Tran et al., 2014). The Vietnamese government is well aware that unless the situation is addressed, an increasing burden will be placed on the country's economic and social development. It, therefore, aspires to lean on an internationalised higher education sector to boost its socio-economic growth, human capacity and competitiveness.

The proliferation in economic wealth also means an increase in household income and the number of affluent Vietnamese who can afford and are willing to pay for quality higher education. Vietnam currently has the fastest-growing middle class in Southeast Asia (Jennings, 2016; Trines,

2017) who can spend generously on education by up to 5.4 times compared with the country's lowest-income groups (GSO, 2016b). The rapidly increasing tertiary enrolment and the expansion of educational provision and capacity still fall short of the large volume of domestic tertiary demand (Pham, 2018a). Statistics from Vietnam Ministry of Education and Training (MoET) for the 2012 intake shows that 1.3 million students applied to universities and half a million applied to colleges while the total capacity at 234 universities and 185 colleges could only accommodate 30% of places. International qualifications and credentials, therefore, tap into the unmet demand and, more importantly, add a competitive advantage to employability and mobility, especially when the massification of higher education also means that it is more challenging for graduates to differentiate themselves in the labour market (Gribble, 2011; Mok, 2013; Van Damme, 2001).

Knight (2014) and Youssef (2014) identify three forms of mobility in an internationalisation process of higher education: people mobility refers to the movement of students across borders; programme mobility covers a range of cross-border partnerships such as franchise, double degrees, virtual distance and joint programmes; and provider mobility includes the establishment of branch campuses and institutions in receiving countries. The internationalisation of Vietnamese higher education is currently dominated by the outbound mobility of students and an inbound movement of partnerships in education provision and is characterised by policy borrowing and importing practices.

Mobility of Students

Data availability on the mobility of Vietnamese students relies mostly on reports by host countries and international institutions such as World Bank, British Council and UNESCO. Information is less systematically collected in Vietnam but often a much larger figure for outward mobility is reported to include students enrolled in vocational, language and short-term courses based on reports from embassies (Ziguras & Pham, 2017). In 2009, Vietnam had around 43,000 students studying abroad and was listed among the countries with the fastest-growing outbound student flows following China, India, Germany and South Korea (British Council, 2012). By 2017, the figure has increased to 70,328 according to data from UNESCO Institute for Statistics (UIS, 2018) (Table 2.1) while MoET's press release quotes a much larger number, with 130,000 Vietnamese students studying overseas in 2016. From OECD's database (Pham, 2018a), Vietnam was placed 14th among sending countries of students in 2010 and has now moved to the top 10 senders (Table 2.2). The outbound mobility ratios also increased from 2.4% to 3.0% in the 2011–2017 period. This ratio is defined as the percentage of students from a given country studying overseas over its total enrolment in higher education and combines four variables, namely household incomes, trend factors, exchange rate and domestic tertiary sector capacity (British Council,

Table 2.1 Student mobility

Indicators	2011	2012	2013	2014	2015	2016	2017
Inbound	3717	3996	3608	2540	2874	5624	–
Outbound	52,396	54,081	55,973	59,356	68,038	70,326	70,328
Outbound mobility ratio	2.4	2.4	2.5	2.2	2.8	3.0	–

Source UIS, data accessed on 2 July 2018

Table 2.2 Top 10 countries of outbound mobile tertiary students

Countries	2011	2012	2013	2014	2015	2016	2017
China	656,205	701,393	719,202	768,278	818,803	847,046	847,259
India	205,650	192,100	190,560	215,103	256,101	277,387	278,383
Germany	113,939	118,025	119,571	117,465	115,900	117,924	117,921
Republic of Korea	128,994	122,046	114,103	110,022	107,836	108,517	108,608
Nigeria	60,171	61,245	65,567	79,337	92,621	95,621	95,619
France	60,333	64,012	76,221	81,580	86,241	90,689	90,708
Kazakhstan	43,364	43,555	54,708	67,012	78,252	89,650	89,660
Saudi Arabia	51,352	64,378	74,855	84,177	86,223	85,288	85,277
Ukraine	37,607	37,425	42,441	49,911	68,279	76,185	76,181
Vietnam	52,396	54,081	55,973	59,356	68,038	70,326	70,328

Source UIS, data accessed on 2 July 2018

2012, p. 41). These rising ratios reflect Vietnam's strong economic outlooks and household incomes, which in turns stimulates greater student mobility overseas.

As shown in Table 2.1, Vietnam experiences a large disparity in the inward and outward flows of students, indicating the strong pull factors of foreign education as opposed to the country's limited appeal to international students. The inflow rose modestly from 3717 to 5624 between 2011 and 2016 (UIS, 2018), though Vietnam International Education Cooperation Department (VIED) (2018b) reported a higher number of 7711 by June 2016, about 93% of which are from ASEAN state members. The two neighbouring countries, Laos and Cambodia, account for the largest share of inbound mobile students, with 1772 and 318 students respectively (UIS, 2016) due to their considerable Vietnamese-speaking communities. MoET ambitiously aspired for 15,000 international students to be enrolled in the national higher education system by 2020 (MoET, 2008b). Given no 'magic' measures undertaken at the governmental and institutional level in the coming years, the target cannot be assumed to be achievable. A combination of issues in relation to legislative and regulatory framework, capacity, quality standards, corruption and language issues have been prohibitive to inbound mobility (Pham, 2018b; L. T. Tran & Marginson, 2018b; L. T. Tran et al., 2014) and apparently the speed at which Vietnam is upgrading and internationalising its higher education still lags far behind the government's aspirations.

The outbound flows of Vietnamese students are highly polarised towards traditional markets. At the Vietnam-Europe Higher Education Forum held in 2016, MoET reported Japan, Australia, the United States, China and the UK, to be the five leading destinations for Vietnamese students, accounting for 29.2%, 23.8%, 21.5%, 10%, and 8.4% respectively, totalling 130,000 students (VietNamNet Bridge, 2016). Both the United States and Japan have reported huge gains in the number of students from Vietnam with an increase of nearly 50% between 2013 and 2015 while other traditional markets have experienced a more stable intake (ICEF Monitor, 2016). By comparison, data from UIS *Global Flow of Tertiary-Level Students* reported half the total number and a different order of leading receiving countries, which are the United States (36.2%), Australia

(27.1%), Japan (19.9%), France (9.1%), and the UK (7.8%); the remaining 31.6% belongs to other destinations (Fig. 2.1). The large difference in the number of Vietnamese students in Japan as informed by MoET and by UIS is noticeable. It is argued that the former includes also the number of students enrolled in non-degree programmes including language training and university preparatory courses (Trines, 2017). According to UIS, Vietnam is the 6th sending country following China, India, Korea, Saudi Arabia, and Canada, while the country is in the 5th primary sources of students to Australia, following China, India, Malaysia and Nepal. A number of factors that contribute to the choices of Vietnamese students include the historical and cultural alliance history, bilateral and multilateral agreements including available scholarships to Vietnamese students, the brand power of higher education institutions overseas, and employment and migration prospects (C. H. Nguyen, 2013). As commented by ICEF Monitor (2016), both the United States and the UK have long been leading attraction for international students due to the ranking and prestige that their educational quality holds.

In the meantime, Vietnamese students are also extending their mobility to institutions within the region. The nature of East Asian societies being hierarchical (Wong & Wu, 2011) and brand-conscious (Ashwill, 2015; ICEF Monitor, 2016) also means institutional reputation and rankings bear significant appeal (C. H. Nguyen, 2013), contributing to this intra-regional mobility of Vietnamese students. Notably, Singapore,

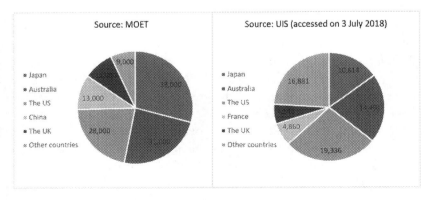

Fig. 2.1 Approximate numbers of Vietnamese students in selected host countries

South Korea, China, Hong Kong and Malaysia are among emerging Asian regional hubs that have been recognised for educational capacity and quality with global top 50 institutions, such as National University of Singapore, Nanyang Technological University Singapore, Tsinghua University China, The University of Hong Kong, Peking University China and The Hong Kong University of Science and Technology (QS World University Rankings, 2018) to name a few. Apparently, the economic prospects in the region's emerging industrialised economies such as China, Singapore and Korea (Pham, 2018a) together with cost differentials and geographical proximity are other factors that further stimulate the shift in the student flow to regional higher education institutions (Gribble, 2011; ICEF Monitor, 2016). Many of these countries are offering attractive incentives in terms of employment and residency for graduating international students. In addition to that, the establishment of the ASEAN Economic Community (AEC) in 2015, and ASEAN's *Common Space of Higher Education* plan, or the *University Mobility in Asia and the Pacific* framework are regional efforts to facilitate student mobility, credit transfers, quality assurance and research clusters (ASEAN Secretariat, 2017; Van Damme, 2001). Vietnam has been active in identifying itself with the ASEAN (British Council, 2017, 2018), and this will stimulate further the growth in the inbound and outbound mobility of its students.

Among the outbound figures, almost all Vietnamese students overseas are self-funded. Statistics from the VIED (2018b) shows that by June 2016, there are 5422 awardees under different state-funded scholarship schemes. The two largest-scale ones are Project 911 *Vietnamese Government PhD Scholarship Programme for University Lecturers for the 2010–2020 Period* (under Decision No. 911/QD-TTg dated 17/6/2010) and Project 599 *Training Cadres Abroad Using State Budget for the 2013–2020 Period* (Decision No. 599/QD-TTg dated 17/4/2013) in addition to scholarship schemes under bilateral government agreements with 19 foreign partners (VIED, 2018b). Project 911 targets to train 1200–1500 doctoral degree holders for universities and colleges annually in such quality education systems as the United States, the UK, Australia, Canada or France, while Project 599 serves to train Vietnamese personnel in bachelor's and master's level of study. Around 1300 key personnel are selected to be sent to countries that Vietnam has long alliance history with; notably around 800–1000 scholarships are offered by Russia each year (VIED, 2018b).

Mobility of Programmes and Providers

While the mobility of programmes and providers in Vietnam has not been as active as that of students, its participation in WTO in particular has paved the way for all the four modes of supply in educational services as specified in WTO's General Agreement on Trade in Services (GATS) (Varghese, 2009) to be present in the national market (Table 2.3) (G. Nguyen & Shillabeer, 2013). Vietnam is mostly characterised as an importing destination adopting 'whole package' Western programmes and standards (Q. A. Le, 2016; Nhan & Nguyen, 2018; Phan, 2017) and educational services and providers have been increasingly diverse in forms and disciplines.

Among educational providers that are mobile to Vietnam, RMIT Vietnam and British University Vietnam are the two cross-border higher education institutions with 100% foreign funds operating in the country at the moment. RMIT Vietnam has one campus in Ho Chi Minh City and another in Hanoi. The newly established British University Vietnam is a

Table 2.3 Forms of cross-border educational programmes and providers in Vietnam

GATS' modes of supply	Forms of presence in Vietnam
Cross-border education: services crossing the border while consumers still inland	E-learning, massive open online courses (MOOCs)
Consumption abroad: physical movement of customers across border	A fulltime, exchange or joint degree programmes
Commercial presence: a commercial presence of providers in a foreign country to render service	Local branches (e.g. RMIT University Vietnam), twinning partnerships, franchising arrangements
Presence of natural persons: temporary travel of academics to provide such services as intensive courses, seminars or workshops	Foreign professors, teachers, researchers working or delivering workshops and seminars in Vietnam (e.g. Carnegie Mellon University providing training and workshops to Vietnamese professionals)

special case as it is supported by a consortium of top UK institutions, such as University of London and Staffordshire University, enabling students to take the same courses and receive the qualifications as those offered in the home institutions. In addition to these cases, four universities were established between 2008 and 2014 under intergovernmental agreements between Vietnam and a foreign partner in the hope of creating new role models of internationalised and research universities (Hoang et al., 2018). These comprise Vietnamese—German University, Vietnamese—Russian University, Vietnamese—Japanese University, and University of Science and Technology of Hanoi. Vietnam—UK Standard State University (currently known as VNUK Institute for Research and Executive Education) will be set up under the support of the governments of Vietnam and the UK (VNUK, 2016) together with Vietnam–Japan, Vietnam–Russia, and Vietnam–United States universities for the same purposes as the four mentioned earlier.

Compared with provider mobility, programme mobility is more common. Programme mobility is in the forms of twinning and joint programmes depending on whether local institutions are involved in conferring qualifications and where students complete their study (see Hoang et al., 2018). By 2018, the total number of collaborative programmes licensed by MoET, the two national universities (Vietnam National University Hanoi and Vietnam National University Ho Chi Minh), three regional universities (The University of Hue, The University of Danang, and The University of Thai Nguyen University) and Hanoi University of Science and Technology is 525 according to VIED (2018a). Among these, courses at doctoral, master's and bachelor's levels represent 2.5%, 42.7%, and 48.8%, respectively. Most of the programmes are offered by local universities in partnership with France (103), the United States (82), the UK (81), Australia (49), China (34), and Taiwan (31). Until 2016, 17,709 students graduated from collaborative programmes at the bachelor level in the total 42,725 enrolments; 23,325 graduated from master-degree programmes among 36,900 enrolments; and there was a total of 459 students enrolled in doctoral programmes (Thanh Nien News, 2017). Business and management related studies are the most popular, making up over two-thirds of the total figure. However, MoET aims to cap the number of graduates of these majors and encourages areas that are vital to the country's economic development, such as technology, engineering and medicine (APEC Secretariat, 2015).

Regarding the viability of programme and provider mobility in Vietnam, collaborative programmes between local and foreign higher education institutions will continue to grow due to their strong potential in facilitating the transfer of knowledge, students and research across borders compared with the establishment of offshore campuses as contended by APEC Secretariat (2015). Meanwhile, online modalities such as MOOCs, despite their advantage of flexibility and affordability, have not prevailed traditional face-to-face learning (APEC Secretariat, 2015) due to their resource-intensive requirements. There is only one MOOC launched in 2013 (RMIT Vietnam News, 2017) which has shown no advances so far.

Practices in the Internationalisation of Higher Education in the National Policy Framework

Internationalising the higher education sector is now among the most commonly cited preoccupation in the strategic agenda of countries around the globe. The British Council has conducted a number of research into national strategies and legislation to identify the level of national support that countries in different regions reserve for internationalising their higher education. In the two most recent publications, *The shape of global higher education: International mobility of students, research and education provision* (British Council, 2017) and *The shape of global higher education: Understanding the ASEAN region* (British Council, 2018), Vietnam is characterised as having a regulatory framework and infrastructure that are highly facilitative to global engagement and institutional success in comparison with its regional counterparts (Fig. 2.2). On a scale of 10, Vietnam scores *very high* in terms of quality assurance and degree recognition, evidencing strong governmental-level commitment in developing, supporting and monitoring transnational higher education activities. The regulatory framework that reflects the government's efforts in elevating its higher education to world-class standards has been extensively reviewed by local and international researchers (see Hoang et al., 2018; A. T. Nguyen, 2009; N. Nguyen & Tran, 2018).

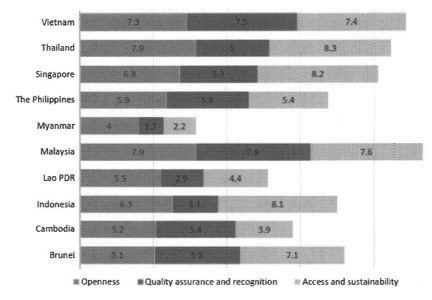

Fig. 2.2 ASEAN countries and the national frameworks for internationalising higher education (adapted from British Council [2012, 2017, 2018])

In 2015, interviews were conducted for the OECD and the APEC Secretariat with policymakers, agencies, and local practitioners from eight APEC economies who are directly engaged in transnational higher education. It is agreed that policies must be in place to facilitate cross-border higher education mobility; however, 'the current situation is one in which policies and regulations are not always conducive' to internationalisation activities (APEC Secretariat, 2015, p. 6). Concerns for quality, for instance, tend to result in complex regulations which can add to practical constraints in the implementation. Key representatives from Vietnam's VIED (MoET), International Cooperation Department (MoET), General Department of Educational Testing and Quality Accreditation (MoET), British Council Vietnam, The University of Queensland, RMIT International University Vietnam, and Hanoi University, who participated in the study, acknowledged the challenges of regulating transnational higher education activities since these involve foreign institutions.

The remaining part of this chapter explores activities across core domains in higher education in the context of Vietnam's policy and regulatory environment. Aspects to be examined include establishing and maintaining international partnerships, internationalising curricula, enhancing research capacity and performing quality assurance.

Expanding International Partnerships

The government of Vietnam places high importance on international partnerships in education as encapsulated in its strategic policies. The Higher Education Reform Agenda (HERA) was introduced in 2005 as a framework for higher education reform until 2020, in which the government strongly aspires to internationalise the sector (The Government of Vietnam, 2005). In its Law on Education 2005 (38/2005/QH11), the state is committed to giving priority to investment in education, including foreign investment (National Assembly of Vietnam, 2005) and the 2012 Law on Higher Education (08/2012/QH13) specifically encourages the mobility of students, academics, and researchers into and out of Vietnam by means of branch campuses, collaborative programmes, representative offices, and promotion events (National Assembly of Vietnam, 2012). For foreign education providers, in addition to a clear, transparent, and consistent procedure for visa granting and educational establishments, the country offers different incentives in the form of tax breaks and land use incentives (The Government of Vietnam, 2005) as seen in the establishment of RMIT University Vietnam. For local institutions, a number of commitments have been articulated by the government of Vietnam, such as increasing institutional autonomy (The Prime Minister, 2006), improving institutional teaching and research capacity through scholarship projects and collaborative partnerships, and mobilising resources, specialists, and finance (National Assembly of Vietnam, 2012; The Government of Vietnam, 2005). MoET is also drafting its 'Internationalisation of Higher Education Strategy (IHES) for Vietnam for the 2017-2025 period', focusing on operationalising those commitments to support institutions in expanding their regional and international network.

The above-mentioned policy environment, in general, has enabled the internationalisation landscape in Vietnamese higher education to be more dynamic. A growing number of institutions have actively formed and expanded cross-border teaching and research partnerships. As of 2015, the state funded 10 partnerships with foreign providers while the remaining 422 ones were self-financed by institutions themselves (Canadian Bureau for International Education, 2017). A sizeable number of foreign providers offering educational services in Vietnam are ranked in the world's top universities, indicating that the quality aspect of international partnerships has been attended to, especially as some institutions are now more selective about who they partner with and for what purpose. Vietnam National University Hanoi, for example, defines strategic partnerships as long-term, intensive cooperation in collaborative research, technology transfer and knowledge exchange (Vietnam National University Hanoi, n.d.). The university, therefore, is consolidating its established relations while at the same time reaching out for institutions, research institutes and organisations that lead the region and in the world. It currently boasts 135 partnerships, including those with top institutions from the United States, the UK, France, Japan, France, Korea and China, and deepens its engagement with the Asia Pacific by expanding its memberships to East Asian Universities Group (BESETOHA), ASEAN University Network (AUN), University Mobility in Asia and the Pacific (UMAP), Association of Southeast Asian Institutions of Higher Learning (ASAIHL), and Southeast and South Asia and Taiwan Universities (SATU). This direction closely aligns with the country's motivation in confirming its presence and engagement in the region.

It is worth noting that Vietnam National University Hanoi is among a very limited number of institutions that enjoy a high level of autonomy and support from the central government (Table 2.4). The current policy environment is still a barrier for a majority of institutions in initiating and maintaining partnerships. The Communist Party maintains a highly state-centric control of educational provision, resulting in a lengthy approval process and complex overlapping functions between overseeing authorities (T. T. Tran, 2014) plus increasing restrictions on foreign providers. For example, to ensure only reputable education providers penetrate the

Table 2.4 Decision-making power in Vietnamese higher education

Types of institutions	Supervising authorities	Decision-making power
2 national universities	Prime Minister	Highest
3 regional and 14 key universities	MoET	High
More than 100 other universities	MoET and line ministries	
Provincial universities	MoET, line ministries, and provincial authorities	

M. H. Do (2014) and Q. M. Le (2011)

national market, Decree 86/2018/ND-CP (The Government of Vietnam, 2018), as a replacement to Decree 73/2012/ND-CP (The Government of Vietnam, 2012), tightens the regulations on foreign cooperation and investment in education in terms of investment capital, programme accreditation and foreign teachers' qualifications. While Vietnam has a comprehensive set of regulations and legal frameworks to monitor foreign providers and international partnerships operating inland, most of the focus so far has been on the quantity and inputs rather than quality and outcomes (Ziguras & Pham, 2017). It is also the case that many Vietnamese institutions lack adequate funding and capacity to initiate and sustain relationships. This has resulted in institutional practices being dominated by narrow, fragmented and intradisciplinary engagement and by expansion in terms of quantity rather than quality, which has scarcely impacted on faculty and institutional capacity. Institutions generally take offerings from foreign providers with great excitement and do not have stringent procedures or criteria to consider the ranking and reputation of partner institutions, causing diploma mills to proliferate in the country.

One policy area that is often neglected is the promotion of the country's educational services and the support for Vietnamese students overseas. Decision 05/2013/QD-TTg identifies one of the responsibilities of Vietnamese representative agencies in foreign countries to be to

> [...] develop and expand the cooperation with educational institutions and governments of host countries; find sources of scholarships for Vietnamese students; study the policies and education system of host countries to advise

the Government and other agencies concerned in the development of Vietnamese education; send students overseas to study in fields of study that meet the needs of human resource development of Vietnam. (The Prime Minister, 2013)

In practice, apart from VIED and International Cooperation Department (MoET), Vietnam does not have dedicated agencies overseas that can organise education exhibitions and marketing events to promote the national education and programmes. Embassies of Vietnam have not been active in this respect and the large cohort of Vietnamese students, alumni, academics and communities overseas has not been targeted as a networking resource for research and teaching activities. Most collaborative programmes are the 'bottom-up' outcome of personal connections between local staff and overseas partners before being institutionalised (APEC Secretariat, 2015).

Internationalising Curricula

Wong and Wu (2011) reiterate Maurice Harari's (1992) claim that curriculum lies at the heart of internationalisation. Essentially, an internationalised curriculum is grounded on institutions' capacity to cater to a diversity of backgrounds and provide graduates with global perspectives and intercultural competencies (Leask, 2009; Yang, 2017). Examples of international perspectives expected of internationalised curricula include the ability to think globally while being aware of one's own and others' cultures and appreciating multicultural diversity to one's professional practice (University of South Australia's graduate quality, cited in Leask, 2001, p. 106). Internationalising the curriculum, therefore, is not confined to the pure inclusion of some international contents (Van Damme, 2001) but embraces the richness of pedagogical and learning strategies (Leask, 2001). Internationalised curricula in OECD's typology (IDP Education Australia, 1995) are characterised as (i) preparing graduates for defined international professions, (ii) leading to internationally recognised professional qualifications, (iii) leading to joint or double degrees in international and language studies, (iv) compulsory components being offered at or by universities abroad, staffed by local lecturers, (v) involving an international subject or area or language studies, (vi) interdisciplinary programmes, (vii) traditional subject area being broadened by international cross-cultural or intercultural approaches, (viii) curricula in foreign languages or linguistics that explicitly address cross-cultural communication issues and that provide training in intercultural skills, and (ix) curricula in which the content is specially designed for overseas students.

Reflecting on these characteristics, tertiary curricula in Vietnam have been narrowly interpreted and practised to be considered internationalised. The spotlight of a so-called internationalised curriculum has always been on several traditional courses now being instructed in a foreign language, whole-package courses imported from foreign curriculum, or joint and double degrees conferred by foreign providers operating in conjunction with a local institution (L. T. Tran & Marginson, 2018a). The government has in place policies to promote cutting-edge knowledge and skills, linguistic competence, and intercultural awareness for students, with the introduction of 'advanced curricula' in 2004 (A. T. Nguyen, 2009), English as a medium of instruction in selected courses, 'advanced programmes', and the 'Vietnam New Model Universities' project in 2008 (Pham, 2018a; L. T. Tran et al., 2014; L. T. Tran & Nguyen, 2018; L. T. Tran, Phan, & Marginson, 2018). The promotion of courses delivered in English is part of the ambitious 'National Foreign Language Initiative 2020', which aspires to train Vietnamese graduates who are able to 'use a foreign language confidently in their daily communication, their study, and work in an integrated, multicultural and multilingual environment' (MoET, 2008b, p. 1). Meanwhile, the task of designing 'advanced curricula', mostly in relation to science and technology disciplines, has been assigned to institutions since 2004 (The Prime Minister, 2004) and operationalised in 37 'advanced programmes' at 24 Vietnamese universities as of December 2016 (Dan Tri News, 2016). MoET (2008a) demands institutions base their 'advanced programmes' on the curricula, teaching methods, training management procedures and language of instruction on courses offered by the top 200 reputed institutions in the world. The most visible benefits for learners directly engaged in these schemes so far are in terms of improved language skills and employability (L. T. Tran et al., 2018). The enrichment in terms of international perspectives is yet questionable, especially when these government-led schemes so far have not been successful in attracting foreign students to allow for the inclusion of internationally cultural richness. After a decade of implementation, a truly internationalised curriculum can be said to remain a goal.

For one thing, students graduating from advanced programmes have commented on the loose connection with their industry and professional network (Dan Tri News, 2016). The lack of stable and quality faculty remains a constant concern, especially as courses are taught by fly-in-fly-out foreign academics who can only undertake very short-term teaching assignments and by local lecturers who themselves find foreign language and pedagogical expertise to develop learners' skills in unfamiliar sociocultural environments a challenge (Dan Tri News, 2016; A. T. Nguyen, 2009; Vu & Burns, 2014). The English-as-a-medium of instruction policy, in particular, has not been accompanied by systematic training and professional development for lecturers to deliver content matter in a foreign language in any higher education institutions. For another, entirely importing foreign curricula without examining cultural relevancy has been argued to result in identity clashes and abstract learners from their local contexts (Chalapati et al., 2015; V. H. Nguyen & Hamid, 2015; Phan, 2017). Observing the implementation of advanced programmes, A. T. Nguyen (2009) contends that 'an Asian dimension is rarely found in this aspect of internationalization of higher education because Vietnam wants to access and capture the so-called source technology in higher education, which is believed to belong to Western countries' (p. 18). It is worth reiterating that internationalising curricula is not only about the delivery of contents but also pedagogies that can cater to diverse cultures, perspectives and experiences (Banks, 2004). Alternatively stated, the Westernised format of delivering lectures, tutorials and learning strategies that are imported together with the subject matter in these programmes can alienate local students who are familiar with the Vietnamese learning expectations and values. 'Advanced programmes' and 'new model universities' so far have only aimed at a small proportion of students who can afford the costs and are competent users of a foreign language (L. T. Tran & Marginson, 2018a). This way of interpreting and practising the internationalisation of curricula is very narrow in contrast with current practices of highly internationalised higher education systems around the world. As emphasised by

Leask (2013), 'universities have a responsibility to provide an internationalised curriculum to *all* students' and 'we must move away from focusing on isolated projects and activities focused on a few students, completely ignoring the fact that all graduates will work in a global setting' (2013, p. 102). Vietnamese institutions need to be aware that not every student will be able to study abroad; 'internationalisation at home' should be practised so that all students will be equipped with the skills and knowledge required of global citizens.

Enhancing Research Capacity

The implication that Horta (2009) and Marginson (2006) draw from leading research universities is that student and faculty structure needs to be built to reflect the primary mission of enhancing institutional research capacity. In other words, teaching activities are geared towards an internationalised student cohort at graduate level, especially doctoral programmes, and faculty members must be identified with international teaching and research profiles. Funding schemes based on performance and equity are also found to be effective in boosting research quality and research capacity (Horta, 2009; World Bank, 2008).

Reflecting on the developed world's strategies, the Vietnamese government can be said to have made sizeable efforts in enhancing the research capacity for the national higher education system. National policymakers are well aware of the two tasks that need to be accomplished, namely massifying higher education services in response to local and national demands and simultaneously building elite universities that can compete globally in terms of teaching, training and research (World Bank, 2008). To assist the allocation of limited state resources, 19 institutions so far have been included in the list of 'key' universities according to the Prime Minister's Decision 37/2013/QD-TTg in the hope that they can model the quality in research and training, especially in priority areas for the development of the country, and then can be enlisted among the top universities in the world. The 'Vietnam New Model Universities' project also reiterates the government's aspirations to upgrade national institutions to become research universities with global standards of excellence (Hoang et al.,

2018). Both key universities and those of smaller capacity are encouraged to cooperate with international researchers and scientists to improve their training and research capacity (Hoang et al., 2018). Between 2016 and 2017, Vietnamese universities signed 2142 agreements with international and regional organisations and institutions and received 3214 foreign experts and lecturers to deliver lectures and conduct research in Vietnam, with Can Tho University, Vietnam National University Hanoi, and Hanoi Medical University among the top host institutions (Daidoanket News, 2017; Nhandannews, 2018). Encouraging academic research output is another national measure and the country has witnessed an annual increase of 20% in the publication volume since 2002 (Manh, 2015). A considerable number of publications were attributed to the government establishing the National Foundation for Science and Technology Development (NAFOSTED) in 2008 (Manh, 2015). NAFOSTED aims to encourage engagement in international research by funding Vietnamese institutions and researchers in a multitude of social and natural sciences areas, hosting international conferences and training programmes, and co-funding bilateral and multilateral research collaboration with other countries and agencies, especially in costly and under-researched areas such as health, medical and biological studies. For instance, NAFOSTED networks with Australian National Health and Medical Research Council (NHMRC) to grant funding to collaborative research projects on infectious diseases, maternal and child health, and public health (NHMRC, 2018) or recently signs a memorandum of understanding with the British Academy and Royal Academy of Engineering to launch mobility grants to support research projects in the field of engineering, social sciences and humanity (NAFOSTED, n.d.). All these examples show that initiatives and funding schemes exist to enable the engagement of Vietnamese institutions in international research.

Despite efforts, ambitious targets are far from being achieved as Vietnam has not been able to elevate the amount of research funding and upgrade its incentive, communication and monitoring system to a decisive level that can generate changes. Examining the volume of Vietnam's publications from Scopus database between 1996 and 2013, Manh (2015) found that 77% of the publications are contributed by primary researchers from Japan, the United States, France, Korea, and the UK, in co-authorship with

Vietnamese ones. While this signifies an increasingly wide network and integration that Vietnamese academics have with the world, it also marks a stage in which national research output still depends much on collaborative research. NAFOSTED receives a modest sum of 10 million USD annually, which comprises only 1.3% of the total government expenditure on science (Manh, 2015). On a national level, the investment in research as a proportion of GDP in Vietnam as of 2013 was 0.4% compared with other economies in Asia and the Pacific, such as Korea (4.2%), Japan (3.3%), Singapore (2.2%), China (2.1%) and Malaysia (1.3%) (Asian Development Bank, 2017, p. 58). Expenditure on research in Vietnamese higher education, in particular, is considerably low, accounting for around 75 million USD for five years between 2011 and 2015 (Saigongiaiphong Online, 2017). As this means inadequate infrastructure for high-tech studies, research projects in Vietnam primarily concentrate on areas that resort to pure mathematics and theories (World Bank, 2008) and the publication output lags far behind countries whose governments spend aggressively on higher education research. The gross domestic expenditure on research in universities of Singapore, Thailand and Malaysia is 28.8% (2010), 24.9% (2009) and 28.9% (2011) respectively (UIS, 2014, p. 35), which corresponds with prolific research output (Fig. 2.3). Vietnam has expanded its graduate education to account for a significant share of the

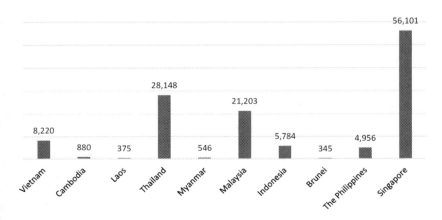

Fig. 2.3 Research output by Southeast Asian countries 2001–2010 (T. V. Nguyen & Pham, 2011, p. 11)

student cohort, with 15,112 students enrolled in 971 doctoral courses at 158 graduate schools and research institutes nationwide and 105,801 students at master's level in 2017 (VietnamNet, 2017a; VietnamNews, 2016). Lenient entry and exit requirements for doctoral programmes are yet argued to have led to a massive rise in the number of doctoral students to the extent of a so-called PhD inflation (VietnamNews, 2016). Graduate programmes, in other words, have not supported the production of new knowledge and scientific research that can contribute to the internationalisation of the higher education sector.

Performing Quality Assurance

Quality assurance has increasingly become a 'brand name' for education systems, providers and programmes (Chan, 2011) as it involves ongoing evaluation of the quality of provision (Q. T. N. Do, 2018). Despite only recently initiating its quality accreditation and assurance system (SEAMEO RIHED, 2012), Vietnam has made important strides in developing a comprehensive framework that can enable it to monitor the operation of foreign providers and programmes inland. The country has also been proactive in participating in regional mechanisms such as the ASEAN Quality Assurance Network, Asia-Pacific Quality Network, or the International Network for Quality Assurance and Accreditation in Higher Education (INQAAHE) (SEAMEO RIHED, 2012). This is among efforts for collaboration on quality assurance and credit recognition that can further facilitate the mobility of students, academics and programmes (H. C. Nguyen, 2017).

Similar to China, Hong Kong and Singapore, Vietnam employs a moderately liberal regulatory model to monitor foreign institutions and programmes operating onshore (G. Nguyen & Shillabeer, 2013). MoET retains control for the fear of low-quality providers and programmes to enter the country. Therefore, it demands foreign institutions to have their programmes accredited in their home country or by Vietnamese accreditation agencies before being offered to Vietnamese students (The Government of Vietnam, 2018). Twining and joint programmes between a local and a foreign institution need to be licensed by either MoET or a few national or regional universities while foreign institutions can establish their own legal teaching and research entities in Vietnam with the approval from the Prime Minister under Decree 86/2018/ND-CP on foreign investment in education and training (The Government of Vietnam, 2018). Following their establishment, licensed providers or programmes are subject to legal regulations, including financial and quality commitment for the life of the courses, a condition that was tightened under Decree 73/2012/ND-CP and recently Decree 86/2018/ND-CP. Another area that Vietnam is paying special attention to in order to support education mobility concerns credentials recognition. According to Decision 77/2007/QD-BGDDT, qualifications from collaborative programmes are recognised on the condition that the programmes are accredited in the home country and approved for operation by Vietnam MoET (MoET, 2007). Foreign providers with branch campuses based in Vietnam can issue qualifications upon satisfying conditions specified in Decree 86/2018/ND-CP (The Government of Vietnam, 2018). MoET has a designated agency, the National Recognition Information Centre (VN-NARIC), which has the function of recognising the qualifications of international students and verifying the qualifications of Vietnamese students graduating from foreign institutions (VN NARIC, n.d.). In a recent move towards degree recognition, the Prime Minister has approved the Vietnam National Qualification Framework (NQF), which describes 8 levels of skills and knowledge that learners are expected to demonstrate from elementary certificates to doctoral degrees, and the National Vocational Qualifications Framework (NVQF). Vietnam designs this reference system to benchmark educational outcomes of its graduates against the ASEAN Qualifications Reference Framework to facilitate mobility in education and employment between the country and other ASEAN member states (VietnamNet, 2017b).

While MoET strives to enforce quality control over foreign providers and collaborative programmes, this remains a challenge due to limited resources and overlapping in the governance between different ministries involved in overseeing cross-border partnerships. The overlapping in the functions of different ministries could be seen in the case of Singapore Melior Business School, which operated under the supervision of MoET,

Ministry of Planning and Investment, Minister of Labour, and Department of War Invalids and Social Affairs, each with its own governance model yet still failing to timely intervene in the school's malpractices (G. Nguyen & Shillabeer, 2013). MoET encourages institutions to set up their own quality assurance centres that serve to assist self-assessing and self-monitoring of quality of provision. However, investigating institutional practices, Q. T. N. Do (2018) comments that institutions tend to view quality assurance as a pragmatic means of enhancing their public image, increasing tuition fees, and raising student enrolments rather than improving their quality or internal capacity. Partnering with Western institutions is deemed more beneficial as these are generally known to have undergone a demanding quality assurance process in their home economy (APEC Secretariat, 2015). Since higher education in Vietnam is still a loosely controlled market, it has become an attractive destination for malpractices that target uninformed consumers who are lured by foreign qualifications offered at affordable prices (Ashwill, 2015; N. Nguyen, 2018; Nhan & Nguyen, 2018). It is worth noting that MoET has only been able to regulate newly opened courses rather than the whole process in which these are run. The approval process also notoriously depends on paperwork rather than the actual examination of foreign providers and programmes (G. Nguyen & Shillabeer, 2013), leaving some institutions to manipulate the system. In fact, despite the inclusion of quality assurance in the 2005 Law on Higher Education and of quality assurance of partnership with foreign providers in Decree 73/2012/ND-CP, scandalous cases of non-compliance have been reported, leaving thousands of victims (Thanh Nien News, 2017).

Conclusion

While recognising the strategic role of internationalising higher education and aspiring to integrate it in the education system, Vietnam has only been able to elevate this goal to the scale of a supplement to unmet demands and domestic thirst for foreign qualifications. Internationalisation in both policy documents and institutional practices is still confined to several facets of student, programme and academic mobility, thereby not yet being able to lift the country out of a peripheral position both in the regional and global higher education landscape. In stark contrast to the story of Vietnam, where most government-led initiatives remain at macro-level intervention, many Asian counterparts such as Singapore, Malaysia, Japan, South Korea and Hong Kong China are investing more aggressively in their educational hubs and have achieved success in moving from an import-oriented to import-intensive state. A lesson Vietnam can learn from these successes is that internationalising the higher education sector needs to be premised on a combination of a facilitative policy environment, adequate government funding, strong institutional commitment, intensive marketing strategies and a developed quality assurance system. Singapore can be a role model in this respect since it especially attends to the quality aspects and enthusiastically competes for the best students. The government of Singapore is highly selective about the reputation of foreign providers (Mok, 2013) and employs an external panel to regularly validate onsite the practices of local universities against their self-assessment reports (Chan, 2011). From this, institutions' strengths and weaknesses can be identified and ameliorated. The country also places heavy weight on research and generously subsidises international students committed to working in Singapore upon graduation. The government of Singapore considers this as a means of investing in the national economy; alternatively stated, Singapore has integrated higher education internationalisation in its nation-building agenda (Mok, 2013). Overall, Vietnam needs to actively promote the sharing of good practices, develop a coherent and transparent policy and regulatory framework, and at the same time place stricter enforcement on the quality aspects of transnational partnerships.

References

APEC Secretariat. (2015). *Enhancing cross-border higher education institution mobility in the APEC region*. Singapore: APEC.
ASEAN Secretariat. (2017). *ASEAN Economic Community (AEC)*. Jakarta: Association of Southeast Asian Nations.
Ashwill, M. (2015). US institutions find fertile ground in Vietnam's expanding higher education market. *International Higher Education, 44,* 13–14.

Asian Development Bank. (2017). *Key indicators for Asia and the Pacific* (48th ed.). Manila: Asian Development Bank.

Banks, J. A. (2004). Approaches to multicultural curriculum reform. In J. A. Banks & C. A. McGee Banks (Eds.), *Multicultural education: Issues and perspectives* (pp. 242–264). Hoboken: Wiley.

British Council. (2012). *The shape of things to come: Higher education global trends and emerging opportunities to 2020.* Retrieved from https://www.britishcouncil.org/sites/default/files/the_shape_of_things_to_come_-_higher_education_global_trends_and_emerging_opportunities_to_2020.pdf.

British Council. (2017). *The shape of global higher education: International mobility of students, research and education provision.* Retrieved from https://www.britishcouncil.org/sites/default/files/h002_transnational_education_tne_ihe_report_final_web_2.pdf.

British Council. (2018). *The shape of global higher education: Understanding the ASEAN region* (Vol. 3). Retrieved from https://www.britishcouncil.org/sites/default/files/h233_the_shape_of_asean_higher_education_report_final_v2_web_1.pdf.

Canadian Bureau for International Education. (2017). *Vietnam: Insights from an international collaboration mission.* Retrieved from https://cbie.ca/wp-content/uploads/2016/05/MarketReport.pdf.

Chalapati, S., Chalapati, N., & Weibl, G. (2015). European influences on Vietnamese higher education: Internationalised curriculum and cultural challenges. *Australian & New Zealand Journal of European Studies, 7*(2), 45–57.

Chan, D. K. (2011). Internationalization of higher education as a major strategy for developing regional education hubs: A comparison of Hong Kong and Singapore. In J. D. Palmer, A. Roberts, Y. H. Cho, & G. S. Ching (Eds.), *The Internationalization of East Asian higher education: Globalization's impact* (pp. 11–40). New York: Palgrave Macmillan.

Daidoanket News. (2017). *Hội nhập quốc tế trong giáo dục đại học: Những bước chuyển mình* [Improvements made in internationalisation of higher education]. Retrieved from http://daidoanket.vn/xa-hoi/hoi-nhap-quoc-te-trong-giao-duc-dai-hoc-nhung-buoc-chuyen-minh-tintuc378051.

Dan Tri News. (2016). *Chương trình tiên tiến: Thách thức hấp dẫn đối với sinh viên* [Advanced programmes and challenges for students]. Retrieved from http://dantri.com.vn/giao-duc-khuyen-hoc/chuong-trinh-tien-tien-thach-thuc-hap-dan-doi-voi-sinh-vien-20160512153543346.htm.

Dang, Q. A. (2011). *Internationalisation of higher education: China and Vietnam—From importers of education to partners in cooperation* (Master dissertation). Copenhagen Business School, Copenhagen.

Do, M. H. (2014). Towards more flexible organisation. In L. T. Tran, S. Marginson, H. M. Do, T. T. T. Le, N. T. Nguyen, T. T. P. Vu, T. N. Pham, H. T. L. Nguyen, & T. T. H. Ho (Eds.), *Higher education in Vietnam: Flexibility, mobility and practicality in the global knowledge economy* (pp. 55–84). Basingstoke: Palgrave Macmillan.

Do, Q. T. N. (2018). Current perspectives on internationalisation of quality assurance at the institutional level. In L. T. Tran & S. Marginson (Eds.), *Internationalisation in Vietnamese higher education* (pp. 43–54). Cham: Springer.

General Statistics Office of Vietnam (GSO). (2016a). *Báo cáo tóm tắt thực trạng và giải pháp nâng cao năng suất lao động của Việt Nam* [Summary report on Vietnam's labour productivity]. Hanoi: General Statistics Office of Vietnam.

General Statistics Office of Vietnam (GSO). (2016b). *Kết quả khảo sát mức sống dân cư Việt Nam năm 2014* [Data results of the Vietnam household living standards survey 2014]. Hanoi: Statistical Publishing House.

Gribble, C. (2011). National policies on skilled labour and the cross-border student market, with a focus on Vietnam. In S. Marginson, S. Kaur, & E. Sawir (Eds.), *Higher education in the Asia-Pacific* (Vol. 36, pp. 291–307). New York: Springer.

Harari, M. (1992). Internationalization of the curriculum. In C. B. Klasek, B. J. Garavalia, & K. J. Kellerman (Eds.), *Bridges to the future: Strategies for internationalization higher education*. Pullman, WA: Association of International Education Administrators.

Hayden, M., & Lam, Q. T. (2007). A 2020 vision for higher education in Vietnam. *International Higher Education, 44,* 11–13.

Hayden, M., & Lam, Q. T. (2010). Vietnam's higher education system. In G. Harman, M. Hayden, & T. N. Pham (Eds.), *Reforming higher education in Vietnam: Challenges and priorities* (pp. 15–30). London: Springer.

Hoang, L., Tran, L. T., & Pham, H. H. (2018). Vietnamese government policies and practices in internationalisation of higher education. In L. T. Tran & S. Marginson (Eds.), *Internationalisation in Vietnamese higher education* (pp. 19–42). Cham: Springer.

Horta, H. (2009). Global and national prominent universities: Internationalization, competitiveness and the role of the State. *Higher Education, 58,* 387–405.

ICEF Monitor. (2016). *America and Japan reporting big gains in Vietnamese enrolment*. Retrieved from http://monitor.icef.com/2016/04/america-and-japan-reporting-big-gains-in-vietnamese-enrolment/.

IDP Education Australia. (1995). *Curriculum development for internationalisation*. Canberra: IDP Education Australia.

International Labour Office. (2016). *Key indicators of the labour market* (9th ed.). Geneva: International Labour Office.

Jennings, R. (2016). *Growing affluence in Vietnam lures foreign brands*. Retrieved from https://asia.nikkei.com/Business/Trends/Growing-affluence-in-Vietnam-lures-foreign-brands.

Knight, J. (2014). Three generations of crossborder higher education: New developments, issues and challenges. In B. T. Streitwieser (Ed.), *Internationalisation of higher education and global mobility* (pp. 43–58). Didcot: Symposium Books.

Le, Q. A. (2016). The impact of globalisation on the reform of higher education in Vietnam. *International Journal of Business and Economic Affairs, 1*(1), 29–35.

Le, Q. M. (2011, November 28–29). *Good governance in higher education: Concepts, implement and training*. Paper presented at the DIES Conference: Strengthening Universities, Enhancing Capacities—Higher Education Management for Development, Bonn.

Leask, B. (2001). Bridging the gap: Internationalizing university curricula. *Journal of Studies in International Education, 5*(2), 100–115.

Leask, B. (2009). Using formal and informal curricula to improve interactions between home and international students. *Journal of Studies in International Education, 13*(2), 205–221.

Leask, B. (2013). Internationalisation of the curriculum and staff engagement: An introduction. In H. De Wit (Ed.), *An introduction to higher education internationalisation* (pp. 91–106). Milan: Centre for Higher Education Internationalisation.

Ly, T. M. C. (2013). *Critical factors of offshore master of business administration education programmes in Vietnam: Multiple perspectives* (Doctoral dissertation). University of Western Sydney, Sydney, Australia,

Manh, H. D. (2015). Scientific publications in Vietnam as seen from Scopus during 1996–2013. *Scientometrics, 105*(1), 83–95.

Marginson, S. (2006). Dynamics of national and global competition in higher education. *Higher Education, 52*, 1–39.

Ministry of Education and Training (MoET). (2007). *Quyết định ban hành quy định về trình tự, thủ tục công nhận văn bằng của người Việt Nam do co sở giáo *dục nước ngoài cấp* [Decision on promulgating the regulation on order of and procedures for recognizing diplomas granted to Vietnamese by foreign educational institutions]. Hanoi: MoET.

Ministry of Education and Training (MoET). (2008a). *Project for training by advanced curricula in some Vietnamese universities: Period 2008–2015.* Hanoi: MoET.

Ministry of Education and Training (MoET). (2008b). *Quyết định về việc phê duyệt đề án "Dạy và học ngoại ngữ trong hệ thống giáo dục quốc dân giai đoạn 2008–2020"* [Decision on "teaching and learning foreign languages in the national education system in the period 2008–2010" project]. Hanoi: Prime Minister Office.

Mok, K. H. (2013). *The quest for entrepreneurial universities in East Asia.* New York: Palgrave Macmillan.

NAFOSTED. (n.d.). *Short-term research fellowship opportunities in the UL under the NAFOSTED and UK academies programme.* Retrieved from http://www.nafosted.gov.vn/en/news/Funding-Announcement/Short-tem-research-fellowship-opportunities-in-the-UK-under-the-NAFOSTED-and-UK-Academies-programme-52/.

Nankervis, A., Prikshat, V., & Cameron, R. (2018). Graduate work-readiness in Asia Pacific economies. In R. Cameron, S. Dhakal, & J. Burgess (Eds.), *Transitions from education to work: Workforce ready challenges in the Asia* (pp. 28–54). Oxon: Routledge.

National Assembly of Vietnam. (2005). *Law on education.* Hanoi: National Assembly.

National Assembly of Vietnam. (2012). *Law on higher education.* Hanoi: National Assembly.

Nguyen, A. T. (2009). *The internationalisation of higher education in Vietnam: National policies and institutional implementation at Vietnam National University, Hanoi.* Tokyo: Waseda University.

Nguyen, C. H. (2013). Vietnamese international student mobility: Past and current trends. *Asian Education and Development Studies, 2*(2), 127–148.

Nguyen, C. H. (2018a). Historical trends of Vietnamese international student mobility. In L. T. Tran & S. Marginson (Eds.), *Internationalisation in Vietnamese higher education* (pp. 141–160). Cham: Springer.

Nguyen, D. P., Vickers, M., Ly, T. M. C., & Tran, M. D. (2016). Internationalizing higher education (HE) in Vietnam: Insights from higher education leaders–An exploratory study. *Education + Training, 58*(2), 193–208.

Nguyen, G., & Shillabeer, A. (2013). Issues in transnational higher education regulation in Vietnam. In P. Mandal (Ed.), *Proceedings of the international conference on managing the Asian century* (pp. 637–644). Singapore: Springer.

Nguyen, H. C. (2017). Impact of international accreditation on the emerging quality assurance system: The Vietnamese experience. *Change Management: An International Journal, 17*(3), 1–9.

Nguyen, N. (2018b). Transnational education in the Vietnamese market: Paradoxes and possibilities. In L. T. Tran & S. Marginson (Eds.), *Internationalisation in Vietnamese higher education* (pp. 77–98). Cham: Springer.

Nguyen, N., & Tran, L. T. (2018). Looking inward or outward? Vietnam higher education at the superhighway of globalization: Culture, values and changes. *Journal of Asian Public Policy, 11*(1), 28–45.

Nguyen, T. V., & Pham, L. T. (2011). Scientific output and its relationship to knowledge economy: An analysis of ASEAN countries. *Scientometrics, 89*(1), 107–117.

Nguyen, V. H., & Hamid, O. (2015). Educational policy borrowing in a globalized world: A case study of Common European Framework of Reference for languages in a Vietnamese university. *English Teaching: Practice & critique, 14*(1), 60–74.

Nhan, T. T., & Nguyen, H. C. (2018). Quality challenges in transnational higher education under profit-driven motives: The Vietnamese experience. *Issues in Educational Research, 28*(2), 138–152.

Nhandannews. (2018). *Giáo dục đại học với nỗ lực hội nhập quốc tế*. Retrieved from http://www.nhandan.com.vn/giaoduc/item/35589602-giao-duc-dai-hoc-voi-no-luc-hoi-nhap-quoc-te.html.

NHMRC. (2018). *NHMRC-NAFOSTED joint call for collaborative research projects*. Retrieved from https://www.nhmrc.gov.au/grants-funding/apply-funding/nhmrc-nafosted-joint-call-collaborative-research-projects.

Pham, H. H. (2018a). International students' choice of destinations for overseas study: A specific push-pull model for Vietnam. In L. T. Tran & S. Marginson (Eds.), *Internationalisation in Vietnamese higher education* (pp. 161–178). Cham: Springer.

Pham, H. H. (2018b). *Vietnam: Struggling to attract international students*. Retrieved from www.universityworldnews.com/article.php?story=2011121617161637&mode=print.

Phan, L. H. (2017). *Transnational education crossing 'Asia' and 'the West': Adjusted desire, transformative mediocrity and neo-colonial disguise*. New York: Routledge.

QS World University Rankings. (2018). *QS world university rankings 2019.* Retrieved from https://www.topuniversities.com/university-rankings/world-university-rankings/2019.

RMIT Vietnam News. (2017). *MOOCs promise to open up Vietnamese higher education.* Retrieved from https://www.rmit.edu.vn/news/moocs-promise-open-vietnamese-higher-education.

Saigongiaiphong Online. (2017). *Các trường đại học nghiên cứu khoa học chưa xứng tầm* [Limited university research capacity]. Retrieved from http://www.sggp.org.vn/cac-truong-dai-hoc-nghien-cuu-khoa-hoc-chua-xung-tam-471588.html.

SEAMEO RIHED. (2012). *A study on quality assurance models in Southeast Asian countries: Towards a Southeast Asian quality assurance framework.* Bangkok: SEAMEO RIHED.

Thanh Nien News. (2017). *Bê bối chương trình liên kết nước ngoài* [Major issues in the operation of joint programmes]. Retrieved from https://thanhnien.vn/giao-duc/be-boi-chuong-trinh-lien-ket-nuoc-ngoai-881378.html.

The Government of Vietnam. (2005). *Government resolution on substantial and comprehensive renewal of Vietnam's tertiary education in the 2006–2020 period.* Hanoi: The Government.

The Government of Vietnam. (2012). *Decree No. 73/2012/ND-CP on foreign cooperation and investment in education.* Hanoi: The Government.

The Government of Vietnam. (2018). *Decree No. 86/2018/ND-CP on foreign cooperation and investment in education.* Hanoi: The Government.

The Prime Minister. (2004). *Tiếp tục hoàn thiện mạng lưới các trường đại học, cao đẳng* [Continuing to improve the network of universities and colleges]. Hanoi: The Prime Minister.

The Prime Minister. (2006). *Decree No. 43/2006/ND-CP on providing the right to autonomy and accountability for performance of duties, organizational structure, staffing and finance of the public institutions.* Hanoi: The Prime Minister.

The Prime Minister. (2013). *Decision 05/2013/QD-TTg of the Prime Minister on the conditions for granting the certificate for oversea study counseling service registration.* Hanoi: The Prime Minister.

Tran, L. T., & Marginson, S. (2018a). Internationalisation of Vietnamese higher education: An overview. In L. T. Tran & S. Marginson (Eds.), *Internationalisation in Vietnamese higher education* (pp. 1–17). Cham: Springer.

Tran, L. T., & Marginson, S. (Eds.). (2018b). *Internationalisation in Vietnamese higher education.* Cham: Springer.

Tran, L. T., Marginson, S., Do, H. M., Le, T. T. T., Nguyen, N. T., Vu, T. T. P., … Ho, T. T. H. (2014). *Higher education in Vietnam: Flexibility, mobility and practicality in the global knowledge economy*. Basingstoke: Palgrave Macmillan.

Tran, L. T., & Nguyen, H. T. (2018). Internationalisation of higher education in Vietnam through English medium instruction (EMI): Practices, tensions and implications for local language policies. In I. Liyanage (Ed.), *Multilingual education yearbook 2018: Internationalization, stakeholders and multilingual education contexts* (pp. 91–106). Cham: Springer.

Tran, L. T., Phan, H. L. T., & Marginson, S. (2018). The 'Advanced Programmes' in Vietnam: Internationalising the curriculum or importing the 'best curriculum' of the West? In L. T. Tran & S. Marginson (Eds.), *Internationalisation in Vietnamese higher education* (pp. 55–76). Cham: Springer.

Tran, T. T. (2014). Governance in higher education in Vietnam—A move towards decentralization and its practical problems. *Journal of Asian Public Policy, 7*(1), 71–82.

Trines, S. (2017). *Education in Vietnam*. Retrieved from https://wenr.wes.org/2017/11/education-in-vietnam.

Trung, T. Q., & Swierczek, F. W. (2009). Skills development in higher education in Vietnam. *Asia Pacific Business Review, 15*(4), 565–586.

UNESCO Institute for Statistics (UIS). (2014). *Higher education in Asia: Expanding out, expanding up: The rise of graduate education and university research*. Montreal, QC: UNESCO Institute for Statistics.

UNESCO Institute for Statistics (UIS). (2016). *Inbound internationally mobile students by country of origin*. Retrieved from http://data.uis.unesco.org/Index.aspx?queryid=172.

UNESCO Institute for Statistics (UIS). (2018). *Outbound internationally mobile students by host region*. Retrieved from http://data.uis.unesco.org/Index.aspx?queryid=172.

Van Damme, D. (2001). Quality issues in the internationalisation of higher education. *Higher Education, 41*(4), 415–441.

Varghese, N. V. (2009). Cross-border higher education and national systems of education. In J. Fegan & M. H. Field (Eds.), *Education across borders: Politics, policy and legislative action* (pp. 33–48). Heidelberg: Springer.

Vietnam International Education Cooperation Department (VIED). (2018a). *Danh mục các chương trình liên kết đào tạo đã được Bộ Giáo Dục và Đào Tạo phê duyệt* [List of collaborative programmes licensed by MOET]. Retrieved from http://lienket.vied.vn/index.php?lang=vi&mid=9.

Vietnam International Education Cooperation Department (VIED). (2018b). *General information on scholarship programs using state budget recruited by the*

Ministry of education and training. Retrieved from http://vied.vn/en/about-vied/vietnamese-government-s-scholarship-schemes.html.
Vietnam National University Hanoi. (n.d.). *Introduction to VNU international cooperation.* Retrieved from https://vnu.edu.vn/eng/?C2522.
VietnamNet. (2017a). *Những con số 'biết nói' về giáo dục đại học Việt Nam* [Vietnamese higher education and figures that can 'talk for themselves']. Retrieved from http://vietnamnet.vn/vn/giao-duc/tuyen-sinh/nhung-con-so-biet-noi-ve-giao-duc-dai-hoc-viet-nam-389870.html.
VietnamNet. (2017b). *Vietnamese qualifications framework's implementation faces challenges.* Retrieved from http://english.vietnamnet.vn/fms/education/173383/vietnamese-qualifications-framework-s-implementation-faces-challenges.html.
VietNamNet Bridge. (2016). *More Vietnamese students study abroad, but few foreigners enroll in Vietnam.* Retrieved from http://english.vietnamnet.vn/fms/education/166725/more-vietnamese-students-study-abroad–but-few-foreigners-enroll-in-vn.html.
VietnamNews. (2016). *PhD training quality needs major improvement.* Retrieved from https://vietnamnews.vn/society/346121/phd-training-quality-needs-major-improvement.html#smz7kMWlyOj6BO8u.97.
VN NARIC. (n.d.). *National recognition information centre mission.* Retrieved from https://en.naric.edu.vn/.
VNUK. (2016). *The VNUK institute for research and executive education.* Retrieved from http://vnuk.udn.vn/about/?lang=en.
Vu, N. T. T., & Burns, A. (2014). English as a medium of instruction: Challenges for Vietnamese tertiary lecturers. *The Journal of Asia TEFL, 11*(3), 1–31.
Welch, A. R. (2010). Internationalisation of Vietnamese higher education: Retrospect and prospect. In G. Harman, M. Hayden, & T. N. Pham (Eds.), *Reforming higher education in Vietnam: Challenges and priorities* (Vol. 29, pp. 197–213). New York: Springer.
Welch, A. R. (2012). Contributing to the Southeast Asian knowledge economy? Australian offshore campuses in Malaysia and Vietnam. In A. R. Nelson & I. P. Wei (Eds.), *The global university: Past, present, and future perspectives* (pp. 55–81). New York: Palgrave Macmillan.
Wilmoth, D. (2004). RMIT Vietnam and Vietnam's development: Risk and responsibility. *Journal of Studies in International Education, 8*(2), 186–206.
Wong, M. S., & Wu, S. F. (2011). Internationalization of higher education in East Asia: Issues, implications, and inquiries. In J. D. Palmer, A. Roberts, Y. H. Cho, & G. S. Ching (Eds.), *The internationalization of East Asian higher education: Globalization's impact* (pp. 197–214). New York: Palgrave Macmillan.

World Bank. (2008). *Vietnam: Higher education and skills for growth*. Retrieved from http://siteresources.worldbank.org/INTEASTASIAPACIFIC/Resources/Vietnam-HEandSkillsforGrowth.pdf.

World Bank. (2013). *Skilling up Vietnam: Preparing the workforce for a modern market economy—Vietnam development report 2014*. Retrieved from http://documents.worldbank.org/curated/en/610301468176937722/pdf/829400AR0P13040Box0379879B00PUBLIC0.pdf.

Yang, R. (2017). Internationalization of higher education in China: A national scenario. In H. de Wit, J. Gacel-Ávila, E. Jones, & N. Jooste (Eds.), *The globalization of internationalization: Emerging voices and perspectives* (pp. 142–152). Oxon: Routledge.

Youssef, L. (2014). Globalisation and higher education: From within-border to crossborder. *The Journal of Open, Distance and E-Learning, 29*(2), 100–115.

Ziguras, C., & Pham, A. (2017). Internationalization of higher education in Vietnam: Moving towards interdependence. In H. de Wit, J. Gacel-Ávila, E. Jones, & N. Jooste (Eds.), *The globalization of internationalization: Emerging voices and perspectives* (pp. 131–142). Oxon: Routledge.

3

History of Quality Assurance in Vietnamese Higher Education

Huong Thi Pham and Cuong Huu Nguyen

Overview of Historical Developments and Context of Vietnam Higher Education

Doi Moi and Higher Education

After the country reunification in 1975, Vietnam applied the Soviet-style central planning model with state ownership and a closed-door policy on international relations. During the period between 1976 and 1986, Vietnam was characterised by poor economic performance and a high level of poverty (Pham, 2013).

In 1986, Vietnam officially announced a policy, which is well known as "*doi moi*", marking the movement from a communist-style planned economy to a market-led economy with socialist orientation (George, 2010;

H. T. Pham (✉)
Ho Chi Minh City University of Education, Ho Chi Minh City, Vietnam
e-mail: huong.pham@ier.edu.vn

C. H. Nguyen
University of Education, Vietnam National University, Hanoi, Vietnam

© The Author(s) 2019
C. H. Nguyen and M. Shah (eds.), *Quality Assurance in Vietnamese Higher Education*, https://doi.org/10.1007/978-3-030-26859-6_3

Madden, 2014). This societal reform has significantly influenced the development of higher education policy.

After *doi moi*, with the introduction of free-market approach, the government decided several implications for higher education reform. Higher education institutions (HEIs) would now have to (a) train manpower for non-state sector jobs; (b) obtain income from outside the state sector; (c) develop their own institutional plans and learning programmes to meet the needs of society as well as the state; and (d) while graduates would be responsible for finding their own work (George, 2010). These would decentralise higher education governance and restructure the system to link education to economic development of the country (Madden, 2014).

The most significant and comprehensive policy on higher education reform is the Higher Education Reform Agenda (HERA). The HERA proposes (a) to confer legal autonomy on HEIs; (b) to eliminate line-ministry control; (c) to call for developing a system of quality assurance and accreditation (QAA) for higher education; and (d) to develop a Higher Education Law (Hayden & Lam, 2006).

Higher Education Governance

Higher education system in Vietnam is very complex and fragmented with many small universities, which are highly specialised, and big universities, such as the Vietnam National Universities, which cover a wide range of disciplines (Niedermeier & Pohlenz, 2016). About 30% of HEIs in Vietnam report to the Ministry of Education and Training (MoET), while the remaining report to their line ministry (e.g. Ministry of Agriculture, Ministry of Finance, etc.). The Department of Higher Education (DHE) and the MoET are the state agencies that manage the quality of higher education (Do, Pham, & Nguyen, 2017). The MoET oversees all HEIs, except for the two national universities, which are under the oversight of the prime minister, in terms of academic matters, including enrolment and admission, curriculum development and organisation, assessment, and quality assurance (QA). The MoET has deployed some measures and instruments for QA and accountability enhancement (Do et al., 2017).

The Development of QA System

Vietnam has been attempting to establish a quality assurance system for higher education that aligns with the global trend (Pham, 2014). This attempt began in the late 1990s with the introduction of development strategies to 2020 for higher education by the MoET. Key figures include completing the organisational and managerial systems of higher education, empowering universities in terms of their training and research, and developing a system to assess and control the quality of higher education and teaching and training, based on a standard set of criteria (MoET, 1998). In particular, in an attempt to gain a national consensus on the concept of quality and to focus on measures to improve the quality of this sector, the MoET organised the first national workshop on QA in higher education in 2000. Consequently, building up a system to assure quality in higher education at the national and institutional level was regarded as an initial step to improve educational quality (Nguyen, Oliver, & Priddy, 2009). This was supported by the government through the establishment of policies and strategies for educational development and the identification of approaches and mechanisms in management via monitoring, inspection, and accreditation of educational quality (Phan, 2001). The Educational Development Plan 2001–2010 legalised the MoET to issue a provisional regulation on higher education accreditation and officially authorised accrediting activities (MoET, 2004).

Accreditation and US Models

Vietnam is one of the countries which do not have a tradition of higher education evaluation and accreditation (Pham, 2014). QA systems in other countries have been examined, and this has led to debates about which models could be most appropriately adapted to the Vietnamese setting. International and national conferences, as well as round-table discussions, have been hosted in Vietnam on this issue between 2000 and 2002. The US accreditation model was the one Vietnam decided to follow (MoET, 2004).

Vietnam's accreditation is a variation of the US model, so the accreditation procedures and evaluation methods, in essential, resemble those in the USA. The process includes registration (for accreditation), self-study, external review, feedback on review results, and final decision. However, the model is significantly different from the US model in a way that accreditation is voluntary and independent of the state in the USA while it is compulsory and state-controlled in Vietnam.

Structure of QA System

The significant and first step to build a QA system in Vietnam is the establishment of the General Department of Educational Testing and Accreditation (GDETA) (renamed as Vietnam Education Quality Management Agency, VQA, since 25 May 2017). It was established in 2003 as a department of the MoET. The department laid the first foundation for Vietnam's national quality assurance system in higher education. Another attention in the history of QA development in Vietnam is the establishment of two centres of quality assurance at the two national universities in Ho Chi Minh and Hanoi (Le & Nguyen, 2009).

The establishment of this agency and other QA centres within HEIs marked the introduction of quality accreditation and the beginning of an accreditation system in the country's higher education. It led the development of legislative frameworks for accreditation, including regulations, standards and criteria, and procedures. It also led the pilot institutional accreditation within the scope of Higher Education Project (HEP) 1 and 2. GDETA has played a major role in constructing and developing the national accreditation system.

In 2009 under the Amended Law, accreditation regulations have more space in the law with three articles added (Vietnam National Assembly, 2009), requiring HEIs to "conduct quality self-evaluation and be subject to accreditation by the competent quality accreditation agency" (Article 58) and the state to "organise and manage the assurance and accreditation of educational quality" (Vietnam National Assembly, 2005, Article 99). Since then, as required by the Education Law, all HEIs in Vietnam have started to establish their own QA units.

The Role of World Bank and International Projects

The World Bank and other international projects have a significant role in the development of higher education and QA policies in Vietnam through their financial support (Madden, 2014; Pham, 2013). The key objectives of these projects are to change the management of the system, moving from "a passive subsidized approach to a forward looking market approach" (The World Bank, 2008, p. 16). Through the international support, the MoET recognised fundamental issues related to higher education quality as a result of several decades of inappropriate quality management and decided to take measures to infuse QA management into the system (MoET, 2009, p. 8).

With support of the World Bank, the first and second Higher Education Projects were carried out (HEP 1 from 1996 to 2006 and HEP 2 from 2007 to 2012). One priority of both projects was QA establishment in Vietnam. The initial focus of HEP 1 was on researching the internal processes of QA, which led to the establishment of the first two QA centres at Vietnam National University Hanoi and Vietnam National University Ho Chi Minh City in 2000 (Thuy Thi & Yi-Fang, 2014, p. 10). The main outcome of the support from the HEP 1 was the establishment of national institutional standards for QA and the creation of a department under the MoET in 2002, which has been renamed to the General Department for Educational Testing and Accreditation in 2003.

However, the World Bank supports neoliberal perspectives to emphasise on decentralisation, institutional autonomy, and accountability. These values are likely incompatible with the tradition of central control in Vietnam. Accreditation in higher education is considered as the best approach because the World Bank and the Vietnamese government both focus on accountability (Madden, 2014).

The Development of Legislative Frameworks

Quality assurance and accreditation in Vietnam has been documented in laws approved by the National Assembly (Education Law, Amended Law, Supplementing a Number of Articles of the Education Law and Higher

Education Law), decrees promulgated by the government, and circulars promulgated by the MoET (Nguyen, Evers, & Marshall, 2017).

In advocacy of the national QA movement in Vietnam, educational quality accreditation was officially brought into the Vietnam Education Law in 2005 and Amended Law in 2009 (Vietnam National Assembly, 2005, 2009), specifically stated in Articles 17, 58, and 99. H. C. Nguyen et al. (2017) reviewed this highest Vietnamese legal framework and noted that the 2005 Law only has one article and one clause related to accreditation as follows:

> Education quality accreditation is the major measure to define the level of achieving the goals, realizing the programs and contents of education by schools and other educational institutions. Education quality accreditation is conducted regularly throughout the country and for every educational institution. Results of the education quality accreditation are publicly announced for awareness and supervision by the society. The Minister of Education and Training shall have to direct the implementation of education quality accreditation. (Vietnam National Assembly, 2005, p. 5)

Quality assurance and accreditation is also officially stated in the Higher Education Law which was approved in 2012. The law gives one chapter (Chapter VII) with five articles (Articles 49–53) specialising in higher education accreditation. In this law, the regulations for accrediting agencies are presented. For instance, "accrediting agencies are responsible for assessing and recognising higher education institutions and programmes that meet quality standards" (Clause 1, Article 52) (Vietnam National Assembly, 2012). Article 51 of the law states that individual institutions of higher education are subject to accreditation whenever required and that the MoET regulates the national standards, evaluation, and accreditation criteria. Accreditation results will be used by the government to identify autonomous rights for the institutions and for budget and investment (Dang, 2013, p. 322).

By law, institutional accreditation is compulsory for all HEIs with a five-year cycle and if not granted can have the consequence of stopping student enrolment. Furthermore, there are plans to use the accreditation results to classify universities and rank them as well as to connect the results with budgetary consequences (Nguyen et al., 2017; Niedermeier & Pohlenz, 2016).

Based on these laws, a number of regulations for accreditation have been promulgated by the government and the MoET. Specifically, regulations on institutional and programmatic accreditation standards, procedures and cycles for quality accreditation, establishment of accrediting agencies, and accreditors were developed and issued by the MoET (2007, 2012a, 2012b, 2012c, 2013b as cited in H. C. Nguyen et al. [2017]). These legal documents are essential instruments to exercise accreditation activities.

Piloting and Experimentation of Accreditation Approach

In 2004, the MoET issued a Decision No. 38/2004/QD-BGDDT on promulgating temporary regulations for accreditation of universities with 10 standards including 53 criteria to conduct the pilot projects with 20 universities. These 20 pilot accreditations were supported by HEP 1 and the Dutch Government's ProfQim project to test the accreditation methodology. One of the results of the pilot was that changes were needed to the accreditation framework and that decision rules for performance definition of the universities needed to be established (Westerheijden, Cremonini, & van Empel, 2010, p. 192).

After the first pilots, the MoET stopped the full accreditation process and required universities to conduct yearly self-assessments based on the revised standards and criteria (10 standards and 61 criteria) and to hand in a self-assessment report to the MoET without undergoing external assessment. By 2009, external reviews were conducted in 40 universities. As of April 2014, 87% of the universities and colleges completed self-evaluation and submitted their self-evaluation reports to the MoET. The MoET used the meantime to update the regulations, procedures, and standards. The major change within the process was the establishment of independent centres for education accreditation, which support the credibility of the accreditation scheme (Niedermeier & Pohlenz, 2016).

Between 2009 and 2016, none of the institutions were reviewed (Do et al., 2017). From 2016 to the mid-2018, a number of HEIs were externally reviewed and recognised based on these standards after the establishment of the four centres. The increasing number of institutions applied for accreditation is perhaps due to the MoET's decision to issue another set of standards which are believed to be harder for institutions to comply with.

This process of piloting is continuing. In 2017, the MoET decided to replace the current accreditation standards by regional QA standards and criteria.

Standards for Quality Assurance and Accreditation for Institutions

As discussed in the previous section, the MoET promulgated a provisional regulation on accreditation in 2004, in which 10 standards with 53 criteria were proposed to cover activities of HEIs:

(1) Missions and objectives of the university (two criteria);
(2) Organisation and management (five criteria);
(3) Study programme (four criteria);
(4) Training activities (five criteria);
(5) Managerial, teaching, and administrative staff (10 criteria);
(6) Learners (nine criteria);
(7) Research, application, development, and technology transferability (five criteria);
(8) International cooperation (three criteria);
(9) Library, learning equipment, and other facilities (seven criteria); and
(10) Finance and financial management (three criteria).

For each criterion, an institution was assessed on two levels, with level 1 considered to be meeting minimal standards. Provisional standards were implemented to pilot the regulation and to revise it (if required), based on the feedback from participating institutions. Many university representatives claimed that the criteria's validity was unreliable and untested (K. D.

Nguyen et al., 2009). The initial ten standards and 53 criteria were revised resulting in an unchanged number of standards but with an increase of criteria to 61.

After a three-year trial of the provisional regulation, a revised regulation was officially signed on 1 November 2007, composing of the same 10 standards but covering 61 criteria; eight criteria were added to the provisional one. There is only one acceptable level of achievement in this new set of standards. K. D. Nguyen et al. (2009) argued that HEIs generally have supported and followed the revised regulation because the new standards are revised in a more qualitative style. Public and private institutions are evaluated against the same set of standards.

Promulgation of the standards was followed by the decision on the procedures and cycle for quality accreditation issued on 14 December 2007, which details steps in the accreditation process and the eligibility of an institution for accreditation status. An institution will be granted an accreditation certificate if it meets (at minimum) 80% of the criteria. In addition, based on an institutional self-study, the National Council for Accreditation will endorse a certificate for accreditation for the institution via blind voting (Tran, Nguyen, & Nguyen, 2011).

Foreign and local scholars have pointed out several issues about the set of standards and criteria. K. D. Nguyen et al. (2009) state that the standards focus on input and process more than outcomes, contain many quantitative criteria although they have been revised to be more qualitative, have a loose connection and consistency among standards and criteria, and lack a clear philosophy of accreditation. This is also noted by Tran et al. (2011) that the standards only require universities to present evidence of their physical and human resources, and contain "no requirements on specifications of course, objectives, and no requirements on the translation of mission statement into objectives at the programme and course level" (p. 136). The standards tend to promote an QA approach of focusing on past and present achievements (Nguyen et al., 2017) which some researchers believed to be opposed to accreditation philosophy: focusing on "fitness for purpose" defined by institutions' missions and objectives, using qualitative criteria, and encouraging future-oriented achievements (Nguyen et al., 2009, 2017). Consequently, the set of standards "tends to be a control instrument rather than a quality improvement instrument"

(Westerheijden et al., 2010, p. 193). They stress the need for improving the standards and provide some recommendations on how to improve them. Nevertheless, there have not been significant amendments to the standards and criteria until the recent completely new set of standards, which are addressed in the next section, presents developments.

Standards for Quality Assurance and Accreditation for Programmes

Together with developing accreditation standards for HEIs, the MoET is also a circular relating to programme accreditation, Circular No. 38/2013/TT-BDGDT. The Circular regulates definition, procedure, and cycle for programme accreditation. Programme accreditation is defined as "an activity to assess and recognise the level that the programme achieves against the accreditation standards issued by the MoET" (MoET, 2013, p. 2). It is important to note that by the time the ministry issued the Circular, accreditation standards for programmes had not been issued. The procedure and cycle for programmatic accreditation are similar to those of institutional accreditation.

There are two types of accreditation standards for programmes in Vietnam: general standards and specialised ones. With the support from international organisations, four sets of standards are developed for specific programmes, including: primary school teacher training programmes (with 7 standards and 37 criteria), high school teacher training programmes (with 7 standards and 40 criteria), vocational teacher training programmes (with 7 standards and 40 criteria), and nursing programmes (with 8 standards and 42 criteria). Similar to institution accreditation, a programme only receives the accreditation certificate if it satisfies at least 80% of all criteria (see more in Nguyen, 2018).

Late in 2016, the MoET promulgated the fifth sets of standards for all higher education programmes (with 11 standards and 50 criteria). The standards are translated from AUN-QA standards with minor changes (with permission from the network). This is the standards that are currently used for all HE programmes.

These sets of specialised standards mainly focus on assessing the quality of a programme covering: programme objectives, learning outcomes, organisation, training management and assessment, curriculum, training activities, faculty, support staff, students and student service, facilities, finance, graduate assessment and career counselling for students.

Current Development of QA System in Vietnam

After 15 years of developments, the QA system in Vietnam has gained certain achievements. The accreditation exercises have been pushed to a next step of the entire accreditation process: external evaluation and recognition with the establishment of five accrediting bodies.

The Establishment of Five Accrediting Agencies in Vietnam

After the establishment of a state agency to manage quality accreditation, GDETA (or VQA recently) as discussed earlier, in October 2008, the National Accreditation Council was established to make accreditation decisions; however, it was abolished with the decision to introduce a decentralised system with independent accreditation agencies (Hoang-Do & Quyen-Do, 2014). This decision was introduced by the MoET in 2010 with the "Project on Developing Educational Quality Accreditation System in Higher Education and Vocational Education period 2010 to 2020". The MoET and VQA are therefore only supervising and granting licenses for accreditation agencies and setting the framework. The government indicated its intention to set up an external QA system with two types of accreditation agencies: from 2011 to 2015, public accreditation agencies set up by the government and at a later stage; from 2016 to 2020, private accreditation agencies set up by the private sector. A new National Council for Accreditation will be established, which will be in charge of accreditation activities and advise the minister on matters of accreditation agencies (Thang & Lee, 2014, p. 13). However, it is still not yet established as planned as of April 2019.

The Circular 61/2012/TT-BGDĐT is the legal document which stipulates conditions for the establishment of accrediting bodies, their functions, responsibilities, and authority, promulgated by the MoET on 28 December 2012 (Do et al., 2017). The Circular laid the foundation for the establishment of two accrediting centres in the two national universities in 2014 (CEA VNU-HN in the North and CEA VNU-HCM in the South), the third centre in Danang University (CEA-UD in central Vietnam) in 2015, and another one under the umbrella of the Vietnam Association of Universities and Colleges early in 2016. Recently, a fifth one was formed as part of Vinh University in 2017. This is believed to be the result of the pressure of international and local experts and funding agencies (Do et al., 2017) in an attempt to separate accreditation responsibilities from governmental management organisations (Nguyen, 2018; Nguyen et al., 2017).

As defined by the Circular, accrediting bodies, including public and private agencies, undertake external assessment and recognise education providers and programs that meet the standards set by the MoET. The Circular also specifies that these agencies be independent of HEIs (MoET, 2012). The MoET licenses, recognises, and oversees accrediting agencies.

Universities are free to choose any of the five centres, except for the four hosting universities of the centres, which cannot be accredited by their own centre. The plan is to have the centres operating independently in three years' time. The centres are fully financed by the universities without funding by the government (Niedermeier & Pohlenz, 2016).

So far, the five centres have conducted first peer-review process according to the 10 standards and 61 criteria set by the MoET (last revision in March 2014) and granted accreditation status to 80 universities as of May 2018.

Five accrediting agencies have been set up so far. As mentioned above, four agencies are based in two national universities and one regional university, and one public university and so report to the presidents of these universities. Private accrediting agencies can be established only after 2016, and there is one under the Vietnam Association of Universities and Colleges which can be independent from HEIs but not private in nature.

The effort to establish these bodies is expected to enhance the quality of Vietnam's higher education, as they act in an independent manner. However, this structure of the accreditation system raises concern among scholars and experts over the "independence" of the accrediting agencies. According to the government plan, the two accrediting centres established in 2014 were supposed to be independent from their hosting universities in 2017 after three years of establishment. However, as of April 2019, none of them are independent. Furthermore, the national accreditation structure also shows the MoET's intensive involvement in the accreditation process. This perhaps could explain the similarity of operations among the four "dependent" accrediting bodies and the "independent" one and raise a concern of negative competition among the five centres.

As regards the shift from a centralised to a decentralised QA approach with more independent agencies, Niedermeier and Pohlenz (2016) claimed that Vietnam is a very interesting case for the region and a good example of how frameworks are continuously changing and under development.

The Current New Sets of Standards for Programme and Institutions

Programmatic Standards

Programme standards that are adapted from the AUN-QA assessment scheme (third version) were published in 2016 by the MoET (2016). The standards cover 11 standards and 50 criteria (Fig. 3.1).

Programme accreditation is compulsory with a five-year cycle, too.

Besides this set of standards, HEIs are autonomous to use other international assessment and accreditation schemes, such as AUN-QA, ABET, CTI as these are also recognised by the MoET.

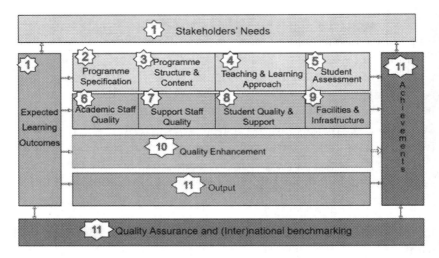

Fig. 3.1 AUN-QA model for programme (3rd version) (AUN, 2016, p. 9)

Institutional Standards

Similar to programme standards, the MoET decided to adapt the institutional assessment model from AUN-QA (Fig. 3.2) for institutional accreditation in Vietnam, and they were translated into Vietnamese. These new standards were issued in 2017.

The issuance of this new set of standards, which are effective from 2018, has somehow contributed to the increasing number of HEIs applied for external assessment during the second half of 2017 from 12 HEIs at the end of 2016 to 63 HEIs at the end of 2017. It is widely believed that the new standards are more difficult than previous ones, in terms of both the number of standards and criteria (from 10/61 to 25/111) and the requirements for compliance.

Vietnam QA Systems in the Region

Niedermeier and Pohlenz (2016) categorised ASEAN countries into three groups based on the maturity of QA systems as follows:

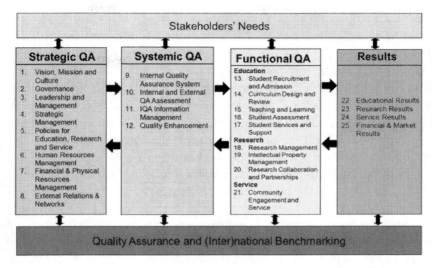

Fig. 3.2 AUN-QA framework for institutional level (2nd version) (AUN, 2016, p. 10)

- Consolidated: Brunei, Indonesia, Malaysia, Thailand, the Philippines, Singapore
- Developing: Cambodia, Lao PDR, Vietnam, and
- Newcomer: Myanmar

Vietnam is seen as a country, on the one hand, to have more experience with QA than the other Cambodia, Lao, Myanmar, and Vietnam (CLMV) countries but, on the other hand, it is still in an emergent and piloting phase. The QA system in Vietnam is currently undergoing major changes with a step-by-step approach to enhancing and developing the framework (Niedermeier & Pohlenz, 2016). Vietnam is believed to be the most advanced country within the CLMV countries regarding its availability and quality of resources. However, it is likely that Vietnam has not yet found a suitable quality approach and means for a steady implementation of QA mechanisms (Niedermeier & Pohlenz, 2016). Also according to Niedermeier and Pohlenz (2016), Vietnam is currently shifting to more independent QA agencies, and a pilot of so-called "autonomous universities" is taking place. Do (2017) agrees with the view stating that QA developments in Vietnam seem to be "awkward and unstable".

In comparison with the Philippines and Indonesia (consolidated QA systems) which have developed quality standards for both institutional and programme levels for a long time, Vietnam has recently issued programme standards and replaced the existing institutional standards which were developed and revised for ten years with a complete new set of standards. In terms of the level and scope of the evaluation/external QA exercise, Vietnam like Cambodia and Lao has focused first on institutional assessment while other countries including the Philippines stressed the importance of programme accreditation.

The QA developments in Indonesia have a longer history than Vietnam; therefore, it would be more mature in terms of structure and achievements. It has a significantly higher number of programmes and institutions accredited. More importantly, it is believed that national accreditation agency for higher education (NAAHE)'s accreditation decisions are independent from governmental interference (Niedermeier & Pohlenz, 2016). The initial government support from the beginning to introduce the concept into the country significantly contributed to the results, perhaps successful in building trust with HEIs. With time, the entire system is becoming more diverse as regards the structure of accrediting agencies, the number of specialised programmes, and wider participation of other stakeholder groups. The accreditation can be granted, denied, or deferred for improvement. Adding another level of being deferred can be an option for Vietnam to consider, encouraging HEIs participating in accreditation without "losing face" in a Confucian country (Pham, 2014). The system also has its own challenges, including the number of HEIs and programmes, the values of accreditation, professionalisation of QA staff as well as the risk of setting too high standards in alignment with regional and international ones (Niedermeier & Pohlenz, 2016); the QA model in Indonesia seems to be successful in building the public trust and gaining support from HEIs.

Although the number of universities undergone external assessment has increased slightly since 2009, higher education accreditation implementation in Vietnam is argued to be too slow when compared with other systems in the region. For example, in Thailand, the Office for National Education Standards and Quality Assessment (ONESQA) (responsible for educational quality assessment) was established in 2000. As of September

2015, they completed the third round of external quality assessment for all HEIs (ONESQA, 2015). One of the Vietnam's neighbouring countries, Cambodia that established the national accreditation organisation at the same year as Vietnam (2003) also accredited all foundation programmes and a number of institutions in 2013. The main reason for the slow pace of accreditation is argued due to the fact that the MoET ceased external assessment activities within six years (from 2009 to 2015) to revise the regulations, procedures, standards, and structure of the higher education accreditation system. This could suggest that the values of a QA system are still vague from the government level to grassroots level.

In sum, it can be seen that the establishment of accrediting agencies in Southeast Asia was influenced by a surge in the establishment of QA agencies around the world (Woodhouse, 2007). Malaysia and Thailand with similar time to establish QA models (few years difference) as Vietnam have gained significant achievements and together with Indonesia are categorised as to have "consolidated" QA systems, while Vietnam is considered to have a developing and young QA system perhaps because of management issues in QA arrangements.

Future Implications for QA Developments in Vietnam

In comparison with other QA systems in the region, Vietnam can learn from others to promote the independence of accrediting agencies and speeding up the pace of accreditation.

Independence of Accrediting Agencies

It can be learned from other countries that independence of these agencies in isolation of any higher education system from the government is not a determinant. Most of ASEAN countries claimed their accrediting agencies are independent from government perhaps in making accreditation decisions, some are successful, and others are not. From the history of consolidated QA developments in the region, it can be observed that they are moving towards establishing private bodies, which were planned to be legally allowed in Vietnam from 2016. However, it did not happen as of April 2019. This may suggest that without a developed and stable QA model at a state level, it is difficult to diversify external quality assurance agencies.

To gradually build trust with other groups of stakeholders, the current functions, responsibilities, and activities of the newly established accrediting bodies in Vietnam should be comprehensively evaluated. Few universities were denied accreditation could be a good signal of independence of these agencies, but this is far away from being sufficient for the purposes of a QA system. Perhaps the major challenge in Vietnam is "unfinished" external QA frameworks (Niedermeier & Pohlenz, 2016).

For future development of QA approach, H. C. Nguyen et al. (2017) suggest Vietnam learns from the countries in the region such as Cambodia (with Accreditation Committee of Cambodia [ACC]), Thailand (with the ONESQA), and Malaysia (with Malaysian Qualifications Agency [MQA]) where the national higher education QA agency in these countries is beyond the ministry of (higher) education, and their accreditation practices have achieved great results although their systems were established at the same time as Vietnam's.

Complete External QA Framework

To move forwards from the current state of affairs of QA development, consistent strategy could be a solution. Niedermeier and Pohlenz (2016) also believed that for countries with unfinished QA frameworks, "'starting small' and developing things over the course of time can be a strategy, but the research outcomes suggest that the main pillars of the QA systems should be set (e.g.: purpose, standards, guidelines for evaluation, procedures, cycles, consequences) in order to avoid uncertainties and ambiguous communications" (p. 44). As discussed above, the QA plans of the government almost were unachievable, which could lead to another issue in Vietnam is how to achieve this set framework or the developed framework is not appropriate in the Vietnamese context because uncertainties and resistances are currently common. Once trust and certainties are confirmed, other challenges of QA in Vietnam can be solved over time, including human resources for QA, HEIs' commitment to QA, and pace of accreditation implementation. Otherwise, Vietnam will have an emergent and piloting phrase after almost 15 years of development (Niedermeier & Pohlenz, 2016).

Conclusion

Over the period of 15 years, Vietnam has been able to establish a QA system for higher education. With international supports and funding, the country has developed legislative frameworks for QAA and is completing its QA structure. Many efforts had been made to develop and revise Vietnamese quality standards for HEIs. Recently, AUN-QA standards for both institutions and programmes, however, have been adapted and translated into Vietnamese as the country standards. This has made Vietnam a unique case in the region to adapt both regional sets of standards as its national ones. Although Vietnam has gained some achievements in developing its QA mechanism and system, the system is still at a piloting and developing stage and far behind some countries in the region. The country can learn from other countries in the region such as Malaysia, Indonesia, and the Philippines to push accreditation activities. Actions are necessary to offer complete independence for accrediting agencies.

References

AUN. (2016). *Guide to AUN-QA assessment at institutional level (2nd version)*. Bangkok, Thailand: The Author.

Dang, H. V. (2013). *A new approach to explain policy reforms in Vietnam during doi moi by developing and validating a major policy change model for Vietnam*. Retrieved from http://pdxscholar.library.pdx.edu/open_access_etds/611/.

Do, T. N. Q. (2017, December 2). Kiểm định chất lượng giáo dục: Nhìn từ góc độ kỹ thuật. *Vietnamnet*. Retrieved from http://vietnamnet.vn/vn/giao-

duc/khoa-hoc/kiem-dinh-chat-luong-giao-duc-nhin-tu-goc-do-ky-thuat-414408.html.
Do, T. N. Q., Pham, T. H., & Nguyen, K. D. (2017). Quality assurance in the Vietnamese higher education: A top-down approach and compliance-driven QA. In M. Shah & T. N. Q. Do (Eds.), *The rise of quality assurance in Asian higher education* (1st ed.). Cambridge, MA: Chandos Publishing.
George, E. (2010). Higher education in Vietnam 1986–1998: Education in transition to a new era? In P. T. Nghi, G. Harman, & M. Hayden (Eds.), *Reforming higher education in Vietnam: Challenges and priorities*. London: Springer.
Hayden, M., & Lam, Q. T. (2006). A 2020 vision for Vietnam. *International Higher Education, 44,* 11–13.
Hoang-Do, M., & Quyen-Do, T. N. (2014). Higher and tertiary education in Vietnam. In L. Tran, S. Marginson, & H. Do (Eds.), *Higher education in Vietnam: Flexibility, mobility and practicality in the global knowledge economy* (p. 260). New York: Palgrave Macmillan.
Le, H. V., & Nguyen, K. D. (2009). Quality assurance in Vietnam's engineering education. In A. Patil & P. Gray (Eds.), *Engineering education quality assurance* (pp. 97–106). Boston, MA: Springer.
Madden, M. (2014). Walking the line: Quality assurance policy development and implementation in Việt Nam. *Higher Education, 67,* 91–104. https://doi.org/10.1007/s10734-013-9642-8.
Ministry of Education and Training (MoET). (1998). *Vietnam.* Paper presented at the World Conference on Higher Education: Higher Education in the Twenty-First Century, Paris, France.
Ministry of Education and Training (MoET). (2004). *Quy dinh tam thoi ve kiem dinh chat luong truong dai hoc, ban hanh kem theo QD so 38/2004/QD-BGD&DT* [Provisional regulation on university accreditation, issued as the attachment of the Decision No. 38/2004/QD-BGD&DT].
Ministry of Education and Training (MoET). (2009). *The report of the development of higher education in Vietnam, the solutions for assuring and enhancing quality of education.* Hanoi, Vietnam.
Ministry of Education and Training (MoET). (2012). *Circular No. 61/2012/TT-BGDDT Promulgating Regulations on Accrediting Agencies.* Hanoi, Vietnam: The Author.
Ministry of Education and Training (MoET). (2013). *Circular No. 38/2013/TT-BGDDT Promulgating Regulations of Procedures and Cycles of Programme Accreditation for Universities, Colleges and Professional Secondary Schools.* Hanoi, Vietnam: The Author.

Ministry of Education and Training (MoET). (2016). *Standards for higher education programmes*. Hanoi, Vietnam: The Author.

Nguyen, H. C. (2018). How to fulfil Vietnam's higher education accreditation strategic plan 2017–2020? *International Journal of Educational Organization and Leadership, 24*(3/4), 17–25.

Nguyen, H. C., Evers, C., & Marshall, S. (2017). Accreditation of Viet Nam's higher education: Achievements and challenges after a dozen years of development. *Quality Assurance in Education, 25*(4), 475–488. https://doi.org/10.1108/QAE-11-2016-0075.

Nguyen, K. D., Oliver, D. E., & Priddy, L. E. (2009). Criteria for accreditation in Vietnam's higher education: Focus on input or outcome? *Quality in Higher Education, 15*(2), 123–134.

Niedermeier, F., & Pohlenz, P. (2016). *State of affairs and development needs—Higher education quality assurance in the ASEAN region*. South Jakarta, Indonesia: DAAD.

Office for National Education Standards and Quality Assessment (ONESQA). (2015). *Quality Assurance in Thailand*. http://www.onesqa.or.th/en/download/1004/.

Pham, T. H. (2014). *Quality culture in Vietnamese universities: A multiple case study of quality assurance and quality culture of business English undergraduate programmes at three universities in Vietnam* (Doctoral dissertation). Victoria University of Wellington, Wellington.

Pham, T. L. P. (2013). *Higher education governance in Vietnam: University action, the state and changing relationships*. University of Kassel, Kassel.

Phan, V. K. (2001). *Chien luoc phat trien giao duc 2001–2010* [Educational development strategies 2001–2010]. Paper presented at the conference on Higher Education, Hanoi, Vietnam.

Thang, T. T., & Lee, Y. F. (2014). Stakeholders' perspectives on quality assurance in Vietnamese higher education. *Higher Education Evaluation and Development, 8*(2), 1–30.

Thuy Thi, T., & Yi-Fang, L. (2014). Stakeholders' perspectives on quality assurance in Vietnamese higher education. *Higher Education Evaluation and Development, 8*(2), 1–30.

Tran, N. D., Nguyen, T. T., & Nguyen, M. T. N. (2011). The standard of quality for HEIs in Vietnam: A step in the right direction? *Quality Assurance in Education, 19*(2), 130–140.

Vietnam National Assembly. (2005). *Luat Giao Duc* [Educational Act]. Hanoi: Giao Duc Publisher.

Vietnam National Assembly. (2009). *Law on Amending, Supplementing a Number of Articles of the Education Law.* Retrieved from http://vanban.chinhphu.vn/portal/page/portal/chinhphu/hethongvanban?class_id=1&_page=3&mode=detail&document_id=92515.

Vietnam National Assembly. (2012). *Higher Education Law.* Retrieved from http://vanban.chinhphu.vn/portal/page/portal/chinhphu/hethongvanban?class_id=1&_page=2&mode=detail&document_id=163054.

Westerheijden, D. F., Cremonini, L., & van Empel, R. (2010). Accreditation in Vietnam's higher education system. In G. Harman, M. Hayden, & P. T. Nghi (Eds.), *Reforming higher education in Vietnam: Challenges and priorities* (pp. 183–195). Amsterdam: Springer.

Woodhouse, D. (2007). *Feedback on the guidelines from the perspective of QA agencies.* Paper presented at the UNESCO 3rd Global Forum on International Quality Assurance, Accreditation, and the Recognition of Qualifications, Dar es Salaam, Tanzania.

The World Bank. (2008). *Implementation and results report: Vietnam higher education project 1.* Washington, DC: The Author.

4

Quality Assurance and Accreditation as a Mechanism for Accountability

Do Thi Ngoc Quyen

National Quality Assurance Arrangements

Commencing with the introduction of accreditation, the national quality assurance 1990s system has been driven by a top-down approach through a variety of centralized mechanisms and regulations with a focus on compliance rather than on continuous improvement. Only until recently have top universities played a greater part in leading quality assurance (QA) activities in the system. Internal quality assurance (IQA) and external quality assurance (EQA) activities are having mutual impact, yet effectiveness is an open question still.

D. T. N. Quyen (✉)
Hanoi University of Business and Technology, Hanoi, Vietnam

Regulatory Framework in Quality Assurance

Laws and Quasi-Law Legal Documents

A legislative framework consisting of such legal documents as laws, decrees, circulars, and decisions has been in place to regulate external QA activities in the local higher education system, among which the Law on Education and Law on Higher Education are the most important.

The first legal stipulation on quality assurance was in the Law on Education 2005 about the instrument selected as the mechanism for accountability. Article 17 of this Law specifies that accreditation is the key mechanism for the assessment of education quality defined as the fitness for preset goals and objectives of higher education institutions (HEIs), that it is to be implemented periodically, and that its results are to be publicized. The revised Law 2009 added regulations on the roles of the state management agency, which include the promulgation of evaluation standards and criteria, accreditation procedures and process, and the establishment of accrediting agencies. The revised Law also specifies the principles of accreditation, which are independence, impartiality, integrity, and transparency. It should be noted that at this stage, all these regulations are about accreditation, not quality assurance. The state management agency that oversees the entire accreditation system between 2003 and 2017 was the General Department of Testing and Accreditation (GDETA).

The concept of QA was legalized for the first time in the Law on Higher Education 2012, in which there is a chapter of regulations for both QA and accreditation. The Law stipulates that accreditation is a mechanism for quality assurance and adds to the regulatory framework the roles of HEIs in QA and accreditation. Specifically, HEIs bear the responsibility for quality assurance, specifically in establishing an internal QA unit, evaluation for accreditation of programs and institution as a whole, quality improvement, and maintenance and development of such QA conditions as academic and non-academic staff force, curricula and materials, physical facilities and services, and financial resources. Especially, the Law 2012 added two important points, one on the linkage between accreditation status and autonomy and another on the national standards of HEIs. That is, in addition to the set of accreditation standards and criteria for both program and institution levels, another set of standards is to be used for evaluating HEIs for the certification of the so-called university meeting national standards of HEIs.

According to the Law on Higher Education, HEIs are also required to make data and information about QA conditions, research and training outcomes, and accreditation status available to the public. The Law also sets out regulations on HEIs' accounting practice, audit, and financial disclosure. For public HEIs that receive state funding, the utilization and allocation of funds are under the regulation of the Law on state budget.

However, after several years of implementation, some stipulations were outdated and could not foster an environment that is advantageous for the development of higher education. The Law was revised, and the revised version of the Law passed on end of 2018 and coming into effect from July 2019 contains a number of significant changes. With regard to QA, the changes address two major issues. One is the independence of accrediting agencies by requesting them to be separated from the universities in which they are operating. The other deals with the role of accreditation as a means for accountability and autonomy by requiring accreditation status as a condition for student recruitment and autonomy in different aspects. It is noteworthy that the new stipulations will also nullify some existing sub-law documents such as Decree 73.

Another important legal document that regulates QA activities in HEIs is the Charter for Universities 2014. The stipulations in the Charter relevant to QA operations are consistent with those specified in both of the aforementioned laws; however, none of them has stated a specific mechanism for linking accreditation with autonomy. This issue is therefore still vaguely defined and the implementation of this policy is still a puzzle.

Decrees and Circulars

In order to implement the regulations set in the laws, an array of decrees and circulars is promulgated to provide a legal corridor for QA activities of HEIs and other actors in the system. With regard to accreditation, four circulars currently active and governing the national accreditation system include Circular 12/2017/TT-BGDDT, passing regulations on the (institutional) accreditation of HEIs, Circular 04/2016/TT-BGDĐT with regulations on programmatic accreditation, Circular 60/2012/TT-BGDĐT on external reviewers, and Circular 61/2012/TT-BGDĐT on the establishment, closure, and operations of accrediting centers. Decree 73/2015/ND-CP was circulated in 2015 to operationalize local ranking and stratification. Also in 2015, the national standards for HEIs were set out together with the issuance of Circular 24/2015/TT-BGDĐT. In addition to these decrees and circulars, two other circulars, 22/2017/TT-BGDĐT and 09/2017/TT-BGDDT, state the conditions, procedures for providing degree programs and suspension of enrollment and revocation of decision on bachelor, master, and doctorate program provision.

Together with the revised Law on Higher Education, a number of sub-law documents including decrees and circulars are expected to be made available to guide the implementation of new stipulations. There are concerns among the local academia over the feasibility of the new stipulations on QA and accreditation due to the limited capacity of existing accrediting agencies.

Vietnamese Qualification Framework and National Education System Structural Frame

After a long time being on the agenda, the development of a national qualification framework was finally accomplished with the promulgation of Decision 1982/QĐ-TTg dated October 18, 2016. The national qualification frameworks of many other countries such as Australia and the UK were points of reference for the development of the Vietnamese Qualification Framework (VQF).

The VQF, aligning with the Association of Southeast Asian Nations (ASEAN) qualification reference framework, sets out 8 levels of qualifications. The 8 levels are as follows:

- Level 1, 2, and 3 are equivalent to Elementary 1, 2, and 3
- Level 4 is Intermediate
- Level 5—College
- Level 6—Bachelor's degree

- Level 7—Master's degree
- Level 8—Doctoral degree.

Decision 1982 stipulates that Ministry of Education and Training (MoET) takes the lead, in cooperation with MOLISA, MoF, line ministries, provincial authorities, and HEIs, in implementing the VQF in higher education and translating the VQF into the learning outcomes of all degree levels in higher education.

At the same time the VQF was promulgated, the national education system structural frame was also issued together with Decision 1981/QĐ-TTg. As per Decision 1981, higher education includes bachelor, master, and doctoral education; therefore, the task of MoET is to translate the skills and capabilities from levels 6 to 8 of the VQF into degree programs.

These two frameworks are expected to provide a corridor directing the development of programs and curricula, teachers and learners, standards and criteria for quality evaluation and management. Yet, after two years, the extent to which these frameworks have been rendered into university curricula and the higher education standards and student learning outcomes remains unnoticeable.

The Lack of a National QA Framework

Despite recent development in the national QA system during the past 15 years, a national quality assurance framework is still absent, and the development of such a framework has not yet commenced. According to the Vietnam Education Quality Management Agency, MoET, there has been a plan for this task, and the ASEAN QA framework issued by ASEAN Quality Assurance Network (AQAN) would be a key point of reference.

Due to the lack of this framework, at present HEIs do not have guidelines for implementing and deploying quality assurance activities. HEIs are carrying out the QA tasks in their own way and at their own pace. A common approach adopted by most HEIs and their QA units is to observe strictly what has been imposed by MoET. That is, HEIs carry out QA activities and adopt QA practices submissively without understandings about the principles underlying those policies and practices. Specifically, many local HEIs take accreditation standards and criteria as guidelines for their QA activities. Many university leaders and managers, as well as QA practitioners, often perceive accreditation as QA and vice versa. In practice, all legislative documents are serving as mixed frameworks for QA. For these reasons, together with the lack of expertise in QA at the institutional level, HEIs can hardly develop a quality culture within their institution.

QA Mechanisms

Accreditation as a Key Instrument

The concept of accreditation was introduced in Vietnamese higher education in the early 2000s even before QA. The pilot implementation of institutional accreditation, organized by the Department of Accreditation and Testing, MoET, took place from 2005 to 2007 using the first version of the evaluation standard set containing 10 standards and 53 criteria. After this stage, the standards were revised, and the second version of the standards (10 standards and 61 criteria) were stipulated (Quyen-Do, Huong-Pham, & Kim-Nguyen, 2017). By 2009, external reviews were conducted in 40 universities against the second version of standards; however, no HEI was granted an accreditation status. As of April 2014, 87% of the universities and colleges completed and submitted their self-evaluation reports to MoET for external reviews. However, between 2009 and 2016, no more universities were reviewed and accredited. The first accrediting centers were established in 2014 and 2015, but did not operate until 2016 (Nguyen, Evers, & Marshall, 2017). The second version of the standards was officially used for evaluation for roughly two years from 2016 to July 2018 (Fig. 4.1).

In 2017, a new set of standards for evaluating institutions, which is essentially a copy of the AUN-QA standards for institutional level, was promulgated by Circular 12/2017/TT-BGDĐT and is effective from July 2018. The new set includes 25 standards, aligning with the AUN-QA framework (see Fig. 4.2).

In terms of program accreditation, even though all necessary regulations on the standard, procedure and process, accreditation cycles, and so

Fig. 4.1 Developments of accreditation in Vietnamese higher education (Compiled by author)

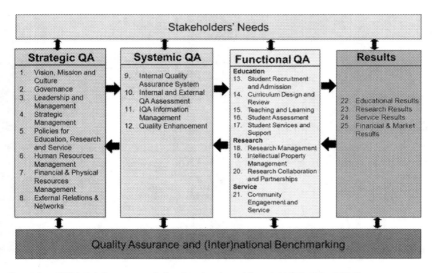

Fig. 4.2 AUN-QA framework for institutional level (AUN-QA, 2016)

on have been promulgated, program accreditation is in essence not yet operational. Only a very small number of programs have been accredited locally (eight of several thousand programs). MoET has encouraged HEIs to go for international and regional program accreditation such as ABET, ACBSP, HCERES, and AUN-QA. As of April 2018, 104 degree programs across the system have been accredited internationally.

Other Instruments in Place for QA Purposes

Apart from accreditation, several other tools, including *Ranking and Stratification, Licensure, Certification*, and *Public provision of data*, are also in place in Vietnamese higher education for QA purposes.

MoET introduced Public provision of data in 2009 under a program called 'three disclosures.' With the promulgation of Circular 09/2009/TT-BGDĐT dated May 7, 2009, replaced by Circular 36/2017/TT-BGDĐT in effect from February 13, 2018, MoET requests HEIs to make information about their institution and operations available to the public. The data include their commitment to actual educational quality, conditions for education QA, and financial operations (Bộ Giáo dục và Đào tạo [Ministry of Education and Training], 2009). Since then, HEIs have responded to this request and make the required data available on their Web sites open for the public; however, the data and information are not verified in terms of accuracy. With this 'three-disclosures' program, the transparency in the system has been enhanced, and the accuracy and integrity of the data provided are still questionable.

Licensure has been employed in the system for long to manage and control the opening of new institutions and educational programs. The decision to establish a HEI is made by the prime minister and deputy prime minister, while the decision to allow a HEI to operate is made by MoET. Decision 07/2009/QĐ-TTg dated January 15, 2009, and Circular 08/2011/TT-BGDĐT dated February 17, 2011, specify requirements on the conditions for minimum standards, for example, teacher–student ratio, minimum campus area, quantity and qualifications of full-time teaching staff, facilities and equipment, and library resources. Most of these requirements are quantitative, fixed, and applicable to all types of institutions and disciplines. Failure to meet these requirements leads to termination and closedown of a program and an institution. In 2012 and 2014, a lot of programs were terminated due to their not meeting these standards.

Stratification and rankings: Decree 73/2015/ND-CP was promulgated in 2015 to mark the launch of the so-called hybrid between stratification and ranking. The Decree specifies the standards for stratification and a framework and standards for ranking HEIs. According to this Decree,

HEIs are classified into three types (1) *research-oriented universities*; (2) *application-oriented universities*; and (3) *practice-oriented universities*. These three types form three layers of universities, and HEIs are ranked within each layer. The Decree also assigns the ranking task to accrediting agencies. However, since 2015, both ranking and stratification have not been implemented; that is, these two tools have not been in use (Quyen-Do, 2018a).

Box 1: Decree 73/2015 and definitions of HEI types

Definitions of three categories of HEIs (brief descriptions extracted from Decree 73/2015/ND-CP)
1. Research-oriented universities: include training and research specializing in theories; providing degree programs at bachelor, master, and doctorate levels, of which doctorate students account for the biggest proportion.
2. Application-oriented universities: train and provide human resources largely in application orientation; focusing on developing basic research outcomes; applying source technologies in technological solutions, management procedures, to meet the demands of human beings; providing applied bachelor and master programs (accounting for the biggest proportion) and a few research programs at master and doctorate levels.
3. Practice-oriented universities: train and develop learner's practical skills, link training with production and local demands, conduct research toward implementing applied research results to solve problems in real life; providing mainly bachelor programs.

Certification of universities meeting national standards: In 2015, MoET promulgated the so-called national standards for universities (Circular 24/2015/TT-BGDĐT), introducing certification as another QA tool from November 2015. According to this, Circular HEIs prepare a report to submit to MoET to apply for certification, and MoET will then assign the certification job to an accrediting agency. The Circular sets out 8 standards on (1) *land, facilities, and equipment*; (2) *faculties, researchers, and managers*; (3) *curricula and training*; (4) *research and international cooperations*; (5) *finance*; (6) *accreditation*; (7) *ranking status*; and (8) *satisfaction of learners and employers*. Apparently, this Circular was a MoET's move to implement Decree 73 by the government.

Inspection: The inspection of HEIs' operations is stipulated by the Law on Higher Education 2012. MoET's inspection unit is responsible for performing the inspection, including both administration and technical inspection. Other ministerial bodies and provincial authorities also share the task as per the government's deregulations. The inspection covers the implementation and observation of higher education policies with a view to identifying, preventing, and addressing violations. The inspection also carried out in response to complaints and appeals about HEIs' operations.

Actors in National QA System

As per stipulations in the Law on HE, MoET oversees the development of HE and acts as a state agency that manages the quality of HE. DoHE and DoQM are two bodies directly implementing these missions. DoHE is responsible for licensing new HEIs and new degree programs, inspection, certification of 'national-standard' HEIs, and the three-disclosure policy, while DoQM undertakes accreditation and testing and assessment. Under the purview of DoQM are five accrediting centers, which are considered as independent agencies directly conducting evaluation for accreditation. These centers work with HEIs to arrange the accreditation process and charge fees for this service. They are also assigned to carry evaluation services for ranking and stratification.

From this structure, it can be seen that there is an absence of an organization acting a buffer agency between MoET and its departments and accrediting centers. While HEIs can be assessed by accrediting agencies, and recognized by MoET on the basis of the external review results, accrediting themselves is not recognized by any organizations. This possibly creates a gap in the management arrangements of QA and, therefore, should be taken into consideration for the improvement in the structure.

Stakeholders Participating in QA Processes

The implementation of the national QA arrangements, in which accreditation plays a crucial part, involves the participation of both external stakeholders to universities and different internal stakeholders. The evaluation process for accreditation including the self-assessment and external reviews requires the participation of managers, staff members, both academic and administration, and students in different stages. Though this process allows the voice of students to be taken into account, the weight of their voice in practice is still unknown.

Beyond the boundaries of universities, the participation of employers, including enterprises and public organizations, has also been enhanced significantly. Experts and scholars are also invited to provide feedback on the curriculum development in response to accreditation criteria. In addition, as part of the external review, alumni and employer representatives are also invited to interviews during site visits. To recapitulate, almost all stakeholders have played a role in QA activities at different degrees; however, the extent to which they have influenced the decision-making process in HE is still a question.

Results and Challenges of the National QA Arrangements

Slow Progress in Accreditation

After fifteen years from the introduction of the accreditation into the national HE, with lots of changes in standards, procedures and process, and the organization of accreditation, the number of HEIs and programs have been accredited is a modest figure. As of April 2018, of the total 235 universities, 120 have been externally reviewed for the first cycle and accreditation status has been granted to 80 of them. Progress in program accreditation is even poorer. Of around 5000–6000 programs, only 8 programs of 3 universities national-wide have been accredited by local accrediting centers. However, the number of local degree programs have been accredited by international accreditors shows a more optimistic picture. 104 programs of 20 universities, both private and public, have been accredited by AUN-QA, ACBSP, CTI, ABET, FIBAA, AMBA, and IACBE.

T. N. Quyen-Do (2018b) reports a trend in which local HEIs prefer international accreditation to local accreditation. While it is advisable to have degree programs accredited by international and regional prestigious specialist accreditors, international institutional accreditation poses questions about the necessity and effectiveness of this choice. That MoET has encouraged HEIs to apply for international accreditation at both levels partly shows its lack of capacity in meeting HEIs' demands for and public expectations in accreditation.

Low Effectiveness of QA

Though several QA instruments are introduced and applied altogether, the quality of Vietnamese HE is essentially not managed and controlled. Furthermore, the combined adoption of many QA instruments raises concerns about two major issues: the overlapping of standards and scope of work, and the effectiveness of such arrangements.

In the first place, prominent problems are related to the different sets of standards and criteria set out for different instruments. With the adoption of *Accreditation, Licensure, Certification, Ranking,* and *Stratification* in the management of higher education quality, four sets of standards for institutional level are concurrently in use. The question of overlapping standards and criteria is obvious since they all cover requirements on such common areas as land space, facilities, and equipment; human resources (faculties and managers); and finance. In addition, the use of generic standards, which do not have subject-specific requirements in terms of learning outcomes and qualifications, also raises another question. Application of 'one set of standards fits all' ignoring the differences across disciplines may lead to issues relating to the effectiveness of the tools.

Another issue is about the collaborations between state management agencies because these tools are managed and operated by different bodies. Accreditation procedures and decision making are managed by DoQM while Certification, Licensure, and Inspection are managed by the Department of Higher Education (DoHE). This arrangement may cause potential conflict among the instruments. For example, an accredited program or institution recognized by DoQM may be terminated by DoHE due to violation of one of the 'Licensure' requirements. This not only creates contradictory outcomes and impact on the system, but also shows a waste of resources in maintaining all these tools.

Lack of Emphasis on Continuous Improvement

It is not hard to see that the top-down approach has been used extensively in the national QA arrangements. First, all QA regulations are set out in legal documents such as laws, decrees, circulars, which require compliance. Guidelines for QA or accreditations are also promulgated in circulars, leave little room for HEIs' autonomy. All QA instruments run by DoHE and DoQM request absolute conformity from HEIs. Too much emphasis on top-down measures leads to the lack of incentives for continuous improvement.

Also, the mixed arrangement of all these tools may worsen the compliance culture and submissiveness in QA activities in local HEIs. Public HEIs tend to closely observe MoET's licensure and accreditation requirements. They participate in national and regional accreditation systems at both institutional and program levels, but their quality assurance activities are mainly for conforming to accreditation standards, and hardly go beyond these preset requirements. The major findings from the self-evaluation reports are hardly used for improvement purposes. This would be a huge waste of resources for HEIs and the entire QA system. A balance between compliance and improvement is an issue that Vietnamese QA system needs to address in the coming years.

Vietnam QA System Versus Neighboring QA Systems

The development of higher education in Asia in the past 15 years has witnessed remarkable progress in QA activities and cooperation among countries in the region, especially between ASEAN member systems and East Asia countries. In the ASEAN region, regional joint QA initiatives focusing on regional accreditation have benefited the member countries, especially such underdeveloped higher education systems as Vietnam, Cambodia, and Laos. In this section, the national QA systems of two neighboring countries, Indonesia and Thailand, are discussed to provide a glimpse of a regional scenario and have implications about where Vietnam HE QA system stands.

Indonesian QA System

Compared with Vietnamese higher education QA system, the national QA arrangements of Indonesian higher education have been well advanced, in both timing and outcomes, more effective thought leaner.

QA activities at the national level in Indonesia started in as early as 1990s, approximately ten years earlier than in Vietnam. Its beginning was marked with the establishment of the National Accreditation Agency for HE (NAAHE) in 1994. NAAHE's original responsibilities included implementing both accreditation and licensure, and licensure was later passed to the Department of Higher Education. Between 1994 and 2003, both institutional and program accreditations were voluntary and were made compulsory by law in 2003 as per stipulations in the Law on the National System of Education. Specialist accreditation of programs started to be developed in 2006 in collaboration efforts between NAAHE and professional associations in engineering, accounting, teacher training, nursing, pharmacy, and veterinary medicine. Accreditation has been undertaken by both NAAHE and private independent accrediting agencies. By 2015, a majority of the programs (18,841 of 23,224) and 852 HEIs (over 3000 are holding a temporary status) were accredited (Sunarto, 2017). So, in terms of both level of development and outcomes of the accreditation system, Indonesian accreditation is well established and much more advanced than this instrument in Vietnam.

In terms of QA instruments, two main tools are in use: accreditation and licensure; however, they are supplementary to each other. Since 2012, licensure has been used to grant operational licenses to HEIs to allow them to be opened and operate. This operational license acts as a temporary accreditation status which is valid for the first five years from establishment. Before this license expires, HEIs must apply for and obtain an official accreditation status (Sunarto, 2017). That is, licensure is used before accreditation can be obtained, assuring the state quality management covers the entire life cycle of an HEI from the opening throughout its life.

In addition to accreditation and licensure, two other important elements of QA development in Indonesian higher education are the adoption of the National Qualifications Framework launched in 2012 and national standards of HE. HEIs are encouraged to develop their own standards.

QA System in Higher Education in Thailand

Within the ASEAN, Thailand is one of the leaders in QA movements and cooperation in HE. Like Indonesia, Thailand established its national QA system relatively early. Thai Ministry of Education regulates and oversees all HEIs, including state and private HEIs, vocational and technical colleges, and teacher training colleges, through the Office of the Higher Education Commission (OHEC) as a buffer body (Rattananuntapat, 2015). Two of the key functions of this Office are licensing of new private institutions, and monitoring and evaluation of HEIs and programs. Under the supervision of OHEC are two public organizations: the Office for National Education Standards and Quality Assessment (ONESQA) and the National Institute of Educational Testing Services (NIETS). ONESQA was established in 2000 as an independent body for compulsory quality certification and external assessment (Pitiyanuwat, Sujiva, & Pitiyanuwat, 2017).

Right from the beginning, the QA focuses are on both external and internal assessments. A Thai QA framework, a combination of QA standards and Thai Qualifications Framework, has been in place as an important reference point for local HEIs. As can be seen, Thailand set up its QA system with focuses on QA activities and the development of a QA framework, while Vietnam started with accreditation. The direction in which the QA system is developed in Thailand is evidently different from that in Vietnam. QA arrangements in Vietnamese HE are still at an infant stage while in Thai QA system has been well established and reached another level of development. According to Pitiyanuwat et al. (2017), their QA activities are now fully web-based.

References

AUN-QA [ASEAN University Network]. (2016). *Guide to AUN-QA Assessment at Institutional level version 2.0*. Bangkok, Thailand: ASEAN University Network.

Bộ Giáo dục và Đào tạo [Ministry of Education and Training]. (2009). *Thông tư Ban hành Quy chế thực hiện công khai đối với cơ sở giáo dục của hệ thống giáo dục quốc dân* [Circular stipulating regulations on the disclosure of information about education providers in the national education system] (09/2009/TT-BGDĐT).

Nguyen, H. C., Evers, C., & Marshall, S. (2017). Accreditation of Viet Nam's higher education: Achievements and challenges after a dozen years of development. *Quality Assurance in Education, 25*(4), 475–488.

Pitiyanuwat, S., Sujiva, S., & Pitiyanuwat, T. (2017). The rise of quality assurance in Thailand. In M. Shah & T. N. Quyen-Do (Eds.), *The rise of quality assurance in Asian higher education*. Oxford: Chandos Publishing.

Quyen-Do, T. N. (2018a). Accreditation, ranking and classification in Vietnamese higher education: The localization of foreign-born QA models and methods. In N. T. Nguyen & L. T. Tran (Eds.), *Reforming Vietnamese higher education: Global forces and local demands*. Dordrecht: Springer.

Quyen-Do, T. N. (2018b). Current perspectives on internationalisation of quality assurance at the institutional level. In L. T. Tran & S. Marginson (Eds.), *Internationalisation in Vietnamese higher education* (Vol. 51). Cham: Springer.

Quyen-Do, T. N., Huong-Pham, T., & Kim-Nguyen, D. (2017). Quality assurance in the Vietnamese higher education: A top-down approach and compliance-driven QA. In M. Shah & T. N. Quyen-Do (Eds.), *The rise of quality assurance in Asian higher education*. Oxford: Chandos Publishing.

Rattananuntapat, M. (2015). *Quality assurance policies in Thai higher education* (Doctorate thesis), University of Pittsburgh. Retrieved from http://d-scholarship.pitt.edu/26482/1/Rattananuntapat_etd2015.pdf.

Sunarto, K. (2017). The rise of quality assurance in Indonesian higher education. In M. Shah & T. N. Quyen-Do (Eds.), *The rise of quality assurance in Asian higher education*. Oxford: Chandos Publishing.

5

Fifteen Years of Accreditation in Vietnam

Nhi Thi Tran and Phuong Anh Thi Vu

Introduction of Accreditation to Vietnamese Higher Education System

The Vietnamese higher education system expanded rapidly in both the number of students and the number of higher education institutions at the beginning of the twenty-first century. This rapid expansion while the conditions of education were still underdeveloped has affected the quality of Vietnamese higher education (Lam & Vu, 2012; London, 2011; X. T. Pham, 2013). Establishment of a quality assurance system to ensure, maintain, and improve the quality of higher education became more necessary for the country than ever. The topic of establishing a national quality

---

N. T. Tran (✉)
The University of Newcastle, Callaghan, NSW, Australia
e-mail: trannhi.sfl@tnu.edu.vn

Thai Nguyen University, Thái Nguyên, Vietnam

P. A. Thi Vu
Nguyen Hoang Education Group, Ho Chi Minh City, Vietnam

© The Author(s) 2019
C. H. Nguyen and M. Shah (eds.), *Quality Assurance in Vietnamese Higher Education*, https://doi.org/10.1007/978-3-030-26859-6_5

assurance system was discussed by Vietnamese administrators and educators through several workshops and conferences between 2000 and 2002 (Do, Pham, & Nguyen, 2017; K. D. Nguyen, Oliver, & Priddy, 2009). During these years, debate among scholars revolved around defining major challenges and choosing an appropriate quality assurance model for Vietnamese higher education. Great effort was exerted in studying the quality assurance systems from other countries (K. D. Nguyen et al., 2009). International experts were also consulted. At the conclusion of the consultations and study, the American accreditation model was adopted to develop a quality assurance system for Vietnam.

The adoption of the American accreditation system has resulted in the growth of Vietnamese literature on the quality assurance system in higher education (K. D. Nguyen et al., 2009). On the one hand, Vietnamese researchers have doubted the suitability and efficacy of the American model in the context of Vietnam given the large gap in their economies and differences in culture, history, perceptions, and politics, especially the different characteristics of the higher education systems. International experts raised their concern about the model that Vietnam adopted. These scholars argued that the essence of quality assurance is to change culture; yet it is not always easy to change culture in any environment. In a country like Vietnam where traditional culture persists, successful management models adopted in other countries are likely ineffective in Vietnam (K. D. Nguyen et al., 2009). On the other hand, there has been an eager embrace of accreditation as a panacea to help solve all quality problems of education. Among the justifications for the adoption of the American model, there are two prominent reasons. First, it is one of the oldest, largest and most diverse systems. Second, American higher education is recognized as a high-quality system due to its effective accreditation system (K. D. Nguyen et al., 2009).

Considered as the key strategy in improving the quality of higher education in Vietnam, accreditation was first introduced in 2003 with the founding of the General Department of Education Testing and Accreditation, a unit that manages and supervises accreditation activities in the national education system. The establishment of the General Department of Education Testing and Accreditation marked a new stage in the quality assurance system of Vietnam (Lam & Vu, 2012; Ministry of Education and Training [MoET], 2010; Q. G. Nguyen, 2016). The formation of a body specializing in accreditation set a foundation for follow-up activities, including the development of policy and legal frameworks, the establishment of quality assurance units at all levels, implementation at higher education institutions, human capacity enhancement, and international cooperation.

Prior to 2003, the concepts of quality assurance and accreditation were unfamiliar to many Vietnamese people. Quality from 1986 to 2003 equated with adequate resources (Lam & Vu, 2012). With the implementation of accreditation in the higher education system, quality has been reconceptualized as meeting standards (Lam & Vu, 2012). For the first time, accreditation was introduced as a quality assurance instrument with potential prospects for improving the quality of higher education in Vietnam. From accreditation, higher education institutions can better define their objectives and standards for their all activities. Accreditation provides opportunities for higher education institutions to evaluate their own activities and status and adapt them to standards. Accreditation promotes public accountability of higher education institutions (Mai, 2018). With the transition of Vietnamese higher education from elite education to mass education (Lam & Vu, 2012; London, 2011), public accountability is very important because it informs stakeholders about the quality of education providers. The information transparency facilitates fair competition among Vietnamese universities and enhances the improvement of quality in the system. Accreditation is also the basis for the formation of quality culture in higher education institutions. With the official introduction of accreditation, terms such as standards, indicators, transparency, and quality culture are familiar and used. They were absent from Vietnamese higher education prior to 2003.

The Nascent Period (2003–2007)

For a few years after Vietnam decided to apply the American accreditation model to its education system, much effort was devoted to preparing conditions for the implementation of accreditation on a large scale. In the period from 2003 to 2007, the main accreditation activities included the development of legal documents and frameworks, and the establishment of an administration structure.

Legal Documents and Frameworks

The development of an accreditation system consists of the promulgation of legal documents. For a country that has adopted accreditation recently, legal documents and frameworks are effective instruments to put the policy into effect and establish a sustainable accreditation system (X. T. Pham, 2013). The government of Vietnam issued core documents in 2004 and 2005 to support the plan of implementing accreditation in its education system. Resolution 37-2004/QH11 approved by the National Assembly on 3 December 2004 states that education institutions conduct accreditation activities annually. Resolution 14/2005/NQ-CP dated on 2 November 2005 by the government of Vietnam on the fundamental and comprehensive renovation of Vietnamese higher education in the 2006–2020 period emphasizes that accreditation is one of the key solutions to improving quality in education. The document also consists of the plan to develop strategies for quality assurance and an accreditation system. The Ministry of Education and Training (MoET) outlined the tasks of the academic year 2004–2005 through Directive 25/2004/CT-BGD&DT on 2 August of the same year, emphasizing that it was urgent to establish the accreditation system and put it into operation. The temporary regulations on the accreditation of universities were promulgated under Decision 38/2004/QD-BGD&DT by the Minister of Education and Training on 2 December 2004 and used as an instrument to implement accreditation in the higher education system. Noticeably, accreditation was documented in the highest level of legal frameworks—the Education Law and the Higher Education Law. The Education Law in 2005 states that all higher education institutions conduct accreditation periodically and they must publicize results to ensure transparency and supervision. The government's Decree 75/2006/ND-CP promulgated in 2006 that specifies and directs the conduct of acts in the Education Law includes one chapter of accreditation.

A pilot implementation of accreditation took place with the participation of 18 public universities and 2 private universities in the years following the issuance of the temporary regulation. The first accreditation round was conducted with the process of self-study, peer-review, and external evaluation. MoET provided universities with several guidelines on how to conduct the pilot accreditation round. The trial program employed a set of 10 standards and 53 criteria. During the trials, experts continued to adjust and supplement this set. After two years of revision based on comments and advice from Vietnamese and international experts and the feedback and discussions from conferences, the first formal national accreditation framework with 10 standards and 61 criteria was promulgated in 2007 (Lam & Vu, 2012; K. D. Nguyen et al., 2009). The ten standards in this accreditation framework consist of (1) mission and goals, (2) organization and governance, (3) curriculum, (4) training activities, (5) managerial, teaching, and supporting staff, (6) students, (7) research and technology transfer, (8) international cooperation, (9) library, learning equipment, and other facilities, and (10) finance and financial management. With this framework, "for the first time in Vietnam's educational history, a transparent and coherent set of standards for universities came into existence" (Lam & Vu, 2012, p. 131). Legal documents and the national accreditation framework provided a foundation for the development of a Vietnamese accreditation system in the next steps.

Formation of Accrediting Bodies and Human Resource Preparation

With the demand for quality assurance in higher education, the first Vietnamese accreditation unit (the Division of Education Accreditation) was established in 2002. This body first resided in the Ministry of Education and Training Department for Higher Education, then it became a separate division supervised directly by the Ministry of Education and Training in 2003. The unit changed its name to the General Department of Education Testing and Accreditation (GDETA) after the separation. The formation of GDETA marked the formalization of a Vietnamese quality assurance system (Do et al., 2017; Lam & Vu, 2012; Le & Tran, 2017;

H. C. Nguyen, Evers, & Marshall, 2017; H. C. Nguyen, Ta, & Nguyen, 2017). Since its establishment, GDETA has played a critical role in the development of the accreditation system. Legal documents (National Assembly, 2005, 2012; Education Law and Higher Education Law, 2005, 2012; Decree 85/2003/ND-CP) mandate that the Ministry of Education and Training is the state management body to supervise and manage accreditation activities in the education system. The MoET's functions regarding accreditation include the promulgation of a quality framework, the regulation of accreditation cycles, and the establishment and supervision of accrediting agencies. GDETA is a key unit of the Ministry of Education and Training that has conducted these tasks. GDETA is the highest accreditation body in the system granted with MoET's functions and authority articulated in Education Law and Decree 85/2003/ND-CP (Lam & Vu, 2012; Nguyen, Ta et al., 2017).

At the micro-level, the two flagship universities, Vietnam National University in Hanoi and Vietnam National University in Ho Chi Minh City, had set up their quality assurance centers before the formal national quality assurance system was established in 2003. In order to enhance its accreditation system, Vietnam cooperated with the Netherlands in a project from 2005 to 2008 to establish five more quality assurance centers for other key universities, including Thai Nguyen University, Hue University, Da Nang University, Vinh University, and Can Tho University. Unlike the quality assurance centers at the two national universities that had been in operation for a long time, these newly established centers lacked accreditation personnel. In the support of these units, GDETA invited international experts to provide training workshops from 2005 to 2009. These training programs helped develop capacity for Vietnamese accreditation personnel, setting the foundation for the next stage of development.

The University Quality Standard Framework promulgated by the Ministry of Education and Training in 2007 mandates that there must be a quality assurance unit in a higher education institution to conduct its quality assurance and accreditation. In response to this mandate, universities formed their departments specialized in quality assurance. The common functions attached to these departments consist of testing, inspection, and accreditation. With the establishment of the department of accreditation within universities, accreditation bodies have been present at all levels in the higher education system. The completion of the accreditation system was an important step for a large-scale implementation after the pilot accreditation round.

The Stagnation Period (2008–2014)

In the 2008–2014 period, Vietnamese policy-makers at the macro-level continued to develop legal frameworks and mechanisms for the operation of the accreditation system. However, compared with the vigorous activities in the onset period, the implementation of accreditation in this period was slow, leading to criticism from many Vietnamese educators, experts, and researchers for its stagnation (Do, 2017a; Do et al., 2017; Khuc, 2014).

Shaping the Features of Vietnamese Higher Education Accreditation

Vietnam needed evaluation research on the efficacy and sustainability of the adopted model after the first five years of implementation. However, there was not sufficient research to confirm if the higher education accreditation of Vietnam was moving in the right direction (K. D. Nguyen et al., 2009). Without sufficient evaluation research, Vietnamese policy-makers were faced with a problem in making plans for the next stage. Despite the challenge, the General Department of Education Testing and Accreditation made a great effort to continue developing strategies and mechanisms for promoting the accreditation system. Policy-makers at the national level continued to develop legal documents and employ them as a tool for the implementation of accreditation. By the law promulgated in 2005, 2009, 2012, accreditation is obligatory for all higher education institutions and programs (National Assembly 2005, 2009, 2012). To put this mandate into effect, MoET and GDETA provided guidelines, support, and instruction to universities (Nguyen, Ta et al., 2017). MoET and GDETA also assisted higher education institutions in preparing for human resources in accreditation through projects supported by the World Bank (Madden,

2014). Quality frameworks and accreditation processes were introduced to educational managers, accreditation staff, and teachers via several workshops, helping them better understand the concepts, the purpose, value, and nature of accreditation (Nguyen, Ta et al., 2017).

Vietnam has implemented both institutional accreditation and program accreditation. The Ministry of Education and Training promulgated Circular No. 62/2012/TT-BDGDT and Circular No. 38/2013/TT-BDGDT in 2012 and 2013 that provide a definition and guidelines, and describe the procedure and cycle of institutional accreditation and program accreditation. According to these documents, the procedure of institutional accreditation comprises four steps. First, the institution conducts self-assessment, which generates a self-evaluation report. Second, the institution registers for external assessment with an accrediting agency. The accrediting agency conducts an external review by a site visit to the higher education institution. The third step also leads to the generation of an assessment report. The external assessment committee established by the accrediting agency decides if the institution meets standards and this process leads to the final recognition of accreditation outcomes. The certification of institutional accreditation is valid for five years (MoET, 2012b, 2013).

The framework of accreditation with 10 standards and 61 criteria promulgated in 2007 has been used nationwide. An institution needs to satisfy 80% of the criteria in the set of standards to be awarded with certified accreditation (MoET, 2007, 2012a, 2014b). The procedure, cycle, and certification condition for program accreditation are similar to those of institutional accreditation. That means program accreditation also comprises four steps; an accreditation cycle lasts five years; and a program must satisfy 80% of the criteria to receive an accreditation certificate. While there is one set of standards for institutional accreditation, five sets of standards for program accreditation have been developed and promulgated by the Ministry of Education and Training. Of these five sets, one with 11 standards and 50 criteria is used for all higher education programs; three sets varying in numbers of standards and criteria are employed for the accreditation of teacher training programs; and the last is implemented for the nursing program.

Although the mandate of institutional and program accreditation began to be documented in the law and other legal documents simultaneously, the former has been more often implemented than the latter. Some researchers argue that program accreditation is more useful because it has a direct impact on the improvement of the quality of teaching and learning—the core activities in higher education institutions (Do, 2017b). There has been a vigorous implementation of institutional accreditation, with 40 leading universities passing the external assessment in 2009 and almost all the higher education institutions completed their self-assessment reports by 2014 (Do, 2017a); yet only a small number of programs have received external evaluation (Nguyen, Ta et al., 2017). There are two reasons for the slow pace in program accreditation. First, since administrators at the national level and managers at the institutional level seem to have been overwhelmed with the first cycle of institution accreditation, they have had neither time nor resources for program accreditation, leaving this sector almost untouched (Do, 2017a). Second, at present Vietnam prioritizes directing and improving universities to meet minimum standards. The set of standards emphasizing input and process rather than the outcomes shows that Vietnam is repeating the path begun by other countries some decades ago (K. D. Nguyen et al., 2009).

The management of accreditation is highly centralized. GDETA is deeply involved in the accreditation system. The unit develops a common accreditation framework, promulgates accreditation procedures and cycles, establishes, licenses, and supervises accrediting agencies. GDETA also selects accreditors and grants certification. In the early stage before accrediting agencies were founded, GDETA formed groups of external reviewers and conducted external evaluation for higher education institutions. However, this body itself is under the management and supervision of MoET. There is an absence of independence and diversity in the Vietnamese accreditation system compared with other countries like the UK or the United States.

A Period of Stagnation and Issues Open to Debate

More than a decade after of its establishment, the accreditation system in Vietnam is not in full operation. Vietnam still lacks a complete and independent education accreditation system (Do, 2017a; Khuc, 2014).

Education Law (2005, 2009) mandates that all higher education institutions and higher education programs must be accredited. However, there were no significant results in the implementation of higher education accreditation (Khuc, 2014). After the trial period of external evaluation conducted with 40 universities in 2009, none of the Vietnamese higher education institutions received an external assessment between 2009 and 2016. By 2014, only 87% of the country's universities and junior colleges had completed self-assessment reports (MoET, 2014a). Meanwhile, the project on the development of the higher education accreditation system in the period of 2010–2020, approved in 2010, set the objective that in the period 2011–2015, 90% of higher education institutions must receive an external evaluation (MoET, 2010). This objective and many other project objectives have not been achieved (Khuc, 2014). Out of thousands of higher education programs, only 117 completed self-assessment reports based on the framework promulgated by the MoET and 14 programs received certification from international accrediting agencies. Similarly, the project aimed to train 350 accreditors in each year of 2011 and 2012. By 2014, no Vietnamese person received an accreditor certificate. Another plan in the project was to establish three state accrediting agencies in 2012. Only two agencies under the two national universities were established in late 2013, but were in waiting for permission to operate until 2016.

The main reason for the stagnation of accreditation in the 2008–2014 period derived from the cessation of external assessment activities imposed by MoET for a period of reflection, the restructuring of the accreditation system, and the preparation of better conditions for implementation (Nguyen, Evers et al., 2017). Shortages in human resources and budget were other reasons for the slow pace of accreditation. Vietnam lacked accreditation personnel at all levels in the system (Lam & Vu, 2012; H. C. Nguyen, 2018). GDETA has small staff. Usually, there are five or six officials (Do et al., 2017; H. C. Nguyen, 2018) but they have to deal with a huge amount of work, including the supervision of the whole accreditation system, building capacity, revising policy, making and revising frameworks, developing plans and managing projects. In addition, they take responsibility for connecting Vietnamese accrediting agencies and universities with international organizations. Such a huge amount of work is an overload for GDETA with limited staff (Madden, 2014). The shortage in human resources is also a challenge for accrediting agencies. For example, in 2014, the Accrediting Agency of the National University, Hanoi trained the first 35 Vietnamese accreditors. At the time, 760 education institutions were waiting for external assessment. On average, the evaluation for each institution needs 5 reviewers working from three to six months. With the personnel that the agency had, they were able to conduct external evaluation for only 10–20 institutions per year. At universities, a large number of accreditation staff have never received training. Many of the accreditation personnel moved from teaching positions or other departments. These people lacked knowledge, skills, and experience to help implement accreditation programs at the micro-level effectively (Khuc, 2014; H. C. Nguyen, 2018). Another factor challenging the MoET's implementation of accreditation in this period was the shortage in finance (Madden, 2014). In the beginning stage, Vietnam received large support from the World Bank and other international organizations. This financial resource facilitated several accreditation projects in the development of the system. The lack of sustainable resources in the later period affected the pace of implementation.

The stagnation of accreditation had a bad effect on the development of the Vietnamese accreditation system. Higher education institutions wasted their resources, money, and time, since after a long wait for an external review self-assessment reports were no longer suitable and needed to be updated (Do et al., 2017). Educators reduced their belief in accreditation as a key strategy to solve the quality problems in higher education. The law mandates that accreditation is compulsory for education institutions, but after more than 10 years, the first accreditation cycle was not completed. That means the law has not come into effect and the reward and sanction mechanisms are impossible to implement (Madden, 2014).

The Revival of Interest and Activities

The Ministry of Education and Training established three independent accrediting agencies based at two national universities and a regional university in 2014 and 2015. The establishment of independent accrediting agencies has created conditions for the revival of accreditation activities in the higher education system after a long delay. When the accreditation center of Vietnam National University, Hanoi received an operation permit from the MoET in 2014, it began the first training course for 35 accreditors. By 2017, Vietnam had about 700 accreditors (Nguyen, Ta et al., 2017). The MoET established another independent accreditation agency that resides in the Vietnam Association of Universities and Colleges in early 2016.

External evaluation on a large scale took place after the independent accrediting agencies came into operation. Since 2016, many of the higher education institutions that completed self-evaluation reports have registered with the accrediting agencies for external review. By 31 July 2018, 217 out of 235 universities in the higher education system have completed self-evaluation reports (MoET, 2018a). The number of accredited higher education institutions increased quickly in those two years. By the end of 2016, only 12 higher education institutions were awarded accreditation certificates, but the number reached 117 by July 2018 (MoET, 2018a).

At present, the Vietnamese higher education system has focused more on institution accreditation than program accreditation. While 117 out of 235 Vietnamese universities (49.7%) have been accredited, the percentage of accredited programs is very small. Vietnamese universities provide 5000 programs, but only 116 programs have been accredited, accounting for approximately 2.3% (MoET, 2018b). Vietnamese universities tend to choose local accrediting agencies for institutional accreditation and invite international quality assurance organizations to accredit programs. Among 117 accredited higher education institutions, only seven universities have been certified by foreign accrediting agencies. In contrast, local quality assurance organizations have accredited only 10 programs while foreign accrediting agencies have certified 106 accredited programs (MoET, 2018b).

With over ninety percent of universities completing a self-evaluation report, the top-down approach that MoET is applying has proved to be effective (Do, 2017b). Together with the compliance culture existing at Vietnamese public universities, the policy and regulations from the government and MoET have helped accreditation to be quickly implemented at the micro-level (Do, 2017b). However, the final purpose of accreditation is to improve quality. If higher education institutions merely continue to undertake accreditation with a compliance-driven purpose, they will waste time and money without gaining long-term benefits in quality improvement. Therefore, after a successful start, a switch from a top-down management approach to a bottom-up management direction is a necessity to turn accreditation into a part of internal quality assurance within higher education institutions (Do, 2017b).

With a huge number of programs but restricted resources of the accreditation system, it is impossible to accredit all programs in a short time. Many Vietnamese universities have found a solution to respond to the mandate from the MoET while meeting their long-term goals by choosing local accrediting agencies for institutional accreditation and international accrediting agencies for program accreditation. This approach seems to be relevant for Vietnamese higher education institutions in the current context (Do, 2017b). Accreditation requires a large investment of financial resources. Choosing a local agency can help universities avoid a cost burden of accreditation programs if conducted by international organizations. On the one hand, they can satisfy the regulations from MoET with institutional accreditation; on the other hand, they can approach international standards through program accreditation and meet their long-term goals of quality. This trend from the micro-level resonates with the direction from policy-makers at the national level. MoET has encouraged higher education institutions to have their programs accredited by international accrediting agencies. MoET and GDETA have facilitated this strategy by connecting universities with international organizations, and building accreditation personnel's capacity through many projects (H. C. Nguyen, 2017; Nguyen, Evers et al., 2017).

The establishment of independent accrediting agencies has helped GDETA switch its function as an implementation unit to a body of macro-level management, policy-making and system capacity building. In the early stages, GDETA selected accreditors and conducted accreditation programs for universities. The department has now transferred this responsibility to accrediting agencies and provided them with more independence. GDETA has continued to promulgate legal documents and revise standard frameworks to facilitate the implementation of accreditation in the higher education system. A new set of standards adapted from the AUN-QA's standard framework was promulgated in 2017 and began to be implemented in the system in 2018 (H. C. Nguyen, 2018). Although many experts and researchers are concerned that some criteria may not be relevant to Vietnamese higher education institutions (Do, 2017a), the new set of standards and criteria for institution accreditation covers aspects related to improving the quality of a university. The implementation of the new set of criteria will familiarize Vietnamese universities with regional and international standards.

The Role of International Organizations in Vietnamese Accreditation Development

International collaboration has been important at every stage during the 15 years of Vietnamese accreditation development. In the initial stage (2002–2003), Vietnam cooperated with other members of the Southeast Asian Ministers of Education Organization (SEAMEO) to develop a common higher education quality assurance framework for ASEAN countries, and began to implement it in the Vietnamese education system. Founded in 1965, SEAMEO is one of the oldest regional organizations (Madden, 2014). Through workshops and seminars sponsored by SEAMEO, Vietnam exchanged ideas and learned about the experiences of quality assurance in higher education from other ASEAN countries.

With the financial support of the World Bank, Vietnam cooperated with the HBO-raad of Holland in a project from 2005 to 2008 to establish five quality assurance centers in key Vietnamese universities. When the pilot implementation of accreditation began in the Vietnamese higher education system, there was a serious shortage of accreditation personnel, both in quantity and quality (Lam & Vu, 2012). Reviewers from Holland and the United States helped to fulfill the pilot external review for 40 universities. Dutch, American, and Indonesian experts also provided advice on the framework for quality standards and helped to train accreditation staff. Other projects granted by the World Bank and the Asian Development Bank helped to complete the accreditation for many teacher training programs in the higher education system.

At the macro-level, the General Department of Education Testing and Accreditation has been an active member of Asia-Pacific Quality Network

(APQN), the International Quality Assurance Agencies in Higher Education, and the ASEAN Quality Assurance Network. The department has actively engaged in the activities of these organizations (Le & Tran, 2017). For example, GDETA held the Annual APQN conference in 2009 and the APQN international conference and roundtable discussion in 2013. With the participation in quality assurance organizations and active involvement in international quality assurance activities, the capacity of Vietnamese accreditation personnel has significantly improved.

At the micro-level, Vietnamese higher education institutions have cooperated with international organizations. The engagement of Vietnamese universities consists of two aspects. Some leading universities have registered members of international quality assurance organizations. Leaders from these universities have been increasingly interested in international quality standards. Some universities have invited foreign agencies to accredit their programs. In 2017, the University of Social Sciences and Humanity was accredited by the AUN-QA, becoming the first higher education institution in an ASEAN country to receive institutional accreditation conducted by this organization. Vietnamese universities pursue international accreditation as a way not only to improve quality but also to gain reputable status in the system; therefore, they can attract local and foreign students (Do et al., 2017). The international agencies conducting accreditation for Vietnamese programs are ASEAN University Network—Quality Assurance, Commission des Titres d'Ingénieur, Accreditation Board for Engineering and Technology, Accreditation Council for Business Schools and Programs, Foundation for International Business Administration Accreditation, Association of MBAs, International Assembly for Collegiate Business Education, European Network for Accreditation of Engineering Education (MoET, 2018b). Choosing international agencies for program accreditation will continue to be a trend in Vietnam.

Conclusion and Recommendations

Achievements

After 15 years, Vietnam has developed a collection of legal documents that govern the operation of the accreditation system. These documents include laws, resolutions, decrees, decisions, circulars, directives, guidelines, plans, projects, and frameworks related to accreditation. Accreditation is a new activity in Vietnam. The development and promulgation of legal documents have helped to introduce it to stakeholders in a rapid way and facilitate its implementation in the higher education system. They are the basis for the sustainability of the accreditation system. The documents are regularly revised, adjusted, and amended to meet the context and demands of each stage of development, keeping the whole education accreditation system moving in the right direction.

The structure of the accreditation system has been completed with the presence of accreditation units at three levels. GDETA is a state management body for policy-making and managing the system at the macro-level. At the meso-level, there are independent accrediting agencies to conduct external evaluation for universities. At the micro-level, each higher education institution has its own unit responsible for quality assurance and accreditation. Before 2014, when accrediting agencies were absent in the accreditation system, the implementation of accreditation in the higher education system encountered many problems, leading to stagnation for a long time. The completion of the accreditation system is an advantage for the implementation on a large scale.

Human capacity has improved. In the early stage, there was a serious shortage of accreditation personnel at all levels in the system, including experts, external reviewers, and accreditation staff. With projects, training programs, and foreign exchange programs, Vietnam's accreditation human resources have significantly improved in both quantity and quality. The number of accreditors has increased to respond to the demand for external evaluation in the education system. The number of Vietnamese experts, researchers, and educators with better knowledge and expertise in accreditation is increasing. Their comments, ideas, and evaluation of the status of the accreditation system have helped Vietnamese policy-makers adjust policies promptly, make better decisions, and manage the system more effectively. For example, the project on the development of the higher education accreditation system in the period of 2010–2020 planned to establish two independent accrediting agencies in 2012 to conduct external review for the higher education institutions. By 2014, this objective had not been completed. The opinions of experts, researchers, educators, and project funders persuaded MoET from taking action to fulfill this plan (Do et al., 2017). Independent accrediting agencies established in 2014 created the conditions for the revival of interest and activities in the following years.

Stakeholders are more aware of the meaning and role of accreditation in the higher education system. Fifteen years ago Vietnamese educators, teachers, and students were unfamiliar with the concepts of quality assurance and accreditation, and related terms such as standards, criteria, evidence, evidence archive, self-assessment, peer-review, external review, accreditation cycle, institutional accreditation, program accreditation, institution accreditation, program institution, ranking, accountability, transparency, quality culture, quality improvement, internal quality assurance, and external quality assurance. These terms have become common concepts in the culture of Vietnamese higher education.

Literature about Vietnamese quality assurance and accreditation is growing. Both local and foreign researchers have conducted policy and implementation studies of the Vietnamese accreditation policy and its implementation in the past decade and a half. Publications in international and local journals, reports at conferences, statistics from higher education institutions, accrediting agencies, and MoET's archive have contributed a huge number of documents about the 15 year development of the Vietnamese accreditation system. Research results, analysis, points of view, evaluation, feedback, comments, criticism, and recommendations from local experts have been a valuable reference source for Vietnamese policymakers during the past 15 years. They enrich the literature and provide a baseline for further research into Vietnamese education accreditation in the future.

Challenges

The national quality assurance and accreditation system of Vietnam still faces challenges. The independence of the accreditation system has been a debated topic since its early days of establishment. Scholars, experts, and researchers express their doubts about its success if it is not independent from a state body (Dao, 2015; Do, 2017a; Do et al., 2017; Hoang, 2017; Lam & Vu, 2012; Madden, 2014; Nguyen, Evers et al., 2017). The legal status of the national accreditation agency GDETA and accrediting agencies has been unchanged despite warnings, advice, urgings, and criticism from local and international educators and experts. GDETA is still under MoET's supervision and governance. Accrediting agencies function as units belonging to universities with heavy dependence on them for finance and management. The lack of independence of accrediting agency has affected the pace and efficacy of accreditation implementation in the higher education system. The progress of accreditation has been less than expected. Independence and transparency will continue to be a challenge for the development of Vietnamese accreditation in the future.

Maintaining the stability and sustainability of the accreditation system is another challenge for Vietnamese policy-makers and administrators. During its operation in the last 15 years, the accreditation system has showed low stability and sustainability (Do, 2017b; Khuc, 2014). A shortage of funding and personnel makes it difficult to maintain the sustainability of the Vietnamese accreditation system. In the initial stage when there were financial support and experts from international organizations, implementation made good progress. When the funding source ended, the system stagnated. Lack of long-term plans and vigorous implementation is another sign of instability. While the first 5 year accreditation cycle was not completed, MoET promulgated a new set of standards to replace the old one. The introduction of the new set of standards while many higher education institutions were still in the first accreditation round caused difficulty for them in coping with standards and criteria under the new framework. Besides, Vietnam faces a shortage of accreditation personnel with expertise and experience at the policy-making level (H. C. Nguyen, 2018). Accrediting agencies also lack accreditors who have sufficient ability to provide effective and persuasive comments and recommendations in conducting their external reviews (H. C. Nguyen, 2018; Khuc, 2014; T. H. Pham, 2018). Higher education institutions do not have qualified accreditation personnel who understand the value of accreditation and make it an effective activity for internal quality assurance within the higher institution.

The incentive and sanction policy is unclear and documented regulations have not come into effect (H. C. Nguyen, 2018). By law, periodic accreditation is compulsory for all higher education institutions. Universities must publicize accreditation results for accountability and transparency. However, after accreditation "whether a university is given more autonomy, more freedom, and more budget to sustain and improve still remains silent" (Dao, 2015, p. 753). Without the imposition of a reward and punishment policy, higher education institutions' compliance and interest have declined (Do et al., 2017). Universities have now begun to evaluate how much benefit they gained from the national accreditation program, examining if the cost in time and money outweighed the benefits (T. H. Pham, 2018). In addition, a lack of satisfaction with the quality of external evaluation reports and low trust in the competence of external reviewers have reduced the higher education institutions' belief in accreditation as a useful instrument to improve quality (Do, 2017a).

Although accreditation has been a part of the higher education system for 15 years, Vietnamese awareness of accreditation is still low. Universities expect that the announcement of their accreditation to the public may help improve their ability to recruit students. However, many parents and students are ignorant of accreditation and do not make choices based on a university or program being accredited; therefore, accreditation hardly brings recruitment benefits to universities. In some higher institutions, accreditation seems to be a story only among leaders and quality assurance staff. To be more effective, accreditation should be an activity that involves all stakeholders. However, many teachers and students—the stakeholders participating directly in teaching and learning (the core activities at higher education institutions) have little involvement and do not understand the meaning and value of accreditation (T. H. Pham, 2018). Accreditation is a ritualistic activity conducted in many Vietnamese higher education institutions to respond to the government's regulations. A large number of universities pursue accreditation for the purpose of ranking instead of quality improvement (Dao, 2015). Accreditation has not reached the stakeholders who should benefit most from it; thus has failed to meet the final purpose of quality improvement.

Proposed Solutions

Vietnam has adopted the American accreditation model, but it has not fully adopted an independent accreditation system. The independence of a national accrediting agency is important because its evaluation and decisions should not be interfered with or influenced by any outside party (INQAAHE, 2005). The long-time dependence of GDETA as the national accrediting agency on the Ministry of Education and Training has prevented its autonomy and slowed down the progress of accreditation. Scholars describe the current Vietnamese accreditation system as "being both a player and a referee in a match," implying that there is no clear role between the two parties with one being education provider and the other being quality evaluator (S. Nguyen, 2017). Independence of accrediting agencies at the macro-level and the meso-level will promote their operation and help to build stakeholders' trust in the fairness, objectivity, and transparency of accreditation.

Policy-makers at the macro-level need to develop and adjust policies and the management approach to meet the expectations and changes of the current context. Despite the slow pace of implementation, almost all higher education institutions have engaged in the first cycle of accreditation. This shows that top-down management from MoET has proved effective (Do, 2017b) in the way that accreditation has been quickly introduced and largely implemented in the higher education system. However, after the first cycle, the excitement and learning from accreditation have subsided. A switch from a top-down management approach to a bottom-up approach is necessary (Do, 2017b). It would encourage higher education institutions to focus on quality improvement and the development of a quality culture, resulting in long-term benefits. A bottom-up management approach combined with appropriate reward and punishment mechanisms and information transparency will encourage higher education institutions to voluntarily participate in accreditation, enhance the efficacy and sustainability of the accreditation system and finally improve the quality of the higher education system.

Human capacity development should be a priority. A shortage of qualified accreditation personnel has restrained the development of accreditation at all levels. Unqualified accreditors have undermined confidence in accrediting agencies. Vietnam needs more trained accreditors to complete the outlined objectives regarding accreditation. With about 5000 programs still waiting for accreditation, the solution may not lie in an increase in the number of accrediting agencies but rather in an increase in the number and the quality of accreditors. External reviewers for program accreditation need to have expertise in the program to be accredited so that they can provide accurate comments and useful recommendations, helping higher education institutions improve their quality. A combination of accrediting agencies and professional associations would be a good solution for the problem of the shortage of program external reviewers.

One lesson from the past 15 years is that international organizations have made a significant contribution to the development of the Vietnamese accreditation system (Nguyen, Ta et al., 2017). Vietnam should continue to enhance international cooperation in accreditation. Many Vietnamese universities have chosen foreign accrediting agencies for their program accreditation as a way to gain reputation and to learn from professional external reviewers. The policy from MoET that encourages higher education institutions to have programs accredited by reputed international accrediting agencies has showed its efficacy. This strategy, on the one hand, helps to reduce the overload for the local accrediting agencies; on the other hand, helps Vietnamese universities to approach regional and international standards.

Vietnamese education policy-makers have employed accreditation as a key solution to improving the quality of higher education for fifteen years. At present, a baseline study that evaluates the efficacy of the accreditation program and its impact on the improvement of higher education is essential. Plans for the future of Vietnamese accreditation that are based on sufficient evaluation research and that consider various stakeholders' perceptions will help to move the system in the right direction.

References

Dao, K. V. (2015). Key challenges in the reform of governance, quality assurance, and finance in Vietnamese higher education—A case study. *Studies in Higher Education, 40*(5), 745–760.

Do, T. N. Q. (2017a). Kiểm định chất lượng giáo dục: Gian nan bước khởi đầu. *Tia Sáng*. Accessed May 10, 2018 from, http://tiasang.com.vn/-giao-duc/Kiem-dinh-chat-luong-giao-duc-Gian-nan-buoc-khoi-dau-10955.

Do, T. N. Q. (2017b). Kiểm định chất lượng giáo dục: Quốc gia hay quốc tế, trường hay chương trình? *Tia Sáng*. Accessed May 01, 2018 from, http://tiasang.com.vn/-giao-duc/Kiem-dinh-chat-luong-giao-duc-Quoc-gia-hay-quoc-te-truong-hay-chuong-trinh–11018.

Do, T. N. Q., Pham, T. H., & Nguyen, K. D. (2017). Quality assurance in the Vietnamese higher education: A top-down approach and compliance-driven QA. In S. Mahsood & Q. Do (Eds.), *The rise of quality assurance in Asian higher education* (1st ed., pp. 191–207). Cambridge: Elsevier.

Hoang, D. (2017). Kiểm định chất lượng giáo dục đại học: Dân vẫn chưa tin vào kết quả. *VOV* (Hanoi). Accessed May 14, 2018 from, https://vov.vn/xa-hoi/kiem-dinh-chat-luong-giao-duc-dai-hoc-dan-van-chua-tin-vao-ket-qua-707709.vov.

INQAAHE. (2005). *Guidelines of good practice*. Wellington: INQAAHE.

Khuc, H. T. (2014, April 11). Kiểm định chất lượng giáo dục còn bị bỏ ngỏ. *Nhân Dân cuối tuần, Thứ Sáu*. Accessed September 10, 2018 from, http://www.nhandan.com.vn/cuoituan/doi-song-xa-hoi/item/22871802-kiem-dinh-chat-luong-giao-duc-con-bi-bo-ngo.html.

Lam, Q. T., & Vu, T. P. A. (2012). The development of higher education and its quality assurance in Vietnam. In D. Acedo, D. Adams, & S. Popa (Eds.), *Quality and qualities: Tensions in education reforms* (pp. 125–143). Rotterdam, The Netherlands: Sense.

Le, M. P., & Tran, H. L. (2017). *An overview of Vietnamese higher education quality assurance and accreditation system*. Hanoi: MoET.

London, J. D. (2011). *Education in Vietnam*. Singapore: Institute of Southeast Asian Studies (ISEAS).

Madden, M. (2014). Walking the line: Quality assurance policy development and implementation in Việt Nam. *Higher Education, 67*(1), 91–104. https://doi.org/10.1007/s10734-013-9642-8.

Mai, V. C. (2018, July 16). *Education accreditation and requirements for higher education institutions* (2018 ed.). Trung tâm Kiểm định chất lượng giáo dục, ĐH Vinh.

Ministry of Education and Training (MoET). (2007). *Decision No. 65/2007/QD-BGDDT promulgating regulations on standards for accreditation of universities.* Hanoi: MoET.

Ministry of Education and Training (MoET). (2010). *Decision No.4138/QD-BGDDT on approval of the project on the development of the higher education accreditation system in the period of 2010–2020.* Hanoi: MoET.

Ministry of Education and Training (MoET). (2012a). *Circular No.60/2012/TT-BGDDT promulgating regulations on education accreditors.* Hanoi: MoET.

Ministry of Education and Training (MoET). (2012b). *Circular No.61/2012/TT-BGDDT promulgating regulations on accrediting agencies.* Hanoi: MoET.

Ministry of Education and Training (MoET). (2013). *Circular No.38/2013/TT-BGDDT promulgating regulations of procedures and cycles of programme accreditation for universities, colleges and professional secondary schools.* Hanoi: MoET.

Ministry of Education and Training (MoET). (2014a). *Accredited higher education institutions statistics.* Hanoi: MoET.

Ministry of Education and Training (MoET). (2014b). *Decision No.3535/QD-BGDDT promulgating the functions, tasks, powers and organisational structures of MOET.* Hanoi: MoET.

Ministry of Education and Training (MoET). (2018a). *Accredited higher education institutions statistics.* Hanoi: General Department of Education Quality Management, MoET.

Ministry of Education and Training (MoET). (2018b). *Accredited higher education institutions statistics.* Hanoi: MoET.

National Assembly. (2005). *Education law.* Accessed September 25, 2018 from, http://vbpl.vn/tw/Pages/vbpqen-toanvan.aspx?ItemID=6918.

National Assembly. (2009). *Amended education law.* Accessed September, 2018 from, http://vbpl.vn/tw/Pages/vbpqen-toanvan.aspx?ItemID=6918.

National Assembly. (2012). *Higher education law.* Accessed September 25, 2018 from, http://vanban.chinhphu.vn/portal/page/portal/chinhphu/hethongvanban.

Nguyen, H. C. (2017). Impact of international accreditation on the emerging quality assurance system: The Vietnamese experience. *Change Management, 13*(3), 1–9.

Nguyen, H. C. (2018). How to fulfil Vietnam's higher education accreditation strategic plan 2017–2020? *International Journal of Educational Organization and Leadership, 24*(3/4), 17–25.

Nguyen, H. C., Evers, C., & Marshall, S. (2017). Accreditation of Viet Nam's higher education: Achievements and challenges after a dozen years of development. *Quality Assurance in Education, 25*(4), 475–488.

Nguyen, H. C., Ta, T. T. H., & Nguyen, T. T. H. (2017). Achievements and lessons learned from Vietnam's higher education quality assurance system after a decade of establishment. *International Journal of Higher Education, 6*(2), 153–161.

Nguyen, K. D., Oliver, D. E., & Priddy, L. E. (2009). Criteria for accreditation in Vietnam's higher education: Focus on input or outcome? *Quality in Higher Education, 15*(2), 123–134.

Nguyen, Q. G. (2016). Improving accreditation of higher education in Vietnam in the integration process. *International Journal of Science and Research, 5*(3), 1978–1983.

Nguyen, S. (2017). 'Kiểm định chất lượng giáo dục đại học vừa đá bóng vừa thổi còi'. Accessed September 1, 2018 from, https://news.zing.vn/kiem-dinh-chat-luong-giao-duc-dai-hoc-vua-da-bong-vua-thoi-coi-post801469.html.

Pham, T. H. (2018). Impacts of higher education quality accreditation: A case study in Vietnam. *Quality in Higher Education, 24*(2), 168–185.

Pham, X. T. (2013). *Overview of quality assurance and accreditation of education in Vietnam. Report to the national committee for communication.* Paper presented at the AUN-QA International Conference 2013, Hanoi.

6

Drivers of Vietnamese Higher Education Quality Assurance

Nhung Tuyet Thi Pham, Thanh Quy Nguyen and Cuong Huu Nguyen

Introduction

Quality management of Vietnam higher education development has occurred in three phases (Lam & Vu, 2012). During the first phase, before 1985, higher education was highly selective. The students were of outstanding caliber, carefully chosen based on highly competitive university entrance examinations. During this time, the method used for quality management was quality control. The quality of input was controlled by applying stringent selection standards. The quality of output was controlled through examinations, as well as approval of graduation status, certifications, and credentialing. Quality control also existed in the form of the inspectorate system which monitored the key operations in the educational process. The second phase, from 1986 to 2003, witnessed

---

N. T. T. Pham (✉)
College of Foreign Languages, Hue University, Hue City, Vietnam
e-mail: pttnhung.hucfl@hueuni.edu.vn

T. Q. Nguyen · C. H. Nguyen
University of Education, Vietnam National University, Hanoi, Vietnam

the beginning of Vietnam's innovation in higher education. One major goal of the innovation was to increase the capacity of Vietnam's higher education institutions (HEIs) by improving educational access for all students. This goal resulted in a significant increase in student enrollments and the number of institutions. The growth demanded an increase in resources (personnel, infrastructure, and finance) and a new governance mechanism. During this time, quality management focused on investment rather than evaluation of the resource allocation to ensure achievement of the goals. Although this innovation had been in place for the previous two decades, there was no evidence of improved quality in higher education.

In the third phase, from 2004 to the present, Vietnam higher education has continued to increase in the number of student enrollments and institutions (Nguyen, Evers, & Marshall, 2017). In the academic year 2015–2016, Vietnam had 223 universities (163 public institutions and 60 private institutions) with over 1.7 million students (1.5 million full-time) (Nguyen, Evers, & Marshall, 2017). Although the government has made efforts to enhance the quality of the higher education system, this rapid expansion of institutions and enrollments, coupled with ineffective financing and governance policies, has had a negative effect on the quality of higher education in Vietnam. The major problems include a low number of doctoral academic staff, limited involvement in research, lower number of publications in peer-reviewed journals than neighboring countries, high student-to-faculty ratio, lack of soft skills among graduated students (e.g., communicating, problem solving, and ethical reasoning), and high unemployment rates (Nguyen, 2015). The government has issued a series of important national-level documents relating to accreditation in Higher Education Law, clearly stating its plan to introduce accreditation as a new mechanism to manage the quality of higher education. This chapter discusses the drivers of Vietnam higher education accreditation, as well as the impact these drivers have had on accreditation development over the past fifteen years and will have in the future.

Drivers of Vietnam Higher Education Accreditation

Massification in higher education and global, international, and regional cooperation have been the major drivers for development of accreditation in Vietnam higher education.

Massification

The first driver of Vietnam higher education accreditation was the significant changes in higher education. To catch up with global trends, Vietnam's higher education has undergone a massification process to ensure all students have equal access to higher education. This process led to diversification of institutions and high student enrollment. Higher education institutions are classified into three major levels: junior college (awarding three-year bachelor's degrees and diplomas), universities and academies (awarding undergraduate and postgraduate degrees), and Ph.D.-granting research institutes (Hoang & Do, 2014). Accordingly, the higher education system now comprises 223 junior colleges, 236 universities and academies, as well as 64 research institutes that are allowed to award Ph.D.s. Also included are two national universities and three regional universities with special institutional governance structures. The system comprises three types of funding: public, non-public, and foreign-owned tertiary education institutions. Non-public institutions are now for-profit private in nature accounting for 27.5% of the total. There are only a few foreign-owned institutions, more commonly referred to as international universities such as the Royal Melbourne Institute of Technology (RMIT).

Rapid changes in the global higher education contexts, greater higher education international cooperation plus the country's fast economic and demographical growth, have posed huge challenges to the local higher education system. To deal with the quality issues in higher education, the previous approach to quality management focused on quality control and investment rather than evaluating the effectiveness of resource allocation. Vietnam began to seek an alternative quality management approach that was more appropriate for the higher education system's development.

Many other countries in the world including the UK, USA, Australia, and those in the European Union experienced the same quality issues and have used multiple quality management instruments to improve higher education quality such as audit, accreditation and recognition, ranking, benchmarking, certification, licensing, program evaluation, (national) student surveys, and public provision of verified data to provide accountable information to stakeholders (Dao, 2014). Vietnam decided to use accreditation as a key component of its quality assurance (QA) system (Do, Pham, & Nguyen, 2017; Nguyen, Evers, & Marshall, 2017). Vietnam's accreditation originally was a variation of US and European models, with process and assessment methods that include an institutional application for accreditation, an institutional self-study, peer review of compliance, and recognition by an agency not belonging to the educational institutions to recognize the institutions or programs which achieve quality standards (Pham, 2018). As Vietnam has further developed quality assurance models, countries in the Asia-Pacific region have been particularly influential as these countries have similar cultural characteristics that facilitate sharing and exchanging practical experiences. Unlike the voluntary nature of the US accreditation system, Vietnam institutional and programmatic accreditations are by law compulsory for higher education institutions (HEIs) and the key instrument in the national QA system (Pham, 2018, 2019). The purpose of quality assurance and accreditation (QAA) is to build a quality culture and to increase "social accountability" to keep stakeholders well informed of university activities (Madden, 2014). Accreditation also serves as a criterion for state funding, rankings, and stratification of the country's higher education system. In addition, institutional accreditation provides a mechanism for the recognition and transfer of academic credits (Ministry of Education and Training [MoET], 2017a, 2017b).

Global Cooperation

Three important theoretical constructs related to the development of higher education accreditation internationally are globalization, internationalization, and policy attraction (Oliver, Nguyen, & Nguyen, 2006).

In education, globalization is the close intertwined economic and education agendas established by major international donor and technical assistance agencies such as World Bank, the International Monetary Fund, and national overseas aid agencies. Internationalization of higher education is the way that a country maintains its own national identity despite the impacts of globalization. International process promotes the process of exchanging external ideas for policy borrowings of the Vietnamese government. UNESCO and the World Bank are the two long-term strategic partners of the Vietnamese government (Hoang & Do, 2014; Nguyen, 2015).

UNESCO has provided support to Vietnamese higher education for improvement in two fundamental areas: (1) promoting lifelong learning and (2) improving QAA mechanisms. The World Bank has supported progress in improving the higher education system in Vietnam through a series of Higher Education Development Policy Programs (HEDPO) and a "new model" university project. The goal of the first HEDPO was to align the higher education system with the market to respond to social and market demands, improve efficiency and resource utilization, and advance the quality of curriculum, teaching, learning, and research. The goals of the second HEDPO were to increase the quality of teaching in universities and to improve research quality and relevance to Vietnam's socioeconomic needs. The goal of new model was to offer a Western-style university experience (e.g., RMIT) for Vietnamese students through the introduction of Western-style higher education management practices, academic program development, quality assurance (QA) structures, and greater institutional autonomy (World Bank, 2013). In 2017, the World Bank funded US$155 Million to support autonomous higher education in Vietnam. One of this project's goals is to strengthen the key components of higher education such as the national accreditation system (10). It is hoped lessons learned from this project can be generalized to inform policies on autonomy and QA for the universities (Le & Hayden, 2017). The influences of these international agencies have made a significant contribution to the development of Vietnam higher education, especially the implementation of neoliberal approaches to QA that support a fitness for purpose definition of quality (Madden, 2014).

These international agencies influenced and facilitated the introduction of QAA in Vietnam. The concept of QA and the need to establish a national and institutional QA system were first discussed among Vietnamese educators and education officials at the beginning of the twenty-first century (Nguyen, Oliver, & Priddy, 2009). Institutional accreditation was first mentioned in the 2005 Education Law, continued to receive more attention in Education Laws of 2009 and 2012 (Dao, 2014) and 2018 (National Assembly, 2018). Major developments in Vietnam higher education accreditation include government QAA regulations that served as guidelines to develop the accreditation system; establishment of the institutional accreditation standards (the first set issued in 2004 and revised in 2007 and the second set, basically the translation version of Asian University University-Quality Assurance (AUN-QA) version 2.0, issued in 2017 and programmatic accreditation standards in 2016); and establishment of five centers for accreditation (four public and one private) to undertake the evaluation and recognition of education providers and programs. The establishment of accrediting centers (agencies) supports achieving the goals of having all higher education institutions externally reviewed and accredited and 10% of academic programs accredited by December 2020. As of September 2018, there were 120 universities and 3 junior colleges that received Vietnamese institutional accreditation and 6 universities had received international institutional accreditation from AUN-QA and High Council for the Evaluation of Research and Higher Education (HCERES). Ten programs received national program accreditation and one hundred and eleven programs received AUN-QA program accreditation (Vietnam Education Quality Management Agency, 2018a, 2018b). At the micro (institutional)-level, internal quality assurance units specializing in quality assurance were also set up in higher education institutions. These units develop guidelines for internal quality assurance; conduct institution and program self-assessment; evaluate teaching and training support activities; and collect feedback from students, graduates, and employers (Ta, 2016). A policy discourse analysis by Madden (2014) revealed that QA development in Vietnam is walking a fine line between neoliberal reforms (minimal state involvement, maximum borderless economic market, and independent state QA agency) and the state-centric traditions (monitored by the state through a standards-based approach) with Confucian values.

The Higher Education Law draft in 2018 mentioned QA agency stands independent of the university. This change moves toward a Western-style neoliberal QA approach.

International and Regional Cooperation

Accreditation developments and policies in Asian higher education are heavily influenced by Western quality assurance such as the US accreditation and Europe Bologna processes (Pham, 2019). QA approaches in support of neoliberalism, managerialism, and corporatization were introduced into Asia both during the period of colonization and later through globalization and international cooperation (Dao, 2014). While the Asian countries may share many cultural characteristics, considerable gaps exist in the development levels of their higher education systems and in other subsystems such as economic and political settings. Major differences in the Asia region are diverse perceptions about the quality concept; purpose of QA systems; methods to promote quality; responsibilities for QA at the regional, national, and institutional levels; voluntary or compulsory nature of QA participation; procedures of reporting; and follow-up activities. Therefore, Hou, Chen, and Morse (2014) as cited in Pham (2019), classified QA structures in Asia either as "glonacal" (QA systems with accreditors at three levels: global, national, and local (e.g., China, Hong Kong, Japan, Malaysia, and Taiwan) or "non-glonacal" with developing agency structures (e.g., Cambodia and Vietnam)). Based on various factors in QA development and implementation, Southeast Asia QA structures are classified into three groups: (a) consolidated (Brunei, Indonesia, Malaysia, Thailand, the Philippines, and Singapore); (b) developing (Cambodia, Lao, and Vietnam); and (c) newcomer (Myanmar) (Pham, 2019).

To keep up with recent international QA trends and to enhance its QA capacity, Vietnam became an active member of Asia-Pacific Quality Network (APQN), International Network of Quality Assurance Agencies in Higher Education (INQAAHE), the AUN, and the Southeast Asian Ministers of Education Organization (SEAMEO) (Madden, 2014). In general, consensus of the members of these regional networks (a) recognizes the need to protect the state's role in QA, (b) supports privatization of higher education, (c) expands the movement of professionals within the region, and (d) encourages free trade. Of the four regional agencies, APQN has had the strongest presence in Vietnam. APQN was established to assist higher education quality assurance to maintain and improve higher education standards in the Asia-Pacific area. It organized activities for Vietnam to establish networks, take part in external review panels, participate in workshops and conferences, and sign memorandums of understanding with other agencies in Asia. SEAMEO supports the internationalization process and transnational education trends and assists member countries to be more competitive in the global knowledge economy, through better human resource management, long-range planning, and policy reforms, especially walking the line between neoliberal and state-centric QA policies. Although the blending of neoliberal reforms and state-centric QA mechanisms is contrary to some international norms of QA, the regional organizations in Southeast Asia may adjust the norms to solve the tensions between neoliberalism practices that foster institutional competition, transparency, accountability, and institutional autonomy and state policies related to tuition, enrollment, and funding that limit the role of the market in institutional competition (Madden, 2014; Nguyen, Ta, & Nguyen, 2017; Pham, 2019).

Another key driver is the aspiration to create education hubs in countries such as Singapore, Malaysia, and Hong Kong (Coates & Shah, 2017). Increased numbers of international students are now considering studying in China, Singapore, Malaysia, and Hong Kong. There is also the growing phenomenon of academics and other practitioners relocating to Asia for employment and business purposes. Increased numbers of multinational firms are now moving into Asia. Cooperation has been promoted by government policies related to higher education, such as growth of student participation, increased mobility of graduates, reliance on new private/commercial providers, attracting donors, and learning from others' experience to determine Vietnam's comparative advantage in the global market (Dao, 2014; Le & Hayden, 2017).

Drivers' Impact on Vietnam Higher Education Accreditation

Massification in higher education, cooperation with global agencies (e.g., UNESCO and World Bank), international agencies (e.g., INQAAHE) and regional agencies (e.g., APQN, AUN-QA, and SEAMEO), and changes in the Higher Education Law have resulted in the improvement in higher education accreditation.

Achievements

Although higher education accreditation in Vietnam is still in an early stage, initial achievements will lay the foundation for future improvement. Six recent QA achievements are the establishment of a national QA agency, general department of education testing and accreditation (GDETA), the development of regulations relating to accreditation activities for Vietnam's HEIs, the completion of a horizontal structure for the QA system, the establishment of four public and one private center for accreditation to be responsible for external reviews, professional development for academic staff to conduct external and internal quality assurance activities, the establishment of QA units within all HEIs, and the implementation of the National Accreditation Plan for higher education in Vietnam to 2020 (Do et al., 2017; Le & Hayden, 2017; Nguyen, Evers, & Marshall, 2017). The implementation of institutional and program AUN-QA standards for higher education has enabled the engagement of QA units within universities to conduct internal quality assurance (IQA) activities such as monitoring institutional performance, including students' progress, pass rates, dropout rates, employers' feedback, and alumni's feedback, and then communicating such feedback into intuitional activities to make quality improvement decisions (Pham, 2019). An IQA system generally has three main functions: monitoring, evaluating, and improving quality. Some HEIs are deploying an ISO quality management system to more effectively manage their documentation and filing system. Some HEIs have adopted the MoET's standards as a guide for quality management (Nguyen, Evers,

& Marshall, 2017). Whichever approach is taken, all the HEIs attempt to improve the quality of student learning.

The second achievement is in making progress toward implementation of a neoliberal QA approach. First, educators and lawmakers have worked on developing a policy that provides more autonomy to the HEIs. In addition, financial support from the World Bank has enabled piloting the implementation of autonomy practices. This aid is aimed at preparing Vietnamese HEIs to be more responsible and accountable for the quality of student learning. Also, since 2018, Vietnamese HEIs have been implementing the translation of AUN-QA standards version 2.0 for institutional accreditation, reflecting further progress in establishing a neoliberal QA approach. This set of accreditation standards follows the conceptual framework of Plan-Do-Check-Act (PDCA). To work on the PDCA process effectively, institutions must have enough autonomy to state their mission, operationalize the mission into strategic planning, set measurable goals and objectives, collect suitable assessment data, and then allocate appropriate resources to achieve the goals. This quality improvement model aligns with the current assessment movement in USA for the past thirty years (Suskie, 2018). Assessment movement served as a milestone in US accreditation standards to move toward outcome-oriented standards (Gaston, 2014). This implied the initial achievements from Vietnam accreditation follow not only with the current trend of accreditation in the regions but also with developed countries.

Although there are no longitude and empirical research studies on the impact of accreditation on the quality of student learning in higher education, two initial case studies reinforced some expected improvement in the accreditation process (Nguyen & Ta, 2018; Pham, 2018). Both studies indicated that accreditation has led to improvement in (a) management of academic programs, teaching activities, lectures and facilities, (b) support of lecturer, staff, and learners (Nguyen & Ta, 2018), and (c) engagement of various stakeholders in the quality conversation (Pham, 2018). The research findings indicated there is no direct evidence that accreditation results in quality improvement. Still, these case study researchers hoped that improvement in management and infrastructure will lead to direct evidence of quality improvement.

Opportunities

Quality is a process; therefore, there are always areas to make improvement. Based on the two initial achievements in Vietnam accreditation (infrastructure of accreditation and PDCA model to improve the quality of student learning), some opportunities for Vietnam higher education accreditation are to build and sustain a culture of assessment similar to USA to maximize the benefits of PDCA, to clarify the level of independence of center for educational accreditation, and to conduct national and empirical study about the impact of accreditation on higher education accreditation.

The fact that Vietnam's higher education accreditation infrastructure has been sustained for more than ten years provides optimism and opportunity for Vietnam accreditation to promote the implementation of assessment meaningfully. Additional trainings for QA staff and faculty on assessment practices and practical experience are essential to conducting assessment effectively. More workshops and conferences on assessment topics will support the effective implementation of outcome assessment across the institutions and enable them to actively make plans for improving the quality of student learning. When institutions have created an effective infrastructure to collect evidence of student learning, it will be necessary for them to promote a culture of assessment to sustain the quality improvement process (Missouri State University—West Plains, 2010). Some criteria for building a culture of assessment are:

1. Faculty members are engaged in interpreting assessment results, discussing their implications, and recommending changes in academic programs and other areas in order to improve student learning.
2. Academic units or programs are collecting, interpreting, and using the results obtained from assessing student learning in general education, undergraduate majors, and graduate programs.
3. Faculty conclusions, reached after reviewing the assessment results, and the recommendations they make regarding proposed changes in teaching methods, curriculum, course content, instructional resources, and in academic support services are incorporated into

regular departmental and/or institutional planning and included in the determination of the priorities for funding and implementation.
4. Assessment findings about the state of student learning are incorporated into reviews of academic programs and into the self-study of institutional effectiveness.
5. Academic unit heads are documenting the changes made in pedagogy, curriculum, course content, academic resources, and support services to improve student learning as a result of the faculty's responses and the assessment.
6. Student learning is central to the culture of the university and finding ways to improve it is ongoing.
7. A "culture of evidence" has emerged, sustained by a faculty and administrative commitment to excellent teaching and effective learning.
8. Explicit statements regarding the university's expectations for student learning are widely publicized.
9. Programmatic benchmarks are established, against which student's learning outcomes are assessed.
10. Demonstrated student learning, performance, and achievement are publicly and regularly celebrated by the university.

Vietnamese policy discourses (Madden, 2014; Pham, 2018, 2019) have defined quality as fitness for purpose, meaning the organization has appropriate procedures for the specified purposes and that there is evidence to show that these procedures are in fact achieving the specified purposes (3). However, the philosophy of outcome assessment relies heavily on student transformation, the "value-added" of knowledge and skills students have gained as of their graduation. Therefore, Vietnam's accreditation experts should revisit the definition of quality, as fitness for purpose relies more on procedures than outcomes.

External donors such as World Bank and UNESCO recommended that Vietnam's QAA system follows the neoliberalism QA approach of Western countries such as the USA, Europe, and Australia. Although discussions related to the Higher Education Law 2018 have considered separating accreditation agencies from the universities, they are still recognized by a governmental agency, GEATA. This dependence has received much concern from Vietnamese educators who question the accuracy of external evaluations under this structure (Nguyen, 2015; Nguyen, Ta, & Nguyen, 2017; Pham, 2018, 2019). At this point, an opportunity exists for Vietnam to establish an independent and not-for-profit accreditation council to recognize the national centers for accreditation. As an example, US regional accreditation agencies are recognized by the Council on Higher Education Accreditation (CHEA), a non-governmental and not-for-profit organization (Brittingham, 2009; Eaton, 2012).

It would be beneficial to conduct an empirical study to evaluate the impact of accreditation on higher education management and quality of student learning across institutions to gain a bigger picture of the processes. A gap analysis would provide evidence for accreditation experts to identify the positive impacts of accreditation and areas where additional support or resources are needed to maximize the benefits for higher education quality. Also, in order to triangulate the accuracy of quality management tools, multiple quality management measures should be used, such as ranking or performance indicators, to evaluate higher education quality.

Conclusion

Massification in higher education has been a major factor in leading to concerns about higher education quality. Most countries use accreditation as a primary quality management tool to ensure the high quality of student learning. In addition to massification, global donors such as UNESCO and World Bank, international cooperation (INQAAHE), and regional cooperation (APQN, AUN-QA, and SEAMEO) have driven the development of higher education accreditation in Vietnam. Through the funding of higher education projects, global cooperation has encouraged Vietnam higher education accreditation to use a neoliberalism QA approach, common in Western QA models, to improve the quality of higher education. However, time is needed for the full implementation of this approach, as Vietnam higher education is based on state-centric management (Pham, 2018). International and regional cooperation has supported Vietnam in improving human resources in accreditation and by sharing the experience of walking the fine line toward a neoliberalism QA approach (Madden,

2014). Three major efforts made by Vietnam in implementing the neoliberal approach have been to make accreditation agencies more independent, granting greater autonomy to higher education institutions, and implementing principles-based accreditation standards. Another step needed to successfully implement this approach in the new accreditation standards is to revisit the existing definition of quality as fitness for purpose. An alternative definition of *quality as transformation*, the growth of students' knowledge and skills gained, should be considered as the major criteria to evaluate quality in higher education. This change in definition would encourage quality assurance units to conduct more meaningful assessment by showing the "value-added" in the teaching and learning processes. In this scenario, accreditation serves as an intrinsic motivation to improve the quality of student learning rather than providing superficial marketing to attract more student enrollment (Pham, 2019).

Acknowledgements This paper acknowledges the assistance of Dr. Do Minh Hoang for the abstract and Dr. Oliver for the review.

References

Brittingham, B. (2009). Accreditation in the United States: How did we get to where we are? *New Directions for Higher Education, 145,* 7–27.

Coates, H., & Shah, M. (2017). The growing prominence of quality assurance in Asian. In *The rise of quality assurance in Asian higher education* (pp. xxi–xxxi). https://doi.org/10.1016/b978-0-08-100553-8.00017-3.

Dao, K. V. (2014). Key challenges in the reform of governance, quality assurance, and finance in Vietnamese higher education—A case study. *Studies in Higher Education, 40*(5), 745–760. https://doi.org/10.1080/03075079.2013.842223.

Do, Q. T. N., Pham, H. T., & Nguyen, K. D. (2017). Quality assurance in the Vietnamese higher education. In *The rise of quality assurance in Asian higher education* (pp. 191–207). https://doi.org/10.1016/b978-0-08-100553-8.00005-7.

Eaton, J. S. (2012). *An overview of U.S. accreditation.* Available at: http://www.chea.org/pdf/Overview%20of%20US%20Accreditation%202012.pdf.

Gaston, P. (2014). *Higher education accreditation: How it's changing, why it must.* Sterling, VA: Stylus Publishing, LLC.

Hoang, M. D., & Do, T. N. Q. (2014). Higher and tertiary education in Vietnam. In T. L. Tran, S. Marginson, M. D. Hoang, T. N. Q. Do, T. T. T. Le, T. N. Nguyen, T. P. T. Vu, N. T. Pham, T. L. H. Nguyen, with T. H. T. Ho (Eds.). Palgrave Macmillan. https://doi.org/10.1057/9781137436481.

Lam, Q. T., & Vu, T. P. A. (2012). The development of higher education, and its quality assurance, in Vietnam. In C. Acedo, D. K. Adams, & S. Popa (Eds.), *Quality and qualities: Tensions in education reforms.* Rotterdam: Sense Publishers.

Le, L. T. K., & Hayden, M. (2017). The road ahead for the higher education sector in Vietnam. *Journal of International and Comparative Education, 6*(2), 77–89. https://doi.org/10.14425/jice.2017.6.2.77.

Madden, M. (2014). Walking the line: Quality assurance policy development and implementation in Việt Nam. *Higher Education, 67*(1), 91–104. https://doi.org/10.1007/s10734-013-9642-8.

Ministry of Education and Training (MoET). (2017a). *Circular 12/2017/TT-BGDĐT promulgating regulations on accreditation for higher education institutions.* Hanoi, Vietnam: The Author.

Ministry of Education and Training (MoET). (2017b). *Plan No. 118/KH-BGDDT on accreditation implementation for higher education institutions in the period from 2017 to 2020.* Hanoi, Vietnam: The Author.

Missouri State University—West Plains. (2010). *The culture of assessment.* Retrieved from http://wp.missouristate.edu/assessment/CultureOfAssessment.htm.

National Assembly. (2018). *Law amending and supplementing a number of the higher education law.* Hanoi: National Assembly.

Nguyen, H. C., Evers, C., & Marshall, S. (2017). Accreditation of Viet Nam's higher education. *Quality Assurance in Education, 25*(4), 475–488. https://doi.org/10.1108/qae-11-2016-0075.

Nguyen, H. C., & Ta, T. T. H. (2018). Exploring impact of accreditation on higher education in developing countries: A Vietnamese view. *Tertiary Education and Management, 24*(2), 154–167. https://doi.org/10.1080/13583883.2017.1406001.

Nguyen, H. C., Ta, T. T. H., & Nguyen, T. T. H. (2017). Achievements and lessons learned from Vietnam's higher education quality assurance system after a decade of establishment. *International Journal of Higher Education, 6*(2), 153. https://doi.org/10.5430/ijhe.v6n2p153.

Nguyen, H. T. (2015). Reviewed work: *Higher education in Vietnam: Flexibility, mobility and practicality in the global knowledge economy* by Ly Tran, Simon Marginson, Hoang Do, Quyen Do, True Le, Nhai Nguyen, Thao Vu, Thach Pham, Huong Nguyen. *Higher Education, 70*(5), 899–901.

Nguyen, K. D., Oliver, D. E., & Priddy, L. E. (2009). Criteria for accreditation in vietnam's higher education: Focus on input or outcome? *Quality in Higher Education, 15*(2), 123–134. https://doi.org/10.1080/13538320902995766.

Oliver, D., Nguyen, K. D., & Nguyen, T. T. P. (2006, November 28–30). *Higher education accreditation in Vietnam and the U.S.: In pursuit of quality*. APERA Conference, Hong Kong.

Pham, H. T. (2018). Impacts of higher education quality accreditation: A case study in Vietnam. *Quality in Higher Education, 24*(2), 168–185. https://doi.org/10.1080/13538322.2018.1491787.

Pham, H. T. (2019). Limited legitimacy among academics of centrally driven approaches to internal quality assurance in Vietnam. *Journal of Higher Education Policy and Management*, 1–14. https://doi.org/10.1080/1360080x.2019.1565298.

Suskie, L. (2018). *Assessing student learning: A common sense guide* (3rd ed.). San Francisco, CA: Jossey-Bass.

Ta, T. T. H. (2016). *Impacts of accreditation policy on training management of two national universities* (Dissertation). Vietnam National University, Hanoi.

Vietnam Education Quality Management Agency. (2018a). *List of higher education institutions, teacher training colleges and teacher training schools completing self-evaluation reports, being accredited (until 30 November 2018)*. Hanoi: VQA.

Vietnam Education Quality Management Agency. (2018b). *List of programmes that were evaluated/recognized (until 30 November 2018)*. Hanoi: VQA.

World Bank. (2013). *Higher education develops policy program: Third operation*. Washington, DC: World Bank.

7

Stakeholders' Engagement in Quality Assurance in Vietnam

Huong Thi Pham

Introduction

Quality assurance in higher education has been introduced and developed in Vietnam for more than 15 years. Based on the Chiba Principles initiated by Asia Pacific Quality Network (APQN, 2008), the QA system in Vietnam is expected to be composed of three components: internal quality assurance (IQA), external quality assurance (EQA), and quality assurance agencies (QAA). The two primary purposes of developing a quality assurance system are to ensure that higher education is accountable to their provision and to help improve higher education quality (Danø & Stensaker, 2007).

There has been an argument that many different groups of stakeholders in higher education may have diverse expectations and experiences towards higher education quality. They have the rights to define quality from their own perspectives (Pham & Starkey, 2016). This has led to

---

H. T. Pham (✉)
Ho Chi Minh City University of Education, Ho Chi Minh City, Vietnam
e-mail: huong.pham@ier.edu.vn

challenges that colleges and universities face to be accountable to various groups of stakeholders. As Santiago, Tremblay, Basri, and Arnal (2008) cautioned that, "These differences in perceptions of quality by different stakeholders are at the root of misunderstandings and conflicts between the different actors of quality assurance systems" (p. 262). One of the positive measures to address these challenges is to engage them in quality assurance system, and stakeholder engagement has become a norm in higher education governance in many countries (Beerkens & Udam, 2017).

The Concept of Stakeholder Engagement

Stakeholder engagement has become a highly visible issue in higher education governance (Beerkens & Udam, 2017). The level of their engagement varies, from offering advises on national policies and supranational initiatives (OECD, 2002), or serving in university boards and other advisory bodies (Stensaker & Vabø, 2013), or providing input for programme design and development as well as quality assurance (Diamond, 2008). Academic interest in the topic has increased over the past years as well. A number of recent articles study issues like stakeholder identification, stakeholder management, and stakeholders' expectations to higher education (Alves, Mainardes, & Raposo, 2010; Mitchel, Agle, & Wood, 1997). These studies have been focused on theories of stakeholders, stakeholders in higher education, and their roles.

Theories of Stakeholders

Mitchel et al. (1997) propose a theory of stakeholder identification and salience, which includes the concepts of power, legitimacy, and urgency (see Fig. 7.1). Power is "a relationship among social actors in which one social actor, A, can get another social actor, B, to do something that B would not have otherwise done" (p. 869). Legitimacy refers to the actions of an organisation that are desirable and appropriate according to the norms, beliefs, and values of the society. Urgency is the concept that refers

7 Stakeholders' Engagement in Quality Assurance ...

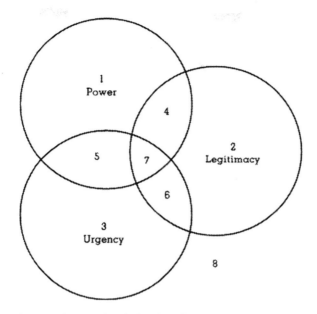

Fig. 7.1 Qualitative classes of stakeholders (Mitchel et al., 1997, p. 872)

to stakeholders' call for immediate attention. The construct salience refers to the claims of the stakeholders and to what extent the leaders prioritize them. All three concepts of power, legitimacy, and urgency are socially constructed phenomena.

From this theory, the authors classify seven types of stakeholders based on the attributes they have (Fig. 7.2). Three of these seven types possess one attribute, other three have two of the attributes, and one has all three of the attributes mentioned in the above section. Latent stakeholders only have one of the attributes. These types are: dormant stakeholder, who has power but not legitimacy or urgency; discretionary stakeholder has legitimacy but not power or urgency; demanding stakeholder has urgency but not power or legitimacy. Expectant stakeholders are those who have two of the attributes. Dominant stakeholder has both power and legitimacy, but not urgency; dependent stakeholder has both legitimacy and urgency but not power; dangerous stakeholder has both power and urgency, but not legitimacy. Definitive stakeholders have all three attributes.

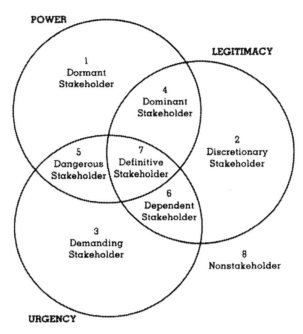

Fig. 7.2 Stakeholder typology (Mitchel et al., 1997, p. 874)

Expectant stakeholders can become a definitive stakeholder if they get the missing attribute.

Stakeholders in Higher Education

Beerkens and Udam (2017) suggested that the views on who should be considered as 'stakeholders' in higher education are different, depending upon the breadth and depth of the definition. By a classic definition, a stakeholder is 'any group or individual who can affect or is affected by the achievement of the organization's objectives' (Freeman, 1984, p. 46). From this definition, Burrows argued that a long list of potential stakeholders could be inspired (Burrows, 1999), and he categorised as internal (e.g. university leaders, employees, potentially also students) and external stakeholders (e.g. employers, various societal actors, media).

Watson (2012), on the one hand, believed that some of the groups are not really a 'stakeholder', having quite a low 'risk' associated with their 'stake'. On the other hand, he agreed that universities as large-scale corporations must be able to balance all voices from these groups.

In the last two decades, two stakeholder groups in particular have gained a widely accepted role in various higher education affairs—students and employers (Smeby & Stensaker, 1999), one as internal and the other as external as identified by Burrows (1999). The trend could be contributed to the typology by Mitchel et al. (1997) adapted by European Standards and Guidelines for Quality Assurance (ESG) considering students and employers as definitive stakeholders who have power, urgency, and legitimacy to engage in higher education (Leisyte & Westerheijden, 2014).

In Quality Assurance

To assure quality in higher education, using this stakeholder approach could be a guideline to identify relevant stakeholders for quality assurance and their potential roles in the QA processes and systems (Matei & Iwinska, 2016). These authors argued the relevance of these stakeholders depends on the extent to which a group of stakeholder takes part in or is in a position that may affect the achievements or performance of higher education institutions (HEIs), and consequently, they should involve in quality assurance.

Matei and Iwinska (2016), based on the different quality assurance approaches, identify several key groups of stakeholders (at different levels of engagement) in quality assurance: academics (both domestic and foreign), students, governments and authorities, employers or industry representatives, professional associations (p. 35).

Srikanthan and Dalrymple (2003) grouped stakeholders into four key categories based on the similarity they may share defining higher education quality: (a) providers (e.g. funding bodies and the community, taxpayers); (b) users of products (e.g. students); (c) users of outputs (e.g. employers); and (d) employees of the sector (e.g. academics and administrators).

Another author, Watty (2003), from the perspective of demand and supply, categorised potential stakeholders into four key groups at each side:

governments, quality assurance agencies, higher education institutions, and individual academics (on the supply side of higher education) and students, employers, parents, and society at large (on the demand side).

The roles and level of engagement of these various groups in quality assurance policies and practices differ across countries (Santiago et al., 2008).

The Role of Stakeholders in Quality Assurance

Beerkens and Udam (2017) reviewed related literature on stakeholder engagement and governance, identifying two theoretical streams of stakeholder engagement. The first stream is *'corporate governance'* seeing universities as autonomous market players. As a result, the strength of stakeholders' claims depends on political norms and an institutional framework (Benneworth & Jongbloed, 2010). The second one is the one covering a *broader governance approach*, redefining the role of government as an (external) stakeholder for universities, as an articulator of its wishes and interests appropriate for influencing (semi-) autonomous universities.

The origins of the current trend towards stakeholder engagement can be drawn to a set of ideas captured in the 'better regulation' agenda and in 'collaborative' and 'participatory' approaches to governance (Beerkens, 2015; Beerkens & Udam, 2017) or turning from collegial governance to managerial and stakeholder and network governance, the role of the internal and external stakeholders, therefore, has increased (Leisyte & Westerheijden, 2014). Some argue that greater reliance on diverse, also non-governmental actors leads to the idea that consulting and engaging stakeholders is an important element in successful governance. In Europe, stakeholder engagement is promoted to respond to increasingly changing higher education governance towards more accountability to society (Leisyte & Westerheijden, 2014). Consequently, institutions of higher education are expected to engage in continual dialogue with relevant groups, while providing accountability, quality, effectiveness, and efficiency (Jongbloed, Enders, & Salerno, 2008).

Beerkens and Udam (2017) identified main contributions that stakeholder engagement can make: contribution to effectiveness, to legitimacy and to appropriateness of a regulation or policy based on various streams of governance theories. A second contribution of stakeholder engagement relates to the notion of 'accountability'. Thirdly, stakeholder engagement can be valuable not only for its outcome but also as a platform for shaping views through a communicative process (Beerkens & Udam, 2017). Similarly, Ulewicz (2017) argued that HEIs as enterprises operate in a dualistic environment. In order to achieve success, the aims of internal stakeholders, the first-degree environment, ought to be compatible with the aims of external stakeholders (the second-degree environment) (p. 99).

Stakeholders in Quality Assurance

The State as a Stakeholder

Government bodies often play an important role in the quality assurance of higher education. In some countries, they are directly in charge of the coordination of quality assurance procedures, while in others this responsibility has been devolved to one or more separate quality assurance agencies/bodies with varying levels of autonomy from government authorities. In the latter case, government authorities sometimes make final decisions regarding accreditation or corrective action on the basis of recommendations of the quality assurance agencies/bodies.

The oldest tradition of accreditation comes from the United States on the basis of voluntary associations rather than government authorities. Quality accreditation in the United States is either regional (institutional assessment) or specialised/professional (programme assessment). These agencies are not government authorities, but the government relies on accreditation by these voluntary associations for establishing eligibility for various forms of state funding. However, the United States Department of Education, a federal agency, and the Council for Higher Education Accreditation carry out the recognition of accrediting agencies (Eaton, 2004). Similarly, the EQA agencies in Japan must be recognised by the Ministry of Education, Culture, Sports, Sciences, and Technology (Kis, 2005).

On the other hand, governments in Europe usually the agencies to set up and fund external quality assurance systems with the involvement of institutions of higher education and other stakeholder groups, including students and business representatives or employers in some cases (Matei & Iwinska, 2016).

Only a few countries (Australia for accreditation, China, Iceland, Japan, Korea, The Netherlands, New Zealand, and the Russian Federation and Switzerland) have government bodies directly in charge of the coordination or implementation of quality assurance activities. The Australian case is peculiar. For several other federal States in Australia, quality assurance is a joint responsibility of the federal and regional levels of government, with the federal State involved in the general steering and harmonisation of the quality assurance system while accreditation is delegated to states and territories for higher education institutions under their jurisdiction. However, the backbone of quality audits is performed by the Australian Universities Quality Agency (AUQA).

But in most countries, quality assurance responsibility is shared between government authorities and one or more agencies coordinating and implementing quality assurance operations. Quality assurance activities are performed by a single agency in Australia (for university audits), Croatia, Estonia, Finland, Greece, Norway, Poland, Portugal, Sweden, and the UK. By contrast, two or more intermediate agencies/bodies are involved in Belgium (Flemish Community), Chile, China, The Czech Republic, France, Japan, Mexico, The Netherlands, New Zealand, the Russian Federation, Spain, and Switzerland. Professional and sectoral agencies are also involved in Korea and Poland.

Among countries where two or more agencies are involved in quality assurance activities, these separate agencies cover different categories of HEIs in Belgium (Flemish Community), The Czech Republic, Japan, Korea, The Netherlands, New Zealand, and Switzerland. In other countries, there are several rationales for having more than one agency. Some intermediate agencies are in charge of specific disciplines and/or levels of study in Chile, China, France, Japan, Korea, and Mexico. Similarly, there are different agencies for different types of approaches in China, Japan, The Netherlands, and the Russian Federation whereas in Spain, the different agencies reflect the federal nature of the quality assurance system. Lastly, Belgium (Flemish Community), Chile, Japan, and The Netherlands have a pyramidal organisation whereby some intermediate agencies are in charge of pre-evaluations which are subsequently examined by another intermediate agency.

Students as Stakeholders

Students have gained a bigger 'stake' through the introduction of (high) tuition fees in the 1970s (Leisyte & Westerheijden, 2014). Over time, today students have become the most important and valuable stakeholder group, especially related to internal quality assessment (Jongbloed et al., 2008; McDowell & Sambell, 1999). Furthermore, students provide essential feedback on teaching. They are increasingly regarded as partners who judge to what extent their personal aspirations are fulfilled (Jongbloed et al., 2008).

Students can participate in quality assurance activities in several ways. The most common form is when they respond to internal evaluation questionnaires as part of HEIs' internal quality assurance procedures. At a second level, students may be consulted by experts during site visits of external reviews. At the next level, students may participate in the external reviews of HEIs and/or programmes themselves, either in expert teams, as observers in expert teams or at the decision-making stage. Finally, at the last level, students may fully participate in the governance of national quality assurance agencies.

Student engagement model in Europe is viewed as successful and as a unique feature of European QA from the global perspective. Students participate in at least three of the four levels of student involvement in more than two-thirds of Bologna participating countries. The students' voice is important for both internal and external QA (Matei & Iwinska, 2016). Students involve in evaluation of courses and participate in IQA via decision-making and quality management processes at HEIs as equal partners (Leisyte & Westerheijden, 2014). They are represented in various governing bodies related to IQA. Students as internal stakeholders are represented at all levels of the institutions, from the overall representative body such as the university senate or board, trickling down to faculty boards, examination committees and programme committees, academic ethics committees (e.g. Latvian cases) or disciplinary commissions (Slovak cases). Yet overall it is observed that there is a tendency to include students in governing bodies and advisory committees related to IQA. Although most of this representation follows national regulations, some additional representation based on institutional rules has been also observed (e.g. in Latvia and Slovakia). Yet, these practices of engaging students highlight various levels across countries. Students participate in QA activities at all four levels in Belgium, Croatia, Estonia, Finland, The Netherlands, Norway, Poland, Sweden, and Scotland in the UK. Students participate in QA activities at three of the four levels in Greece, Iceland, Portugal, the Russian Federation, Switzerland, and the rest of the UK. However, the level of student participation in QA activities is more limited in the Czech Republic, France, and Spain, with students involved at only two levels of participation (Bologna Secretariat, 2007).

For activities related to EQA, as confirmed by ENQA (2014), one of the collateral benefits of the implementation of ESG has been the wide involvement of students in EQA practices. An example of this can be seen in the ENQA Board's decision to involve student representatives—appointed by the European Students' Union (ESU)—in the expert panels of ENQA-coordinated external reviews of agencies and has served as a stimulus for involving students in the work of many QA agencies throughout Europe. Further, in the UK, policy makers increasingly perceived students as legitimate stakeholders who should participate in evaluation processes, e.g. students are members of external review committees (as expected in the ESG). National student surveys in the UK and the Netherlands have boosted legitimacy of the student voice in quality matters.

It can be noted that student participation varies significantly across European countries (Table 7.1). They can be categorised as definitive stakeholders, having gained power thanks to university management and to national student surveys (as in the UK, Netherlands), as expectant stakeholders (Latvia, Poland, Slovakia), or latent stakeholders (as in cases of Portugal and Czech Republic) as they fulfil the legitimacy criterion only.

One particular example of student engagement in QA processes in Scotland is illustrated in Fig. 7.3.

Table 7.1 Results found by Leisyte and Westerheijden (2014, p. 89)

Country	Latent stakeholders	Expectant stakeholders	Definitive stakeholders
Latvia		Students (legitimacy and power)	
The Netherlands			Students (power, urgency, and legitimacy)
Poland		Students (power and legitimacy)	
Slovakia		Students (power and legitimacy)	
Czech Republic	Students (legitimacy)		
Portugal	Students (legitimacy)		
UK			Students (power, urgency, and legitimacy)

Outside of the Bologna area, there is also evidence of student involvement in quality assurance activities, through course evaluation questionnaires in Australia and China while in New Zealand students are represented on academic boards of most HEIs and are consulted or participate in the quality audits of universities and polytechnics. There is by contrast no evidence of significant involvement of students in quality assurance activities in Japan, Mexico, and Korea where they have a minimal role in evaluations in spite of nearly universal course ratings. Indeed, these ratings are more symbolic than anything else and do not seem to have much influence on faculty promotions, attempts to improve quality, nor on HEIs' rankings.

Illustrating best practice, students in the Netherlands have an opportunity to be involved in an annual overview of all programmes aimed at future students. For this purpose, they complete a questionnaire to assess the quality of their programmes on a standardised number of topics. The results are published together with other independent information on all programmes in an annual report—the Keuzegids (Higher Education Guide)—which is also made available through the Internet since 2006. In this way, the Keuzegids not only gives information to prospective students

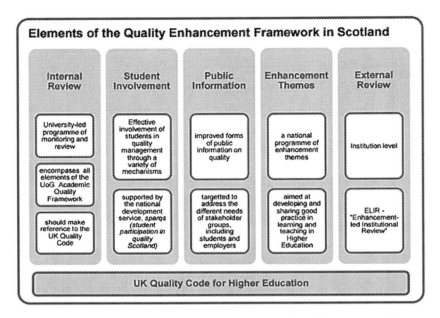

Fig. 7.3 Student engagement in QA processes in Scotland (University of Glasgow Academic Quality Framework as cited in Matei and Iwinska [2016])

on various aspects of the quality of a programme, but the information can also be used by HEIs as a benchmark instrument. The National Student Survey (NSS) in the UK serves similar purposes and has a like effect. Iceland and Poland are other interesting examples of student involvement. In Poland, the president of the students' parliament is by law a member of the State Accreditation Committee and student experts also participate in site visits. In Iceland, regulations stipulate that students must be involved in HEIs' self-evaluation teams as well as in site visits, typically through interviews of 8-12 students by peer-review groups. Evidence suggests that Icelandic students are active participants in the development of internal quality systems.

Employer as a Stakeholder in QA

There is much less evidence of a significant involvement of employers and industry stakeholders in the governance of quality assurance agencies or in their activities, other than the role of some professional associations in the accreditation of some vocational tertiary programmes.

Employers tend to have a more ambiguous role in Europe (ENQA, ESU, EUA, & EURASHE, 2015). Their role is emphasised in quality assurance standards as stated in ESG in programme development (Standards 1.1, 1.2) (ENQA et al., 2015). EQAs agree that employers and professional associations are key actors with regard to employability. Their direct participation in programme design is believed to help HEIs develop better labour-oriented programmes. For EQAs, most of the EQAs in Europe include representatives of professional bodies or practitioners in their evaluation panels, and some agencies include representatives in their boards or advisory bodies.

Within HEIs, the representation of employers in their governance is defined by national regulatory frameworks and by institutional ordinances. The Quality Code of the national Quality Assurance Agency in the UK has guided the inclusion of external stakeholders into UK institutions. External stakeholders are included in university courts or boards of trustees in the UK as well and as in the Netherlands, Slovakia, and the Czech Republic (Leisyte & Westerheijden, 2014) and in the governing boards in the US. At the programme level, programme accreditation rules are often seen as an important impetus for involving employers in programme design and revision. This could be a requirement in some countries or an implicit suggestion in others. Therefore, it is noted that the extent to which employers represent in the governance is various, depending on different types of institutions (Leisyte & Westerheijden, 2014). In the Netherlands, for example, universities of applied sciences are *explicitly expected*, because of their specific profile, to include employers and members of professions (including alumni) in programme committees as well or on scientific boards (in Czech). Similar tendencies related to the character of the institutions are noted in Latvia, The Netherlands, and the UK.

Diverse approaches can be observed towards formal representation of employers in the governance of quality (Leisyte & Westerheijden, 2014).

While a set of countries' national regulations see employers as legitimate stakeholders participating in the strategic development of the institutions, others let institutions decide how these stakeholders should contribute to the programme development and employability of graduates rather than strategic directions of the institutions. In these instances, accreditation rules guide the representation, and stakeholders can gain urgency and power depending on the managerial preferences of the institutions.

For employers' impact on curriculum and programme design, Leisyte and Westerheijden (2014) found that in all case studies, employers are included in institutional processes related to quality assurance in the sense that they are consulted in curriculum design on an ad-hoc basis. However, despite the formal presence of employers is ensured on various boards, their contribution and dedication are not always witnessed (Table 7.2).

Based on the findings, Leisyte and Westerheijden (2014) suggest that the expectations implicit in the ESG are not fulfilled. Without active, self-motivated engagement from actors within HEIs, whatever promoted in policies and regulations (as in the ESG and the Bologna Process) can never be achieved. This also suggests that institutional managers as mediators

Table 7.2 Results found on employers as stakeholders in QA in Europe by Leisyte and Westerheijden (2014, p. 92)

Country	Latent stakeholders	Expectant stakeholders	Definitive stakeholders
Latvia			Employers (power, urgency, and legitimacy)
The Netherlands		Employers (legitimacy and power)	
Poland		Employers (power and urgency)	
Slovakia	Employers (legitimacy)		
Czech Republic	Employers (legitimacy)		
Portugal	Employers (legitimacy)		
UK		Employers (power, urgency, and legitimacy)	

play a key role in giving (or not) power and urgency to various stakeholder categories. Matei and Iwinska (2016) agreeing with this view, indicate that in terms of formal involvement of this stakeholder group in the QA design and implementation process, the reality is challenging.

Outside Europe, employer surveys are only used in China and Korea where the government has systematised surveys to monitor employers' satisfaction as part of a broader endeavour to improve the overall quality of higher education. However, external stakeholders play a minimal role or are ambiguous in QA activities. It is expected in the Netherlands and New Zealand that the views of industry and employers are built into the quality management system, but their actual impact is less clear (OECD, 2008).

Academic Staff as a Stakeholder in QA

For IQA, academics staff are key players in the quality of education at individual higher education institutions. They are claimed to be able to transform quality assurance policies into actual measures. They design up-to-date education methodology and curricula and contribute to the development of a quality culture.

Teaching staff was found in many studies to be involved but merely on an individual basis (expert panel members) and in a rather indirect way (ENQA, 2014; Leisyte & Westerheijden, 2014). Compared to HEIs, there is more distance between the quality of higher education and teaching staff. Often they are represented in umbrella organisations, conferences, or labour unions. However, teaching, and thus teaching staff, seems to have a direct relation to educational quality.

In Germany academic staff is represented in both internal and external quality assurance. They are involved in internal and external evaluation, particularly in accreditation procedures. Accreditation procedures are seen as an appropriate instrument of monitoring whether the level of teaching and learning is being maintained. With regard to this monitoring, surveys are seen as an appropriate instrument for receiving feedback from students (internal feedback) and employers (external feedback). From the feedback, institutions can learn whether the aims of their programmes can be assured and if external requirements are implemented.

In Lithuania, the involvement of teaching staff is quite extensive. At the Centre for Quality Assessment in Higher Education—Lithuania, the accreditation organisation of Lithuania, teaching staff is mainly involved in expert teams, within which they comprise the majority. In both internal and external quality assurance procedures, different HEIs are represented.

Higher Education Institutions as a Stakeholder in QA

HEIs are considered as one of the most important groups of stakeholders. They are primarily responsible for higher education and its quality, quality enhancement, and quality assurance.

In the UK, all publicly funded universities and colleges are reviewed every four to six years. All these institutions subscribe to QAA and pay an annual fee. These subscriptions enable QAA to fulfil its role in protecting the reputation of UK higher education. Representatives of these colleges join a Quality Strategy Network in which they discuss quality issues. Private higher education also contains a substantial and important area of QAA's work. The British government has announced that private providers in England wishing to recruit students who will be drawing on public finance in the form of student loans will need to be reviewed by QAA. Moreover, the public education sector is represented in the Board of QAA.

In the Netherlands, all programmes are assessed every six years. During an accreditation procedure, a lot of communication between NVAO and the relevant university takes place. At a broader level, NVAO often has contact with the umbrella organisations of both private and funded institutions, which have regular meetings with NVAO. Finally, and similar to the UK, HEIs are represented in NVAO's Advisory Board.

ACSUG, the quality assurance agency in Galicia, involves institutions in quality assurance because they are represented in the Board of Directors. At a more practical level, their participation in the evaluation activities of ACSUG has contributed to the design and the implementation of quality improvement processes in Galician universities. For instance, quality improvements have been made in teaching staff, the following up of degrees, and in internal quality assurance systems.

Stakeholders' Engagement in QA in Vietnam

After *doi moi* in 1986, from a highly centralised country, Vietnam has been looking forward to reforming higher education in line with its socio-economic changes to allow private higher education, grant more autonomy to HEIs and develop appropriate accountability mechanisms. With open policy and impact of globalisation, Vietnam has taken several steps to move from central planning in higher education governance to neoliberalism which promotes the corporate governance. This has urged the government to redefine the role of different stakeholders in higher education governance as seen in other countries (Leisyte & Dee, 2012). This section discusses the changing role of related stakeholders and the changing governance in higher education in Vietnam in quality assurance.

Government—Definitive Stakeholder

The government in Vietnam through the Ministry of Education and Training (MoET) is directly in charge of developing the quality assurance system for higher education, including quality assurance policies, standards, cycles for accreditation, guidelines for external accreditation, and requirements for setting up an accrediting agency, training programs, and criteria for assessors (Nguyen, 2018; Nguyen, Evers, & Marshall, 2017).

As of May 2019, Vietnam currently has five accrediting agencies: The first two centres for education accreditation were established within the two national universities: CEA VNU-HN in the North and CEA VNU-HCM in the South, the third centre in Danang University (CEA-UD in central Vietnam), the fourth one under the umbrella of the Vietnam Association of Universities and Colleges early in 2016, and the fifth one of Vinh University. These all five agencies are established by the MoET and under the control of MoET.

For external quality assurance, four out of five accrediting bodies established are part of public universities. These agencies are both reporting to the government and their host institutions. The model is claimed to be a pilot model in the country (DAAD, 2016).

It can be observed that the government in Vietnam has power and legitimacy in quality assurance in Vietnam. They also make laws, regulations, or policies; they would possess urgency as well, having all three attributes to be definitive stakeholders in quality assurance. This has limited the voices of other stakeholders in quality assurance.

Employers and Representatives of the Professional Bodies—Latent Stakeholders

Higher Education Law approved in 2012 requires employers to be members of institution governing boards. The Law has been effective for more than five years. However, not all universities established the board as required. For some with the governing boards, their involvement is still very symbolic and not sufficient; even there are still debates about the roles and responsibilities of this board, leading to current revision of the law which redefines the board, its functions and power in higher education governance.

Currently, their involvement in assuring quality comes from certain accreditation standards in programme development and evaluation in which they provide their feedback and comments on programme learning outcomes or evaluation of graduates they employed through personal contacts with academic staff and survey. Their involvement significantly varies across HEIs. As far as the employers' involvement is concerned, it is still vague about how their feedback is used to improve the quality of education. There is not yet a culture for cooperation established between universities and the business sector that will contribute to identifying the needs of the economy and increase employment of university graduates.

Several representatives from enterprises and the professional bodies are members of Accreditation Boards of accrediting bodies in Vietnam; the Boards will make final decision on accreditation and recognition. In fact, formal accreditation in Vietnam has recently been conducted at large since 2015; the role of employers or professional bodies has not been witnessed or significant in the Vietnamese context.

They perhaps have one attribute of legitimacy in quality accreditation activities to become latent stakeholders. Their role at individual institutions likely depends on HEIs' willingness to respond to employers' contribution to programme design and revision. They do not contribute to any strategic direction or formal role in any committees of any institutions.

Managers of Higher Education Institutions—Latent Stakeholders

One of the most important groups of stakeholders is the providers of higher education. They are primarily responsible for higher education and its quality, quality enhancement, and quality assurance. However, in Vietnam they are not given full autonomy to operate. They have to comply with national regulations and requirements. They are currently not accountable to public. On the other hand, they are at large implementers of national laws and regulations.

For EQA, all HEIs whether public or private are required to apply for accreditation every five years for both institutions and programmes. As of May 2018, only 80 universities out of 235 institutions have been recognised officially for the first time since the government introduced the QAA approach. Therefore, they have one attribute of legitimacy, being a latent stakeholder in any attempts to assure quality in Vietnam.

Students—Latent Stakeholders

The role of students in quality assurance processes is limited to surveys on teaching quality, the most popular activity in all HEIs. The popularity is attributed to one of the government regulations and accreditation standards. They are also involved in evaluation of the entire programme upon graduation, surveys on libraries, and services offered at the institutions. Students are not members of academic council or study programme committees. It can be noted that the results of various student surveys in HEIs are not taken seriously or that students' opinions have no impact on decisions. Students do not receive feedback on what were the results and how they were used.

Currently, the Higher Education Law under revision is considering students as members of the governing board. The debate is still going on whether or not to include them in the board and what their role is as well as the power of their voice.

Although representatives of students are required to be members of a university council to self-evaluate the institution, the reality is opposite.

In Vietnam, the current practice of involving students in quality assurance is limited to teaching evaluation and programme evaluation. However, their contribution to quality assurance and improvement to close a feedback depends on individual HEIs. They are perhaps the least power group with limited legitimacy and without any urgency.

Academic Staff—Sometimes Latent Stakeholder, Sometimes Expectant Stakeholder

Academic staff are considered to be crucial in any attempt to assure quality. They take part in internal quality assurance processes through its members in each HEI (boards, academic council, study programme committees, etc.). Their voice in these committees is also limited because HEIs in Vietnam have to comply with regulations from the top. They do not have power to change immediately what are believed to be inappropriate in their context.

For programme accreditation, it is observed that they are involved in the process. However, the practices are also varied, depending on the middle management of the institution. Some require the wider community of their academic staff; others focus on a group of selected academics. For institutional accreditation, not many academics are directly involved in any working groups during self-study. The majority of members are university administrators and service staff. Faculty staff are required to help with collecting evidence for institutional self-study, and representatives of faculty staff are interviewed during site visit. There is a wide opposition to the current practices of self-assessing from academics (Pham, 2014).

For EQA, academics can be accreditors/peer reviewers if they meet the requirements issued by the MoET, are trained and passed an examination also held by the MoET. After that, they are eligible to serve in peer-review committees.

Conclusion—A Way Forward for Stakeholders' Engagement in QA in Vietnam

Different stakeholders in Vietnam started to participate in quality assurance. Students and employers are currently being redefined their role in the governing board of HEIs. However, the extent of engagement and the impact of stakeholders on study programme development and evaluation as well as governance of quality in the higher education institutions are blurred (Nguyen & Ta, 2018). As Vietnam is strengthening its governance model in the new era of *doi moi*, perhaps seeking 'corporate governance' which considers universities as autonomous market players, there is still much for the government to be done to find appropriate measures for the model. For corporate governance, the strength of stakeholders' claims will depend on political norms and an institutional framework.

The role of different other stakeholders, except the government, as latent stakeholders is currently being promoted. There is sufficient room for improvement so that they can be fully engaged as legitimate participants and who hold urgency and power in decision-making processes around quality of education. Higher education institutions themselves are implementers of top policies and rules. Academic staff are part of higher education institutions, they are also traditionally considered as implementers of top-down policies and institutional polices (in compliance with national policies) if any in a centralised country such as Vietnam (Pham, 2014) rather than as equal partners in deciding aspects of higher education quality assurance, not to mention their roles in teaching and learning process. Students' evaluation and feedback in programme and courses as requested by accreditation standards are still being considered as culturally inappropriate in a Confucian heritage country such as Vietnam (Pham, 2014). The practice of asking them for feedback was somehow conducted in a tokenistic manner, resulting in superficial compliance (Westerheijden, Epping, Faber, Leisyte, & De Weert, 2013). So are other stakeholders (employers and professional bodies).

Whenever their voices are heard, and they have power in decision-making processes, it will be time for Vietnam to learn from other countries' experience in how to balance between different views of higher education quality and measures to improve quality. This issue still challenges attempts of other countries to develop a comprehensive and credible quality assurance system for higher education (Matei & Iwinska, 2016). Still, as recommended by Green (1994) it would be important to 'define as clearly as possible the criteria that each stakeholder uses when judging quality, and for these competing views to be taken into account when assessments of quality are undertaken'. Although challenging, it might be a worthwhile exercise to try to map out all the stakeholders' views and perceptions of quality of higher education as suggested by Matei and Iwinska (2016) for Myanmar, a country with less mature QA system in south-east Asia (DAAD, 2016).

It is also important to consider suggestion by ENQA (2014) that although stakeholders are part of the higher education process and have to participate in a regular and regulated way, their role depends on the national context in different layers: the national legal framework, the academic tradition, and the higher education dynamics (public/private balance, role played by the government, professional bodies, etc.). In attempt to reform higher education in Vietnam and in particular to redefine the roles of different stakeholders in quality assurance, these following findings from ENQA (2014)'s study could be considered:

- Stakeholders' participation in quality assurance practices in QA agencies has a big impact on their transparency and accountability.
- Stakeholder participation in the quality assurance policy results in co-responsibility and legitimacy of the process (and outcomes) of the QA agency and the higher education system.
- The incorporation of new stakeholders requires a need to structure the relationships among the different stakeholders in higher education.
- QA agencies can act as a catalyser: roles clearly defined (respecting the division of responsibility among stakeholders).
- Stronger involvement of stakeholders could result in a potential clash with independence and the balance between them: the so-called involvement's dilemma.

– The development of a database of good practices. While the Vietnamese government is completing a regulatory framework of higher education governance to clearly state the role between the government and institutions, the role of QAA in this system, endeavours initiated from institutions to involve diverse categories of stakeholders to improve their educational quality could be promoted and shared. This can be done via accrediting bodies. The showcase of these good practices would help institutions to identify possible negative local cultures as suggested by Westerheijden et al. (2013).

References

Alves, H., Mainardes, E. W., & Raposo, M. (2010). A relationship approach to higher education institution stakeholder management. *Tertiary Education and Management, 16*(3), 159–181.

Beerkens, M. (2015). Quality assurance in the political context: In the midst of different expectations conflicting goals. *Quality in Higher Education, 21*(3), 231–250.

Beerkens, M., & Udam, M. (2017). Stakeholders in higher education quality assurance: Richness in diversity? *Higher Education Policy, 30*(3), 341–359. https://doi.org/10.1057/s41307-016-0032-6.

Benneworth, P., & Jongbloed, B. (2010). Who matters to universities? A stakeholder perspective on humanities, arts and social sciences valorisation. *Higher Education, 59*(5), 567–588. https://doi.org/10.1007/s10734-009-9265-2.

Bologna Secretariat. (2007). *Bologna process stocktaking—London 2007.* Retrieved from www.dfes.gov.uk/londonbologna/uploads/documents/6909-BolognaProcessST.pdf.

Burrows, J. (1999). Going beyond labels: A framework for profiling institutional stakeholders. *Contemporary Education, 70*(4), 5–10.

DAAD. (2016). *State of affairs and development needs—Higher education quality assurance in the ASEAN region.*

Danø, T., & Stensaker, B. (2007). Still balancing improvement and accountability? Developments in external quality assurance in the Nordic Countries 1996–2006. *Quality in Higher Education, 13*(1), 81–93.

Diamond, R. M. (2008). *Designing and assessing courses and curricula: A practical guide* (3rd ed.). San Francisco: Jossey-Bass.

Eaton, J. S. (2004). Accreditation and recognition of qualifications in higher education: The United States. In *Quality and recognition in higher education* (pp. 63–74). Paris: OECD.

ENQA. (2014). *Report of the ENQA working group on stakeholder involvement in quality assurance practices*. Retrieved from http://www.acsug.es/en/documentacion/publicacions/3144.

ENQA, ESU, EUA, & EURASHE. (2015). *Standards and guidelines for quality assurance in the European Higher Education Area (ESG)*. Brussels, Belgium.

Freeman, R. E. (1984). *Strategic management: A stakeholder approach*. Boston: Pitman.

Green, D. (1994). What is quality in higher education? Concepts, policy and practice. In D. Green (Ed.), *What is Quality in Higher Education?* (pp. 3–20). Buckingham: SRHE/OU Press.

Jongbloed, B., Enders, J., & Salerno, C. (2008). Higher education and its communities: Interconnections, interdependencies and a research agenda. *Higher Education, 56*, 303–324.

Kis, V. (2005). *Quality assurance in tertiary education: Current practices in OECD countries and a literature review on potential effects*. Paris: OECD.

Leisyte, L., & Dee, J. (2012). Changing academic practices and identities in Europe and the US: Critical perspectives. In J. C. Smart & M. B. Paulsen (Eds.), *Higher education: Handbook of theory and research*. Dordrecht: Springer.

Leisyte, L., & Westerheijden, D. F. (2014). Stakeholders and quality assurance in higher education. In H. Eggins (Ed.), *Drivers and barriers to achieving quality in higher education*. Rotterdam: Sense Publishers.

Matei, L., & Iwinska, J. (2016). *Quality assurance in higher education: A practical handbook Budapest*. Hungary: Central European University.

McDowell, L., & Sambell, K. (1999). Fitness for purpose in the assessment of learning: Students as stakeholders. *Quality in Higher Education, 5*(2), 107–123. https://doi.org/10.1080/1353832990050202.

Mitchel, R. K., Agle, B. R., & Wood, D. J. (1997). Toward a theory of stakeholder identification and salience: Defining the principle of who and what really counts. *Academy of Management Review, 27*, 853–866.

Nguyen, H. C. (2018). How to fulfil Vietnam's higher education accreditation strategic plan 2017–2020? *International Journal of Educational Organization and Leadership, 24*(3/4), 17–25.

Nguyen, H. C., Evers, C., & Marshall, S. (2017). Accreditation of Viet Nam's higher education: Achievements and challenges after a dozen years of development. *Quality Assurance in Education, 25*(4), 475–488.

Nguyen, H. C., & Ta, T. T. H. (2018). Exploring impact of accreditation on higher education in developing countries: A Vietnamese view. *Tertiary Education and Management, 24*(2), 154–167.

OECD. (2002). *Responding to student expectations.* Paris: OECD.

OECD. (2008). *Tertiary education for the knowledge society.* Paris: OECD.

Pham, T. H. (2014). *Quality culture in Vietnamese universities: A multiple case study of quality assurance and quality culture of business English undergraduate programmes at three universities in Vietnam* (Doctoral thesis), Victoria University of Wellington,

Pham, T. H., & Starkey, L. (2016). Perceptions of higher education quality at three universities in Vietnam. *Quality Assurance in Education, 24*(3), 369–393. https://doi.org/10.1108/QAE-07-2014-0037.

Santiago, P., Tremblay, K., Basri, E., & Arnal, E. (2008). *Tertiary education for the knowledge society, Volume 1. Special features: Governance, funding, quality.* Paris: OECD.

Smeby, J.-C., & Stensaker, B. (1999). National quality assessment systems in the Nordic countries: developing a balance between external and internal needs? *Higher Education Policy, 12*(1), 3–14. https://doi.org/10.1057/palgrave.hep.8390104.

Srikanthan, G., & Dalrymple, J. (2003). Developing alternative perspectives for quality in higher education. *International Journal of Educational Management, 17*(3), 126–136.

Stensaker, B., & Vabø, A. (2013). Re-inventing shared governance: Implications for organisational culture and institutional leadership. *Higher Education Quarterly, 67*(3), 256–274.

Ulewicz, R. (2017). The role of stakeholders in quality assurance in higher education. *Human Resources Management & Ergonomics, 11,* 93–107.

Watson, D. (2012). Who runs our universities? *Perspectives: Policy and Practice in Higher Education, 16*(2), 41–45.

Watty, K. (2003). When will academics learn about quality? *Quality in Higher Education, 9*(3), 213–221.

Westerheijden, D. F., Epping, E., Faber, M., Leisyte, L., & De Weert, E. (2013). Stakeholders and quality assurance. *Journal of the European Higher Education Area, 4,* 71–85.

8

Access and Equity in Vietnamese Higher Education

Thi Tuyet Tran

Introduction

In the knowledge economy era, higher education (HE) is increasingly viewed as key marker for social inclusion and exclusion (Bourdieu, 2006; Noble & Davies, 2009). The investment in HE study is considered as a process of cultural capital accumulation, or in other words, of developing high-status cultural signals such as attitudes, preferences, formal knowledge, behaviours, goods and credentials (Lamont & Lareau, 1988, p. 156). Thus, HE participation offers a route for students from disadvantaged backgrounds to develop cosmopolitan identities for social inclusion (Beck, 2004). It potentially provides students with competitive advantages to get access to better employment opportunities, better income and richer networks to base on not only at work but also in life in the future.

T. T. Tran (✉)
RMIT University, Melbourne, VIC, Australia
e-mail: june.tran@rmit.edu.au

© The Author(s) 2019
C. H. Nguyen and M. Shah (eds.), *Quality Assurance in Vietnamese Higher Education*, https://doi.org/10.1007/978-3-030-26859-6_8

However, in the mass HE era, when graduates are often oversupplied in many disciplines and many graduates end up unemployed or underemployed (Tran, 2019), the intention is now going beyond HE access to equity and quality in HE. Mass HE or the expanded access does not necessarily mean increase of equity. Resources may be privileged for a few and not equitable in benefiting marginalized groups. In many cases, disadvantaged groups cannot reach quality HE, either because they have dropped out of the system earlier or they cannot afford it financially. In such situations, government's equity policies play an important role to decide who to privilege and who get excluded in getting access to the resources provided (Pereira, 2016).

This chapter aims to discuss the issue of access, equity in relation to quality and external quality assurance (QA) in the Vietnamese higher education system (HES). Vietnam is a middle-income country who is seeking ways to escape the middle-income trap, and educational reforms are considered the key battlefield. Although education quality is the decisive factor for boosting the economic outcomes (Hanushek & Wößmann, 2007; Pereira, 2016), in the context when the gap between the rich and the poor is widening, it is also important as who gets benefits from the education renovation. This is a crucial consideration in Vietnam where the HES has expanded extensively recently, but the student equity issue is virtually left unaddressed (Duong, Wu, & Hoang, 2017).

Considering the relationship between equity and QA is often considered as 'a marriage of two minds' as although they are both long-standing and continuous policy strands on HE agendas, they are usually 'separated strands that use different spheres for implementation' (Martin, 2010, p. 175). This chapter aims to discuss the interface between equity and QA for two reasons: (1) quality has become one of the key-driven factors for education equity because getting access to mass HE is no longer a big problem, but getting access to quality HE study which will potentially lead to higher economic outcomes is what matters now; and (2) unless the external QA system reflects equity explicitly in its criteria, educational equity will still be left unaddressed in a resource-lack country like Vietnam.

This chapter will first pull up the overall picture of the Vietnamese HES with its expansion recently and examine HE inequality based on three characteristics, namely gender, living area and income quintile. Various data sources (i.e. from Ministry of Education and Training—MoET, General Statistics Office—GSO and International Labour Office—ILO) will be used to illustrate the discussion in this section. Then, based on these sources of data and on the findings in the literature, this chapter will explore the reasons behind the inequality in Vietnamese HE. It then looks at the equity policies and the relationship between equity policies and the objectives of the QA system to see how far the QA process is equity sensitive. The conclusion will approach some recommendations for HE policy makers about the relationship between equity policies and QA in HE and how to make the QA system as a tool for the implementation and monitoring of equity policies.

The Expansion of Vietnamese HE and the Issue of Educational Equity

Vietnam was invaded by the Chinese for more than 1000 years (from 207BC to 938), and the Confucian Heritage Culture had been strongly and deeply absorbed in the country. Confucius is in favour of men and considers that men are the owners of the family and women's responsibility is only having babies and taking care of the housework. Thus, like China, Vietnam is considered a masculinity dominated society where gender prejudice was strong. The first university in Vietnam—Van Mieu Quoc Tu Giam—was established in 1076, first for the royal family and their children, but female students were not allowed to attend. Later, it was also open for outside students, who all had to take and pass a regional Huong exam (thi Hương), but, again, female students were prohibited to take part in the exam.

Vietnamese education system has been heavily affected by outsiders. Apart from the earlier influences of the Chinese, the evidence of French and Soviet's influence in Vietnam is also clear. During 87 years of invasion (1858–1945), the French colonial regime, with obscurantism policy (Chính sách ngu dân) to maintain power in the colony, invested very little in education in Vietnam. During this whole period, only one university was established in 1907—Dong Duong University, and some small colleges and with the main aim to provide labour force for the colonial regime. In 1945, when Vietnam gained independent and claimed to be a socialist country, the HES started to develop following the former Soviet model, which consisted of mono and highly specialised institutions, all were public universities. Although universities were open for both boys and girls, from either urban or rural areas, regardless whether they come from a rich or poor family (there was no tuition fees, students were offered scholarships and places to stay free of charge), all students needed to pass the University Entrance Exam—a very high-stake test in order to be able to enrol in a university/college. Universities had a very privileged status where only less than 10% of high school graduates could enter colleges and universities.

The development of the Vietnamese HES after gaining independent is associated with the *Doi Moi* reform—the reform adopted by the Vietnamese Government and the Communist Party in 1986 to abolish the centrally planned economy and adopt a market-led economy. With this replacement, the internal economic developed very fast. The government saw the need to reform and expand the HES to meet the new needs of the economy after *Doi Moi* (Le Thac Can & Sloper, 1995); thus, in 1993—few years after *Doi Moi*, the HES in Vietnam had undergone a significant reform. The first large and comprehensive national or regional universities (e.g. two National Universities) were established on the basis of merging several mono disciplinary universities. Tuition fees were introduced in the system, and students who did not pass the University Entrance Exam were allowed to enter universities but had to pay fees (Hayden & Lam Quang Thiep, 2010). Most significantly, two new sectors (in addition to the state HE sector), a 'semi-public' sector and a 'non-public' sector were formed. As a result, the HES has expanded rapidly. In the school year 1986–1987, there were only 101 public HEIs with 133,136 students. In the school year of 2015–2016, the number of HEIs had increased more than four times (442) and the number of students had climbed to 2,202,732, 16.5 times bigger the size of the system in 1987 (See Table 8.1).

The above expansion of the system is also boosted by the Higher Education Reform Agenda (HERA) promulgated by the Vietnamese Government in 2005 which aimed to expand further the system and opened widely the door for new universities to be established, private and regional

Table 8.1 Number of HEIs and the students (MoET, 2012, 2015, 2018)

School year	Number of HEIs			Number of students		
	University	College	Total	University	College	Total
1986–1987	63	38	101	–	–	133,136
1996–1997	62	63	126	–	–	715,231
2001–2002	77	114	191	763,256	210,863	974,119
2006–2007	139	183	322	1,173,147	367,054	1,540,201
2007–2008	140	206	346	1,180,547	422,937	1,603,484
2008–2009	146	223	369	1,242,788	476,721	1,719,509
2009–2010	149	227	376	1,358,965	597,263	1,956,228
2010–2011	188	226	414	1,435,887	726,219	2,162,106
2011–2012	204	215	419	1,448,021	756,292	2,204,313
2012–2013	207	214	421	1,453,067	724,232	2,177,299
2013–2014	214	214	428	1,461,839	599,802	2,061,641
2014–2015	219	217	436	1,824,328	539,614	2,363,942
2015–2016	223	219	442	1,753,174	449,558	2,202,732
2016–2017	235	–	–	1,767,879	–	–

universities included. This is considered a good signal of equity in HE when the HES became more accessible and students from rural areas can also attend universities or colleges located in their provinces.

Nonetheless, there is still much to do to ensure equity in HE in Vietnam. First, the development of private universities has been facing many obstacles, both financially and in terms of their status in the system. HERA aims to achieve the proportion of 40% students enrolling in private HEIs by 2020, but in 2016, Vietnam had 90 private HEIs with 289,900 students, only about 13% of the total enrolment.

Table 8.2 also indicates that the number of private HEIs has increased more than 4 times in the school year 2015–2016 compared to the school year 2000–2001, but the increase in number of students enrolling in private HEIs is much lower, only 2.8 times. One of the aims of boosting the private sector is to create more choices for students and provide more opportunities for those students who do not pass the University Entrance Exam to study in HE. However, these choices and opportunities do not seem to be open for the poor when the tuition fees in the private universities are much higher than in the public HEIs and the support from the government, if any, is too little compared to the expenses students and their families have to afford to study in private HEIs (Hayden & Thi Ly, 2015).

Table 8.2 Number of HEIs and the students in non-public sector (MoET, 2015, 2018)

School year	No. of private HEIs	No. of students
2000–2001	22	104,265
2001–2002	23	100,990
2002–2003	23	111,856
2003–2004	27	137,122
2004–2005	29	137,760
2005–2006	34	160,420
2006–2007	47	193,471
2007–2008	64	188,838
2008–2009	74	257,117
2009–2010	77	279,373
2010–2011	80	333,921
2011–2012	82	331,595
2012–2013	83	312,652
2013–2014	85	269,636
2014–2015	88	313,620
2015–2016	90	289,900

In Vietnam, the gap between the rich and the poor is getting bigger, and the chance for the poorer to get HE qualifications is also much more limited than the rich (Table 8.3).

Table 8.3 shows a noticeable difference in HE accessibility among different population groups. Specifically, people from rural and lower-income quintiles have much less access to HE than those from urban and richer families. While 18.6% of the target urban population had completed HE degrees, that proportion among rural population is only 4.5%. Similarly, while only 0.6% of the population aged 15 or older of the poorest group achieves HE qualifications, 24.5% of the similar ageing people in the richest group gains HE degrees. Statistically, the share of population aged 15 or older with HE qualifications of the poorest quintile was 40.8 times lower than that of the richest quintile.

In terms of region, the highest accessible to HE is among residents in Red River Delta and South East, the two regions with the highest-income per capita in Vietnam. By contrary, in the poorest regions in the country, i.e. North West and Mekong River Delta, not only the accessibility to HE is limited, but the access to upper secondary is also limited.

Table 8.3 Proportion of population aged 15 and older by highest certificate levels (General Statistics Office, 2016)

	Primary or lower	Highest certificate levels				
		Lower secondary	Upper secondary	Vocational/professional study	College/university	Postgraduate
Whole country	40.3	27.9	14.5	8.3	8.5	0.4
By area						
Urban	27.4	22.5	18.7	12.8	**17.4**	**1.2**
Rural	46.3	30.4	12.5	6.4	4.4	**0.1**
By region						
Red River Delta	20.2	37.2	17.7	11.9	12	0.9
North East	39.1	29.7	13.5	10.4	7.4	0.1
North West	52.7	25.1	10.1	7.3	4.7	0.1
North Central Coast	32.6	33.8	17.7	8.9	7.1	0.1
South Central Coast	42.3	22.7	13.9	7.6	8.6	0.5
Central Highlands	47.2	26.6	13.4	5.7	6.8	0.3
South East	42.1	22.3	16.5	7.7	10.9	0.6
Mekong River Delta	64.7	17.7	8.3	4.7	4.7	0.1
By income quintile						
Quintile 1	64.3	25.9	7.6	1.7	**0.6**	**0**
Quintile 2	50.9	30.4	12.5	4.5	1.9	0
Quintile 3	40.4	31.1	15.4	8.3	4.9	0.1
Quintile 4	29.6	29.3	17.9	12.8	10.3	0.2
Quintile 5	20.7	29.9	18.1	13.8	**22.9**	**1.6**
By gender						
Male	35.7	29.1	15.3	10.7	8.8	0.5
Female	44.5	26.8	13.8	6.4	8.3	0.3

In terms of gender, there seems to be not much difference between male and female access to HE (9.3 and 8.6%, respectively). Indeed, recent data show that female students outnumber male students in the Vietnamese HES. In 2015, there were 1,033,900 male students, while the number of female students studying in the HEIs in the same year was 1,084,600 (General Statistics Office, 2018). In the school year 2016–2017, among 1,767,879 university students, 934,476 of them were female (General Statistics Office, 2018). The overall data seem to show that Vietnam has already achieved gender equality in access to HE. However, looking deeper into the composition of students in HE, picture of gender equity in Vietnamese HE does not seem to be that rosy. Female students are normally over-represented in social science study, but under-represented in science, technology and other disciplines which often lead to better job outcomes and career prospects. The investigation of the Vietnam National University, Ho Chi Minh City in 2016, for example, reveals that proportion of female students studying in the University of Information Technology was only 12.6% (compared to 87.4% male), while in Ho Chi Minh City University of Technology, that proportion was 19% (81% of students were male). Conversely, 80.6% of the students at the University of Social Sciences and Humanity were female (Dang Nguyen, 2016).

Obviously, access and equity has remained a significant problem in the Vietnamese HES that seems to be in favour of the urban, rich and male students. Students who live in rural mountainous areas (where reside most minority groups in Vietnam) from low-income families and female students have remained vulnerable groups and their doors to the HE route to develop cosmopolitan identities for social inclusion (Beck, 2004) have been critically narrow. The following section will discuss the reasons behinds these barriers.

Barriers to Access to HE in Vietnam

There are different reasons limiting the access to HE among youth in disadvantaged groups in Vietnam. This section will discuss the major barriers that significantly influence access to HE in Vietnam.

Economic Barriers

Higher education is getting more expensive in Vietnam, especially for low-economic background families. The tuition fees in several prestige universities/programmes are getting double or triple when these universities are allowed to be financially accountable. Apart from tuition fees, students also need to pay many other expenses such as books, living expenses, food, transportation and other educational expenses. The result of the Vietnam household living standards survey 2014 (General Statistics Office, 2016) shows that the school fee is accounted for only 32% of education expenditure, other expenses are also huge (e.g. fee on extra classes: 16%, other education expenditures 26%). Thus, the increasingly high cost of pursuing HE in Vietnam has become one of the main reasons for the unequal access to HE between the rich and the poor (Pereira, 2016).

In addition to this, the opportunity cost has also become a barrier since graduating from the HES has no longer been a guarantee for these young people to find a job, let alone quality jobs with high income (Tran, 2018); the prospective students can start earn money for their families without attending HE study (Suryadarma, Widyanti, Suryahadi, & Sumarto, 2006). The school-to-work-transition survey data indicate that economic reasons (could not afford/too poor/needed to earn money to support family) are the most significant reason (35.5%) for students to drop out of schooling before completing at all levels (See Table 8.4). Thus, the children from the lower-economic background often miss the chance to sit in the upper secondary school final exam/University Entrance Exam to

Table 8.4 Reasons for stopping education/training before completing (ILO, 2016)

Reasons for stopping education/training before completing	
Failed exams	9.1%
Not interested in education/training	31.9%
Wanted to start working	15.7%
To get married	1.9%
Parents did not want me to continue schooling	1.5%
Economic reasons (could not afford/too poor/needed to earn money to support family)	35.5%
No school near by	0.9%
Other	3.4%

consider HE study. This somehow explains why the proportion of the HE graduates of the rich quintile was 40.8 times higher than that of the poorest quintile (Table 8.3).

Nonetheless, the inequality in education access does not start at HE level but much earlier than that. Table 8.3 indicates that 76.7% of rural population has only lower secondary certificates or lower (compared to 49.9% of the urban population). More seriously, 46.3% of the people living in rural areas could not complete even lower secondary schooling. In terms of income quintile, 90.2% of the people in the poorest group have only lower secondary certificates as the highest educational level. These people all render themselves ineligible for HE.

Similarly, people who live in poorer regions of the country also have much more limited opportunities to pursue HE, 82.4% of the population in Mekong River Delta do not complete upper secondary schooling (Table 8.3) and virtually have no way to consider HE. This proportion among richer regions such as Red River Delta is much lower (57.2%). This indicates that general education, which is considered much cheaper than HE, has already become a burden for many poor families, and they cannot afford to pay fee for their children in upper secondary schooling.[1]

Lack of Access to Quality Education

Vietnam education system still has many internal problems which directly or indirectly affect the teaching quality in the system: low teacher quality, too outdated and old infrastructure, poor class facility and poor teaching and learning material. The 'educational socialization' (xã hội hoá giáo dục) which calls for the contribution from students' families has helped many schools boost up their teaching facilities and attract better quality teachers. Nonetheless, most of these schools are in urban and rich areas. Schools located in remote areas and in the minority communities where most families are poor could not make much use of 'education socialisation' to facilitate learning and thus can hardly be able to increase teaching and learning quality.

---

[1] In Vietnam, primary and lower secondary schools are free and compulsory; students who attend upper secondary schools have to pay school fees.

Looking at the proportion of students attending people-founded and private schools, the indicators also indicate clearly that the lack of access to quality education is much more severe among poor household members. People-founded and private schools are normally much more expensive than public school, and they attract students mainly by their teaching quality and modern teaching and learning facility and infrastructure. At the current stage, the overall proportion of students attending people-founded and private schools in Vietnam still accounts for a small percentage (4.4%) (General Statistics Office, 2016). However, the share of household members attending private schools in urban areas was much higher than in rural areas (9.4% versus 2.5%) and among the richest quintile was also much higher than among the poorest quintile (11% versus 1.1%). The future tendency for the rich household group sending their children to private schools is also 12.8 times higher than for the poorest household group (General Statistics Office, 2016). These indicators all support Fry's (2009) claim that rural students and students from low-economic background families have much more limited access to quality secondary education, and thus, they are seriously disadvantaged in terms of opportunities for HE.

Table 8.4 also shows that there is very high proportion of students dropping schooling because they are not interested in education and training (31.9%). Although these data are not enough to conclude that students left schools because of low-quality education they can are able to get access to, a clear gap between education and learners' needs and interests are revealed. Not only HE, but the Vietnamese education system in general seems to have much to do to achieve the aim of providing inclusive education and quality education for all, given the fact that their practices are largely not aligned with students' needs and interests.

Other Barriers

Apart from economics reason and the lack of access to quality education, family background, cultural factors and place of living also seem to have a certain impact on the issue of education equity in HE in Vietnam. Table 8.5 shows clearly that students whose fathers are better educated have better access to HE. Most children who have university-educated

Table 8.5 Children highest education certificate levels by father's qualifications (ILO, 2016)

Highest certificate levels of father	Highest certificate levels of children							
	Primary and lower (%)	Lower secondary (%)	Upper secondary (%)	Professional study (%)	College (%)	University (%)	Postgraduate (%)	Total (%)
Primary and lower	31.2	37.1	17.1	5.7	3.8	5.1	0.0	100.0
Lower secondary	11.3	**33.0**	23.3	13.8	9.7	8.7	0.3	100.0
Upper secondary	4.6	11.5	23.8	14.6	22.3	22.3	0.8	100.0
Professional study	8.5	7.1	21.4	30.0	11.4	20.0	1.4	100.0
College	0.0	11.1	11.1	11.1	33.3	22.2	11.1	100.0
University	2.0	0.0	4.0	6.0	2.0	**78.0**	8.0	100.0
Postgraduate	0.0	0.0	0.0	0.0	0.0	50.0	50.0	100.0

fathers get access to HE, whereas the majority of students whose fathers have only lower secondary certificates or lower also end up with lower secondary schooling.

The over-representation of male students in scientific and technological fields and the over-representation of female students in social science can come from social and cultural factors. Gender stereotypes are still very strong in Vietnam. The roles of women in society are even reinforced in school textbooks that they are supposed to take care of housework and men are out to earn money (Vu, 2008). There are still cases where parents fear that it will be hard for their daughters to get married with 'too much education' (Mak, 2007). Gender-based choice of study fields also strongly reflects gender stereotypes in Vietnam, where girls are supposed to be suitable for office and teaching jobs while science and technology are the areas of boys. This somehow explains why female students are over-represented in social sciences and under-represented in science in the survey of VNU, Ho Chi Minh City.

Place of living can also have a certain impact on HE equity in Vietnam. Although the Vietnamese HES has expanded extensively recently and almost all cities and provinces in Vietnam each has at least one university, most prestigious HEIs are still located in some central cities such as Hanoi, Ho Chi Minh, Da Nang, Thai Nguyen, Can Tho and Hue. When many students graduated from prestigious universities in urban areas face difficulties in job findings, graduates from local universities who are often not at all competitive compared to those from prestigious universities face even bigger challenges in the labour market after graduation. This discourages provincial students from participating in local HEIs. Thus, while students from poor and rural areas are under-represented in the HES, many provincial universities are struggling in attracting enough students into their universities.

Efforts to Improve Higher Education Equity and Access in Vietnam

Realising the existing inequity in HE, the Vietnamese Government has employed different measures to reduce it. The first measure needed to mention is the differential admission scores adopted in the system. Vietnam applies the HE intake quota system which limited the number of seats offered for upper secondary school students in the HEIs each year, so, in general, only students who achieve high scores in the University Entrance Exam can get access to HE. Nonetheless, the Vietnamese Government adopts a differential admission policy which places different admission scores for four regional categories: big cities, suburbs and towns, rural areas and mountainous areas. The admission scores are half mark apart between two adjacent categories, e.g. the admission scores for students from towns, and mountainous areas are half mark and 1.5 marks (respectively) lower than the score for students in the big cities (Ngo, 2006). On top of it, students whose parents are war martyrs or veterans and ethnic minority students can add one mark on their overall mark before comparing their scores to their regional admission scores. Ngo (2006) suggests that these special admission criteria have increased access to HE for students from rural and mountainous areas and those from lower sociocultural background families by about 70%.

Vietnam also provides different types of financial assistance for students of disadvantaged groups. These include: tuition exemptions, reductions, subsidies, scholarships and postponement of tuition payment for ethnic minority students, orphans, war martyrs or veterans' children, mountainous children and children from very poor families. These students are also allowed to get access to student loan programmes with low interest rates to support their daily expenses. Nonetheless, the effectiveness of the student loan programmes is considered modest because the paperwork takes much time, and in many cases, it prevents many students from low sociocultural background families to get access to these programmes.

The above-mentioned policies do not seem to be enough for students from disadvantaged background families to get access and succeed in HE study. Ongoing academic support during their university time is also essential, as special admission criteria allow them to enter university when their achieved scores are lower than their classmates. They need more support and assistant, not only financially, but also academically, in order to catch up and mingle with other students and become competitive when they finish university and join the labour market. Otherwise, they will still be inferior wherever they are, and be left marginal again at work and in life after graduation.

Quality Assurance and HE Equity Issue

Different countries with different contexts and histories have different equity concerns. Thus, the importance of equity issue in QA frameworks also varies from country to country (Martin, 2010). In South Africa for example, the overall aim of QA framework is to unify the HES and make it more equitable in terms of access and outcomes, and thus, equity concerns are strongly and explicitly addressed in South Africa's QA framework (Lange & Singh, 2010). The whole QA system and processes in this country, including self-assessment, external assessment and follow-up activities strongly reflect equity concerns.

Nonetheless, not all HESs are primarily geared to equity, the linkage between equity policies and QA is normally looser than that in South Africa. It is still argued that strong national equity policies can be reflected in the QA system, equity concerns could become visible in several standards within the QA framework (e.g. Brazi (Ristoff, 2010)), or in quantitative benchmarks and associated grades (in India, (Gupta & Patil, 2010)). The presence of equity concerns in the national QA framework provides strong guidance for not only each HEI to adopt stronger means to promote equity in their institutions, but also for external reviewers to use QA criteria as a tool for making equity expectation explicit to HEIs (Martin, 2010).

Vietnam's QA framework has been created recently and is still in the process of being revised. The first quality assurance framework implemented by MoET in 2005 that involved 53 quality-related criteria used for assessing only public universities. After several times revising, in 2017 MoET issued the current QA framework which consists of 25 quality standards and 111 quality-related criteria, and is used to all HEIs in Vietnam, regardless they are public or private institutions. The Vietnamese QA system is considered young and is put in place with the main aim to respond to the need of quality controlling for an expanding HES (Nguyen, Evers, & Marshall, 2017). Although many more quality-related criteria have been added to the first QA framework in 2005, debates are still lively about the suitability of the current framework as well as the practical and tangible outcomes of the QA mechanism in Vietnamese HE. Most insiders consider QA processes in Vietnam as a means for quality control from the Central Ministry with very little tangible outcomes such as increasing the real quality of teaching and learning or attracting more investment (Duong et al., 2017).

Although the QA framework has been extended to 111 quality-related criteria, it is hard to see any explicit reference for national equity policies as one of its objectives (See MoET, 2017). Access and student enrolment is explicitly addressed in one Standard (No. 13), but the focus is mainly only on how to recruit 'quality students' into HEIs. Equity in access is left unassessed in both institutional and programme QA in the Vietnamese HES. In other words, the current QA framework in Vietnam does not take into account how HEIs address equity issues in their own policies and processes. The linkage between QA framework and equity policies is, thus, very loose.

Conclusion and Recommendations

It is clear from the above discussion that access and equity in Vietnamese HE has remained a significant problem given the context where the gap between the rich and the poor in Vietnam is widening. Several efforts have been made, i.e. expanding the HES to accommodate more students, providing students with more opportunities/choices (public and private universities), applying differential admission scores to welcome more students from rural and mountainous areas, and providing different types of financial assistant for students of disadvantaged groups. Nonetheless, the impact of these efforts has been rather modest. The financial burden that poor families have to bear for their children to stay in the educational system, the lack of access to quality education and cultural perception have all contributed to paint a dark picture of equity in HE in Vietnam. Students who live in rural areas, who are poor and from low sociocultural background are often drop schools earlier (often before they enter upper high school). These students make themselves ineligible for HE.

In this context, the efforts to improve access and equity in Vietnamese HE (i.e. differential admission scores or financial assistant) seem to be too late and not sufficient, as the majority of the disadvantaged students have rendered themselves ineligible for HE and, thus, cannot be benefitted from the government equity policies. Even those who can manage their way to come to HE cannot benefit much from the policy as the financial assistant that they are eligible for is both too little and not easy for them to reach. The policies are there, but there seems to be no means for the government to control how successful the financial support schemes work for the target students so far.

The loose relationship between equity and QA in Vietnam adds the darkness to the picture of HE equity in Vietnam. The current QA framework with 25 standards and 111 criteria has virtually no link to the equity agenda. When the access criteria put a strong focus on 'quality student', but ignore equity concerns, in the context of time-short and resource-poor universities, equity concerns have often been neglected in the system. Students from low sociocultural background families may be able to get access to HE thanks to the special admission scored policy, but they may also be left struggling in their study, as they need more academic support than other students but their universities do not have enough resources to provide them with the support they need.

Equity in HE has remained a critical issue in Vietnamese HE. The HE expansion and HE renovation have mainly brought benefits for students from rich families and in urban areas. Most disadvantaged background children have still been left vulnerable, now in the process of developing their knowledge and skills, in other words, of developing their cultural capital, and later, in finding decent work to earn good income for themselves and for their families. There seems to be little chance for these children for developing cosmopolitan identities for social inclusion (Beck, 2004).

The primary goal of QA system in Vietnam is not for monitoring and implementing of equity policies, but to ensure certain quality standards across the system. Nonetheless, in order to reduce the gap between the rich and the poor and to provide equitable opportunities for student access and success in HE, it is suggested that the QA framework needs to be revised in a way to explicitly reflect equity concerns in its criteria. An explicit linkage between the objectives of the QA system with equity policies will hopefully create a certain positive effect on the process of developing and implementing equity policies in Vietnamese HE. It is also suggested that support, encouragement and assistant for disadvantaged background students should start since much earlier stages than at HE. In addition to the assistant, governments should also initiate different programmes to promote economic growth in rural areas, and place a special effort to provide and promote quality education for all, in order to achieve exclusive education and to provide a means for the students from low sociocultural background to achieve HE study, to be able to get access to better job opportunities and have a better future prospects.

References

Beck, U. (2004). Cosmopolitical realism: On the distinction between cosmopolitanism in philosophy and the social sciences. *Global Networks, 4*(2), 131–156.

Bourdieu, P. (2006). The form of capital. In H. Lauder, P. Brown, J.-A. Dillabough, & A. H. Halsey (Eds.), *Education, globalization and social change*. Oxford: Oxford University Press.

Dang Nguyen. (2016). *Thống kê thú vị về sinh viên nam - nữ của ĐH Quốc gia TP.HCM* [Male-female student ratio in Vietnam National University, Ho Chi Minh City—Interesting statistics]. Retrieved from https://thanhnien.vn/giao-duc/thong-ke-thu-vi-ve-sinh-vien-nam-nu-cua-dh-quoc-gia-tphcm-776276.html.

Duong, M.-Q., Wu, C.-L., & Hoang, M.-K. (2017). Student inequalities in Vietnamese higher education? Exploring how gender, socioeconomic status, and university experiences influence leadership efficacy. *Innovations in Education and Teaching International, 56*(1), 1–11.

Fry, G. W. (2009). Higher education in Vietnam. In Y. Hirosato & Y. Kitamura (Eds.), *The political economy of educational reforms and capacity development in Southeast Asia: Cases of Cambodia, Laos and Vietnam* (pp. 237–261). Netherlands: Springer.

General Statistics Office. (2016). *Result of the Vietnam household living standards survey 2014*. Hanoi, Vietnam: Statistical Publishing House.

General Statistics Office. (2018). *Giáo dục đại học và cao đẳng* [Higher education statistics]. Retrieved from https://www.gso.gov.vn/SLTK/Selection.aspx?rxid=1fcd9551-176f-46c5-b0fb-9dcc84666777&px_db=10.+Gi%C3%A1o+d%E1%BB%A5c&px_type=PX&px_language=vi&px_tableid=10.+Gi%C3%A1o+d%E1%BB%A5c%5cV10.16.px.

Gupta, A., & Patil, J. (2010). The contribution of the National Assessment and Accreditation Council. In M. Martin (Ed.), *Equity and quality assurance: A marriage of two minds* (pp. 145–174). Paris: UNESCO and International Institute for Educational Planning.

Hanushek, E. A., & Wößmann, L. (2007). *The role of school improvement in economic development*. National Bureau of Economic Research.

Hayden, M., & Lam Quang Thiep. (2010). Vietnam's higher education system. In G. Harman, M. Hayden, & Pham Thanh Nghi (Eds.), *Reforming higher education in Vietnam* (pp. 15–30). London: Springer.

Hayden, M., & Thi Ly, P. (2015). Higher education access and inclusion: Lessons from Vietnam. In R. T. Teranishi, L. B. Pazich, M. Knobel, & W. R. Allen (Eds.), *Mitigating inequality: Higher education research, policy, and practice in an era of massification and stratification (Advances in education in diverse communities: Research, policy and praxis, Volume 11)* (pp. 19–33). Bingley: Emerald Group Publishing Limited.

ILO. (2016). *School to work transition survey*. Vietnam: International Labour Office.

Lamont, M., & Lareau, A. (1988). Cultural capital: Allusions, gaps and glissandos in recent theoretical developments. *Sociological Theory, 6,* 153–168.

Lange, L., & Singh, M. (2010). Euity issues in quality assurance in South Africa higher education. In M. Martin (Ed.), *Equity and quality assurance: A marriage of two minds* (pp. 37–74). Paris: UNESCO and International Institute for Educational Planning.

Le Thac Can, & Sloper, D. (1995). Higher education in Vietnam: The door opens—From the inside. In D. Sloper & Le Thac Can (Eds.), *Higher education in Vietnam: Change and response* (pp. 1–25). Singapore: Institute of Southeast Asian Studies.

Mak, G. C. (2007). Women in East Asian education and society: Whose gains in whose perspectives? In W. T. Pink & G. W. Noblit (Eds.), *International handbook of urban education* (pp. 333–358). Dordrecht: Springer.

Martin, M. (2010). *Equity and quality assurance: A marriage of two minds*. Paris: UNESCO and International Institute for Educational Planning.

Ministry of Education and Training (MoET). (2012). *Higher education statistics 2012*. Retrieved from http://www.moet.gov.vn/?page=11.10&view=4446.

Ministry of Education and Training (MoET). (2015). *Education and Training Statistics Report 2011–2015*. Retrieved from Hanoi, Vietnam.

Ministry of Education and Training (MoET). (2017). *Circular No 12/2017/TT-BGDĐT: Thông tư ban hành quy định về kiểm định chất lượng cơ sở giáo dục đại học* [Higher education institutions quality assurance criteria]. Hanoi: MoET.

Ministry of Education and Training (MoET). (2018). *Higher education statistics school year 2016–2017*. Retrieved from https://www.moet.gov.vn/thong-ke/Pages/thong-ke.aspx.

Ngo, D. D. (2006). Higher education in Vietnam. In M. N. N. Lee & S. Healy (Eds.), *Higher education in South-East Asia* (pp. 219–250). Bangkok: The UNESCO Asia and Pacific Regional Bureau for Education.

Nguyen, H. C., Evers, C., & Marshall, S. (2017). Accreditation of Viet Nam's higher education: Achievements and challenges after a dozen years of development. *Quality Assurance in Education, 25*(4), 475–488.

Noble, J., & Davies, P. (2009). Cultural capital as an explanation of variation in participation in higher education. *British Journal of Sociology of Education, 30*(5), 591–605.

Pereira, J. D. (2016). *Equity, access and educational quality in three South-East Asian countries: The Case of Indonesia, Malaysia and Viet Nam*. The HEAD Foundation.

Ristoff, D. (2010). Equity and quality assurance in Brazilian higher education. In M. Martin (Ed.), *Equity and quality assurance: A marriage of two minds* (pp. 75–108). Paris: UNESCO and International Institute for Educational Planning.

Suryadarma, D., Widyanti, W., Suryahadi, A., & Sumarto, S. (2006). *From access to income: Regional and ethnic inequality*. Jakarta: SMERU.

Tran, T. T. (2018). Youth transition to employment in Vietnam: A vulnerable path. *Journal of Education and Work, 31*(1), 59–71.

Tran, T. T. (2019 forthcoming). Graduate employability: Beyond the skills agenda. In H. T. M. Bui, D. Cole, & H. T. M. Nguyen (Eds.), *Innovative higher education and graduate employability*. London: Roughley.

Vu, P. A. (2008). *Gender stereotypes in story textbooks for primary school students in Vietnam* (Master of Education), University of Oslo, Oslo, Norway.

9

Institutional and Programme Accreditation

Hien Thu Thi Ta, Huong Thu Thi Nguyen and Tuan Van Pham

Higher Education Accreditation in Vietnam

Vietnam's higher education currently faces many opportunities for development along with several large and urgent challenges, especially in improving the quality of education to achieve regional and international standards. Facing globalization, international integration is widespread in the field of not only economics but also education, including the liberalization and privatization of the education market, especially higher education (HE). This trend has resulted in the need to develop a common standard of HE quality for mutual comparison, accreditation, and recognition (Do, Pham, & Nguyen, 2017). To develop a common quality

---

H. T. T. Ta (✉) · H. T. T. Nguyen
University of Education, Vietnam National University, Hanoi, Vietnam
e-mail: tahien@vnu.edu.vn

T. Van Pham
University of Science and Technology,
The University of Danang, Danang, Vietnam

standard, it is necessary to have standardized measures to ensure the education quality and accreditation of education quality. The education quality assurance in Vietnam is defined as identified systems, policies, procedures, actions and attitudes to achieve, maintain, monitor, and improve quality. The education quality accreditation is an external evaluation process that aims at providing a decision to accredit an educational institution or a training programme that meets the established standards (Nguyen, Evers, Marshall, 2017).

Legal Framework for the Quality of Education in Vietnam

To implement an education accreditation system in general and specific in HE, Vietnam has set up a legal document system on the education quality accreditation, including the important role of the Communist Party's guidelines and resolutions, and legal documents of the government and MoET. Some key documents can be named, such as the Decision No. 201/2001/QD-TTg dated December 28, 2001 by the prime minister on adopting the Education Development Strategy 2001–2010, which required the education and training sector to urgently build and implement a quality accreditation system at all levels and modes of training (Prime Minister, 2001). The Resolution No. 37-2004 QH11 of the National Assembly, Session XI, adopted on December 3, 2004, clearly stated: "To take quality management as the central task; to conduct the annual education quality accreditation." The Education Law of 2005 (Article 17) affirmed: "The Education quality accreditation is the major measure to define the level of achieving the goals, realizing the programmes and contents of education by schools and other educational institutions; the education quality accreditation is conducted regularly throughout the country and for every educational institution. Results of the education quality accreditation are publicly announced for awareness and supervision by the society" (National Assembly, 2005). The amended Education Law in 2009 added regulations on the education quality accreditation that clearly identified the content of state management, principles, and organizations for the education quality accreditation (National Assembly, 2009).

In addition, other important documents, such as the Resolution No. 14/2005/NQ-CP dated November 2, 2005, by the government described the fundamental and comprehensive reform of higher education in Vietnam during the period of 2006–2020, the Decree No. 75/2006/ND-CP dated August 2, 2006, and the Decree No. 31/2011/ND-CP dated May 11, 2011, of the government, and the Resolution No. 50/2010/QH12 dated June 19, 2010, of the National Assembly, which also instated regulations directly related to the education quality accreditation (Government, 2005).

Specifically, on June 18, 2012, the Law on Higher Education passed by the National Assembly was marked as a breakthrough for the development of higher education in general, and quality assurance and accreditation in particular. This created favorable and unified legal corridors to comprehensively address issues related to HE, including quality assurance and accreditation. The Law on Higher education devoted 1 chapter with 5 articles to discuss quality assurance accreditation of higher education, in which the quality accreditation activities of higher education were regulated specifically, including the objectives, principles, and objects of the quality accreditation to the accreditation organizations and the use of the results of quality accreditation (National Assembly, 2012).

The Resolution No. 29-NQ/TW dated November 4, 2013, by the Party Central Committee (XI) instated fundamental and comprehensive reform of education and training, seeking to meet the requirements of industrialization and modernization in the context of a socialism-oriented market economy and international integration. It also directed the education sector to "complete the education quality accreditation system; to periodically accredit the quality of education and training institutions and programmes and publicize the results of the accreditation results; to establish centers for the education quality accreditation and centers for assessment of national vocational skills" (CCCP, 2013).

In addition to the legal documents promulgated by the government and the National Assembly, MoET has also issued legal documents regulating the process and period of the education quality accreditation, as well as criteria for assessing and implementing the quality of higher education and training institutions. Although not yet completed, this system of documents has greatly helped direct higher education quality accreditation activities in Vietnam to achieve the goal of ensuring and improving the quality of education.

Key Policy Issues for Higher Education Quality Accreditation in Vietnam

State Management in Higher Education Quality Accreditation

Under the Education Law and the Law on Higher Education, the task of state management of higher education quality accreditation is assigned to MoET. Accordingly, MoET is responsible for: "*1. To promulgate regulations on criteria for evaluating education quality: processes and periods of education quality assessment at each educational grade and training level; and operation principles of conditions and criteria for organizations and individuals conducting education quality assessment; to license education quality assessment: and to grant and withdraw certificates of education quality assessment; 2. To manage activities of institution and training programme accreditation; 3. To guide organizations, individuals and educational institutions to conduct self-evaluation and accreditation of education quality; 4. To examine and evaluate the implementation of regulations on education quality accreditation*" (Clause 4, Article 99 of the Education Law (Law No. 38/2005/QH11); Clause 31, Article 1, amending and supplementing a number of articles on the Education Law (Law No. 44/2009/QH12), Article 52, Law on Higher education (National Assembly, 2005, 2009, 2012).

The Objective of Higher Education Accreditation

The education quality accreditation is defined as a special management mechanism that allows the state and society to monitor education quality in order to provide solutions that improve the quality of education. Accreditation aims to ensure, for the community and society, that an educational institution or programme can meet quality standards based on a clear definition of educational missions and goals and ensures the conditions to sustainably achieve those goals. Quality accreditation has two main purposes: (i) To assess an educational programme or institution to determine if it meets quality standards and (ii) To support and promote educational programmes and institutions for continuous improvement of quality. Quality accreditation also provides educational programmes and institutions with an analysis and assessment that identifies strengths and shortcomings in order to improve quality as well as increase the accountability and commitment of the educational programme and institution for quality. The goals of the education quality accreditation were clearly stated in Article 49, Law on Higher Education 2012: "*a) Assuring and improving the higher education quality; b) Verifying the fulfillment of the higher education duties in each period of the higher education institutions or the programmes; c) Forming the bases for higher education institutions to provide explanation for competent State management agencies and for the society in terms of the actual training quality; d) Forming the basis of students to choose higher education institutions, programmes for the recruitment of employers*" (National Assembly, 2012).

Principles of the Education Quality Accreditation

The general principles of the education quality accreditation in Vietnam were defined as: "*1. Independent, objective and lawful; 2. Honest, open and transparent*" (Law No. 44/2009/QH12 amending and supplementing several articles in the Education Law in Article 110b) and "*Equitable, compulsory and periodic*" (Law on Higher education, Article 49) (National Assembly, 2009).

While other countries consider the policy of the education quality accreditation as either compulsory or voluntary or both compulsory and voluntary (compulsory for the private sector and voluntary for the public one), Vietnam considers the policy of higher education quality accreditation as compulsory for the whole system. Thus, it is compulsory for legalized educational institutions and programmes to regulate higher education quality accreditation, establishing a legal framework for educational institutions to implement. This ensures that educational institutions to commit to the society in terms of training quality.

Regulations Related to the Organization of the Education Quality Accreditation

Article 110c of the law, which amended and supplemented a number of articles from the Education Law (Law No. 44/2009/QH12—Law), stated: "*1. Education quality accreditation organizations include: a) Education quality accreditation organizations established by the State; b) Education quality accreditation organizations established by organizations or individuals; 2. The Minister of Education and Training shall decide or permit the establishment of education quality assessment organizations; and provide conditions to establish and dissolve tasks and powers of education quality accreditation organizations.*" The requirements related to education quality accreditation organizations were also detailed in Article 52 of the Law on Higher Education and specified by Minister of Education and Training in the Circular No. 61/2012/TT-BGDDT dated December 28, 2012, which specified the conditions for the establishment, dissolution, tasks, and powers of the education quality accreditation organizations.

Responsibilities and Rights of Higher Education Institutions in Terms of Quality Accreditation

According to regulations, higher education institutions in Vietnam "have the responsibility to conduct quality self-assessment and be subjected to the accreditation by the competent quality accreditation agency" (Education Law 2005, clause 8 Article 58); "*subjecting to the education quality assessment at the request from State management agencies in charge of education; Implementing the regulations on information and reporting on higher education quality assessment; Being entitled to choose an education quality assessment organization among the education quality accreditation organizations accredited by the Ministry of Education and Training to carry out the assessment of the higher education institution quality and the training programme quality; Being entitled to complain and denounce to competent agencies about the decisions, conclusions and illegal acts of organizations and individuals that carry out higher education quality accreditation*" (Law on Higher Education, Article 51) (National Assembly, 2012).

Education Quality Accreditation Process in Vietnam

According to the Circular No. 62/2012/TT-BGDDT dated December 28, 2012, which described the regulations of the process and frequency of the education quality accreditation for universities, colleges, and professional intermediate schools; the Circular No. 38/2013/TT-BGDDT dated November 29, 2013, discussed the process and frequency of quality accreditation for programmes of universities, colleges, and professional intermediate schools; and the Circular No. 12/2017/TT-BGDDT dated May 19, 2017, promulgated regulations on the accreditation of higher education institutions by the Minister of Education and Training. The education quality accreditation process consisted of three basic steps that can be summarized as follows: (i) Internal assessment is the process during which educational institutions and programmes examine and assess themselves based on the education quality assessment standards promulgated by the MoET in order to report on their education quality, efficiency of training, scientific research, personnel, facilities, and other relevant issues so that educational institutions can adjust their resources and implementation to meet education quality standards; (ii) External assessment is a survey and assessment conducted by education quality accreditation organizations based on education quality assessment standards promulgated by MoET in order to determine the extent of conformity of educational institutions and programmes to education quality standards; and (iii) Verification and recognition of education quality occur when education quality accreditation organizations recognize the quality of a training programme or educational institution (Ministry of Education and Training, 2017).

Using Results of Higher Education Quality Accreditation

The results of the higher education quality accreditation shall be used to determine the quality of higher education, status, and prestige of educational institutions and programmes; exercise the right of autonomy and self-responsibility; facilitate investment and task assignment; be the basis on which the government and society supervise the operation of higher education institutions.

Penalties for Violations Against Regulations on Quality Accreditation

The Decree No. 138/2013/ND-CP dated October 22, 2013, of the government described the penalties for administrative violations pertaining to education and education quality accreditation (Article 26, section 7). It further specified fines for misreporting results of self-assessment of educational institution quality; failure to conduct self-assessment education quality according to regulations; forgery of documents when applying for accreditation from education quality accreditation organizations; and illegal establishment of education quality accreditation organizations.

Based on the above information, it is clear that policies on higher education quality accreditation in Vietnam have been implemented based on a system of perspectives, objectives, and implementation methods of the higher education quality accreditation as proposed by the government, as illustrated in documents on the higher education quality accreditation promulgated by the government. Major characteristics of the higher education quality accreditation in Vietnam are summarized as follows: (i) Quality accreditation is a compulsory process; (ii) Quality accreditation is conducted at training programme level or educational institution level; (iii) Quality accreditation is accompanied by self-assessment, external assessment, and verification and recognition of education quality; and (iv) Higher education quality accreditation standards are promulgated by MoET (not by education quality accreditation organizations); and (v) Accrediting educational institutions and programmes evaluates the whole system of quality assurance including students' entry level, progress, and learning outcome.

The primary objective of the higher education quality accreditation in Vietnam is to assure and improve the quality of higher education. In order to realize the objectives of the education quality accreditation, the government has promulgated specific regulations for process, procedures, and implementation tools. The policies that Vietnam is currently adopting are in line with worldwide development trends of higher education, according to which higher education accreditation must follow 4 steps: planning, self-assessment, external assessment, and improvement. However, the state regulatory authority on the education quality accreditation in Vietnam has not established adequate penalties that require all educational institutions to participate and improve operation quality for quality accreditation. In addition, although the education quality accreditation organizations are currently adopting the same set of standards provided and guided by MoET, in practice there are inadequacies and inconsistencies in assessment perspectives and balanced assurance in the assessment results.

Quality Assessment and Standards for Higher Education Accreditation in Vietnam

The Establishment and Development of Higher Education Accreditation and Quality Assurance Organizations

In 1995, the Center for Education Quality Assurance and Research Development (currently known as the Institute for Education Quality Assurance) was established by the Vietnam National University in Hanoi (VNU). This was the first specialized unit to conduct the quality assurance and education quality accreditation within a higher education institution, marking the first steps in developing a system of the quality assurance and education quality accreditation in Vietnam. In 1999, the Center for Educational Testing and Quality Assessment was established by the Vietnam National University in Ho Chi Minh City (VNU-HCM). In 2003, MoET was founded by the General Department of Education Testing and Accreditation—GDETA (currently known as Vietnam Education Quality Management Agency—VQA) and served as an office for consultation with the Minister of Education and Training on the quality assurance and education quality accreditation. The establishment of state regulatory agencies to manage the quality assurance and education quality accreditation marked a new development period for the country as a whole (Nguyen et al., 2017).

Next, specialized units were founded and placed in charge of the education quality assurance within higher education institutions based on legal normative documents such as: Regulations on standards for education quality assessment of universities according to the Decision No. 65/2007/QD-BGDDT, which stated that "*universities shall have a higher education quality assurance organization, including specialized centers or departments; competent staff in charge of conducting assessment activities to maintain and improve the quality of universities' performance*" (MoET, 2007a). The Directive No. 46/2008/CT-BGDDT dated August 5, 2008, by the Minister of MoET on the increase of assessment and education quality accreditation stated that the main mission of education quality assurance was to "*build and enhance a system of units in charge of assessment and education quality accreditation in universities, academies, colleges, professional intermediate schools, departments of education and training*" (MoET, 2008). The Clause 1, Article 15 Decision No. 58/2010/QD-TTg dated September 22, 2010, by the Prime Minister on promulgating a University Charter required educational institutions to "*establish specialized units in charge of education quality assurance of the university*" Clause 1, Article 33 Circular No. 62/2012/TT-BGDDT dated December 28, 2012, of the MoET (replacing Decision No. 76/2007/QD-BGDDT) required educational institutions to "*develop a plan to meet education quality standards for each period. Establish a specialized unit for education quality assurance to host and coordinate with other units conducting this plan.*" The Clause 1, Article 50 from the Law on Higher Education 2012 specified the responsibilities of educational institutions regarding the development of an internal quality assurance system. After developing a quality assurance system for 15 years, approximately 90% of higher education institutions in Vietnam have founded specialized units for internal quality assurance. The staff in charge of education quality assurance at educational institutions have actively participated in building and developing an internal quality assurance system of educational institutions, developed quality culture, and positively contributed to education quality accreditation in Vietnam (National Assembly, 2012).

VNU and VNU-HCM have attached great importance to the development of an internal quality assurance system. VNU has incorporated a set of documents on quality accreditation by MoET, AUN-QA and the United States in developing its own documents to conduct quality assurance and quality accreditation. This system of documents has been implemented simultaneously from the VNU level to the member and affiliated unit level, operating step-by-step as an internal quality assurance system in VNU. VNU-HCM and regional universities, including Thai Nguyen University, Hue University, Da Nang University, and Can Tho University, which have carried out self-assessment and external assessment of the quality of educational institutions and programmes, developing a standard for institutional education quality. Two VNUs are the core units in developing a system of quality assurance and higher education quality accreditation in Vietnam.

Meanwhile, following the popular development trend, the foundation of independent quality accreditation agencies has been deemed necessarily by the government (prescribed in the Law on Higher Education) to conduct quality accreditation and recognize qualified educational institutions and programmes. In particular, in 2010, MoET approved a project to build and develop an education quality accreditation system for higher education and professional intermediate education from 2011 to 2020 (Decision No. 4138/QD-BGDDT dated September 20, 2010). This decision had four main objectives: (1) Reinforce and complete a system of legal normative documents on education quality accreditation for higher education—professional intermediate education to create an environment and legal framework for the stable development of an education quality accreditation system; (2) Develop an education quality accreditation system to assess the quality of higher education programmes and professional intermediate schools, contributing to the assurance and improvement of the quality of higher education and professional intermediate education; (3) Develop policies to create a qualified and adequate team of external assessment experts to conduct education quality accreditation for higher education and professional intermediate education; and (4) Increase international cooperation with countries in the region and around the world in education quality accreditation for higher education to be the professional intermediate education. According to regulations implemented by the Education law, two types of education quality accreditation organizations can be established in Vietnam, including: (i) Education quality accreditation organizations founded by the government and (ii) Education quality accreditation organization founded by individuals or organizations (MoET, 2010). In 2013, the first higher education quality accreditation organization founded in Vietnam was the Center for Education Quality Accreditation—VNU (VNU-CEA). So far, five Centers for Education Quality Accreditation have been established and licensed, four of which were founded by MoET, including the Center for Education Quality Accreditation—VNU (VNU-CEA), Center for Education Quality Accreditation—VNU-HCM (VNU-HCM-CEA), Center for Education Quality Accreditation—University of Da Nang (CEA-UD), Center for Education Quality Accreditation—University of Vinh (CEA-UV), and the Center for Education Quality Accreditation under the Association of Vietnam Universities and Colleges (CEA-AVU&C). These centers are stable in terms of organizational structure and performance of assigned functions and tasks (performance results shall be described specifically in section 2.4). This initially has created a remarkable change in awareness and operation methods of self-assessment and quality improvement of educational institutions and programmes, building societal trust and becoming a management tool for education quality for Vietnam regulatory authorities.

Tools to Conduct Education Quality Accreditation

In order to implement education quality accreditation, MoET has promulgated a sufficient system of legal normative documents from legal documents to ministerial-level circulars and department-level guidelines; founded education quality accreditation organizations that serve their specialized tasks; and trained and recruited a highly qualified team of accreditors. In order to train teams of assessors and accreditors for the education quality accreditation, MoET has assigned this mission to three units: VNU, VNU-HCM and the University of Da Nang. Until December 2017, these three units had organized 33 accreditor-training courses and granted certificates of training completion to 965 people. VQA also organized four exam sessions to certify accreditor cards, selecting and certifying 346 qualified participants. This source of accreditors ensures the implementation of education quality accreditation while contributing significantly to the development of quality assurance systems within higher education institutions (MoET, 2018).

The first set of standards for higher education quality accreditation was comprised of 10 standards and 53 criteria (promulgated by Decision No. 38/2004/QD-BGDDT dated December 2, 2004), then adjusted to 10 standards and 61 criteria (promulgated by the Decision No. 65/2007/QD-BGDDT dated November 1, 2007) (MoET, 2007a). This set of standards was adopted for education quality accreditation from 2014 to June 30, 2018, by 122 educational institutions out of 234 total educational institutions in Vietnam (excluding 31 military academies and 5 foreign-invested educational institutions) (MoET, 2018). Seeking to improve higher education quality for quick regional and international integration, on May 19, 2017, MoET promulgated regulations for quality accreditation of higher education institutions, in which a set of education quality accreditation standards was comprised of 25 standards and 111 criteria based on quality assessment standards for higher education institutions at AUN-QA (Circular No. 12/2017/TT-BGDDT) (MoET, 2017). This took effect in July 2017 and was accompanied by detailed guidelines on implementation, marking the first step in global integration. The remaining higher education institutions in Vietnam (which have not been accredited and recognized for quality as of June 30, 2018) shall adopt this new set of standards for education quality accreditation. This new set of standards consisted of quality assurance components from 4 perspectives: strategy (8 standards), system (4 standards), function (9 standards), and results (4 standards), to be assessed on a 7-level scale, from Level 1—completely incompliant to Level 7—perfectly compliant, which is the level of the world's leading educational institutions.

Regarding the education quality accreditation of programmes, from 2007 to 2014, MoET had issued four sets of assessment standards for programmes with particular characteristics: (1) a set of assessment standards for college-level elementary programmes with 7 standards and 37 criteria (enclosed with the Decision No. 72/2007/QD-BGDDT dated November 30, 2007); (2) a set of assessment standards for university-level industrial technique teacher education programmes with 7 standards and

40 criteria (enclosed with the Circular No. 23/2011/TT-BGDDT dated June 6, 2011); (3) a set of assessment standards for university-level high school teacher programmes with 7 standards and 40 criteria (enclosed with the Circular No. 49/2012/TT-BGDDT dated December 12, 2012); and (4) a set of standards for assessment of college-level nurse programmes with 8 standards and 42 criteria (enclosed with the Circular No. 33/2014/TT-BGDDT dated October 2, 2014). These sets of assessment standards mainly focused on programme outcome standards, programmes, training activities, the staff implementing the programmes, learners and activities to support learners, facilities, equipment, and financial work to support the training programme. The rating for each criterion was achieved/not achieved (MoET, 2007b, 2011, 2012, 2014).

In 2016, MoET issued a set of assessment standards for the higher education programmes with 11 standards and 50 criteria (enclosed with the Circular No. 04/2016/TT-BGDDT dated March 14, 2016). This set of standards had an approach based on the quality of AUN-QA and was applied by education institutions in Vietnam for self-assessment and preparation for upcoming education quality accreditation of programmes. Apart from the general aspects mentioned above, the content of these evaluation standards also focused on other aspects, such as the programme description, the approaching methods in teaching and learning, study outcomes evaluation, enhancing quality and training programme outcomes. The rating for each criterion ranged from Level 1—not meeting the criterion to Level 7—excellent performance, typical model of the world (MoET, 2016).

Thus, for over 10 years, MoET has developed and issued a comprehensive set of assessment tools along with self-assessment and external assessment guidelines and required the education quality accreditation activities of education institutions and programmes to meet quality standards.

Outcomes of the Implementation of Higher Education Accreditation in Vietnam

Outcomes of Education Quality Accreditation Activities in Vietnam

Outcomes of Participation in Quality Accreditation by Quality Accreditation Commissions in Vietnam

From 2005 to 2010, actively supported by the Higher Education Project, the Vietnam education quality accreditation system was gradually established. The quality assessment activities were carried out in accordance with the standards issued by MoET. According to statistics from GDETA, by October 2011, 130 universities nationwide had completed self-assessment reports on the quality of support by education quality accreditation, of which 40 had been externally assessed and evaluated by the National Committee of Quality Assurance and 100 programmes for university-level high school teachers had completed the self-assessment report (GDETA, 2011).

With that foundation and the decisive direction of MoET, from 2015 to 2018, the education quality accreditation activities were highly promoted by higher education institutions in Vietnam. By June 30, 2018, 217 universities (81.6%) and 33 colleges and pedagogical intermediary schools (91.7%) had completed the self-assessment report. Of these, 122 educational institutions had been externally assessed and 117 were recognized as meeting quality standards. Of the 33 colleges and pedagogical intermediary schools that had completed the self-assessment report, three had been externally assessed and recognized as meeting quality standards. Regarding the education quality accreditation for programmes, 10 programmes were externally assessed according to the set of quality assessment standards for programmes at higher education levels (enclosed with the Circular No. 04/2016/TT-BGDDT dated March 14, 2016), eight of which had been recognized as meeting quality standards. Table 9.1 lists the number of education institutions and programmes that have been externally assessed and recognized as meeting quality standards set by four education quality accreditation centers (MoET, 2018).

Table 9.1 The number of institutions and programmes externally assessed and accredited by MoET standards

No.	Name of the education quality accreditation center	Education institutions				Programmes	
		Externally evaluated		Recognized to meet the quality standards		Externally evaluated	Recognized to meet the quality standards
		University	College	University	College		
1	VNU-CEA	51	2	50	2	7	5
2	VNU-HCM-CEA	28	–	24	–	3	3
3	CEA-AVU&C	34	–	34	–	–	–
4	CEA-UD	9	2	9	2	–	–
	Total	122	4	117	4	10	8

Outcomes of Participation in Quality Accreditation in Accordance with the Standards Set by Regional and International Quality Accreditation Commissions

Although Vietnam higher education has only recently begun establishing quality assurance and quality accreditation, it has been actively participating in international and regional quality assurance networks and organizations such as the International Network for Quality Assurance Agencies in Higher Education (in which Vietnam has 3 representatives: GDETA/VQA, the Institute for Education Quality Assurance—VNU and VNU Center for Education Accreditation (VNU-CEA); ASEAN Quality Assurance Network (of which GDETA is an official member and VNU-CEA is an associate member); ASEAN University Network (Vietnam also has 3 representatives: VNU, VNU-HCM, and Can Tho University); and ASEAN University Network-Quality Assurance (AUN-QA) (of which 23 Vietnamese higher education institutions are associate members).

In addition to participate in the activities of these quality assurance networks and organizations, higher education institutions in Vietnam have actively registered for the education quality accreditation in order to achieve the recognition of regional and international education quality accreditation commissions in terms of quality (Nguyen, 2017). As of June 2018, four Vietnamese universities had been recognized by High Council for Evaluation of Research and Higher Education (HCERES) as meeting quality standards; two universities had been evaluated and recognized as meeting quality standards by AUN-QA (Table 9.2); 106 programmes had been evaluated and recognized as meeting the quality standards of AUN-QA, CTI, ACBSP, FIBAA, and ABET (Table 9.3).

Analyzing the Outcomes of Quality Accreditation at Higher Education Institutions

As stated previously, as of June 30, 2018, 122 higher education institutions in Vietnam had been assessed in accordance with the set of quality standards issued by MoET (10 standards and 61 criteria). The evaluation indicated that the education quality accreditation has made positive changes

Table 9.2 Educational institutions evaluated and accredited by overseas agencies (VQA, 2018a)

No.	Name of university	Education quality accreditation organization	Time of accreditation	Certificate Issue date	Expiry date
1	Hanoi University of Science—VNU	AUN-QA	1/2017	February 20, 2017	February 19, 2022
2	HCM University of Technology, VNU—HCM	HCERES AUN-QA	2/2017 9/2017	June 13, 2017 October 10, 2017	June 13, 2022 October 9, 2022
3	University of Science and Technology—The University of Da Nang	HCERES	2/2017	June 13, 2017	June 13, 2022
4	Hanoi University of Science and Technology	HCERES	2/2017	June 13, 2017	June 13, 2022
5	National University of Civil Engineering	HCERES	2/2017	June 13, 2017	June 13, 2022

Table 9.3 Number of programmes accredited by overseas agencies (VQA, 2018b)

No.	Name of education quality accreditation commissions	Number of programmes that have been accredited
1	AUN-QA	78
3	Accreditation Council for Business Schools and Programs (ACBSP)	05
4	Commission des Titres d'Ingéni (CTI)	16
5	Foundation for International Business Administration Accreditation (FIBAA)	05
6	Accreditation Board for Engineering and Technology (ABET)	02

and dramatic alterations in the quality assurance activities of higher education institutions, especially in terms of awareness and school management methods. Many higher education institutions had made strong commitments and improved their quality after evaluation. Through this, society's belief in the conditions of education institution quality assurance had been gradually developed.

From the results of 117 accredited education institutions accredited that hade been published on education quality center electronic information Web sites, it can be seen that 100% of the institutions met 09/61 criteria (Criteria 1.1, 2.4, 5.2, 5.3, 6.1, 6.4, 6.6, 8.1, and 9.4). The connotations of these criteria are related to issues concerning the missions of the education institutions, activities of party organizations, mass organizations, democratic issues in education institutions, the dissemination of learner ethics and lifestyles and the provision of IT equipment for learners. However, there are several critical issues that these universities must address, as shown in Fig. 9.1.

The specific issues are as follows:

i. University administration and management are a matter of concern. 36% of the accredited education institutions did not have an organizational structure that met the regulations and other relevant laws (school council, faculty council, and other organizations had not yet been established as regulated). Several higher education institutions

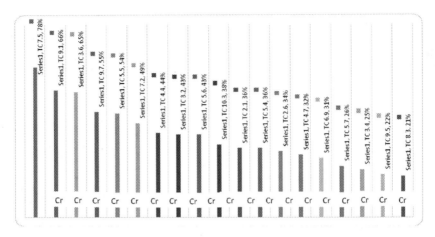

Fig. 9.1 Criteria that 20% or more of the 117 accredited universities throughout the country had failed to fulfill (*Note* Criterion = Cr (TC))

had not been updated and had not developed the regulations on organization and operation in compliance with current regulations. 34% of education institutions did not meet the requirements of strategy formulation, development plan, method monitoring, and evaluation of implemented plans and strategies.

ii. Regarding the programmes: 15.4% of the evaluated education institutions did not have training programmes designed as regulated and did not ensure the quality of non-formal programmes. 65% of the education institutions had not carried out periodic assessments of their programmes and improved the quality based on evaluation results. Review and adjustment of programmes had not been fully and seriously implemented in accordance with the regulations of MoET. 24% of education institutions did not meet the requirements of periodic supplementation and adjustment from the referential basis of advanced international programmes, feedback from employers, graduates, educational institutions, and other organizations to meet the demand for human resources for the socioeconomic development of the locality or the whole country. 43% of education institutions had programmes that did not have clearly defined objectives and an appropriate curriculum structure, had not been systematically designed, did

not meet the knowledge and skills standards of higher education, and did not flexibly satisfy the demands for human resources by the labor market.
iii. Regarding training activities: 44% of the educational institutions had not appropriately ensured that the methods and procedures for evaluating learner results were serious, objective and fair. Consultation with learners, employers, and other related parties was not used as a basis for adjusting teaching activities. Up to 33% of the educational institutions did not meet the requirements of this criterion.
iv. Regarding lecturers and researchers: 55% of the evaluated education institutions did not meet the required number of lecturers to implement programmes and research. The average ratios of students/lecturers in some training sectors were too high (over 60 students/lecturer for some programmes). Lecturers and researchers at 16% education institutions did not ensure the balance of professional experience and rejuvenation as regulated. Particularly, 43% of the evaluated education institutions had lecturers who were not qualified as regulated. Some lecturers did not teach in line with the profession in which they had been trained and had not yet fulfilled professional structure and qualifications as regulated; their foreign language and computer skills did not meet the requirements of training and scientific research tasks. In addition, up to 35% of the institutions did not have a management staff that met the requirements of ethical qualities, professional management capacity, profession, and fulfillment of the tasks assigned.
v. Regarding scientific research: The biggest existing problem for many educational institutions is that many topics and projects had not been completed and inspected as planned (49%). In addition, the applicability and transferability of the technology and science topics are low, indicated by low revenue from scientific research and technology transfer, and educational institutions had not invested in scientific research in accordance with the regulations (this requirement was not met by 78% of the evaluated educational institutions).
vi. Regarding finance: The rational, transparent, and effective allocation and deployment of financial resources for different departments and the operation of higher educational institutions were not guaranteed.

This requirement was not met by 38% of the evaluated educational institutions. In particular, most of the educational institutions had not allocated sufficient finances to scientific research activities as required.
vii. Other existing problems were related to libraries and the area of land used by educational institutions. 66% of the evaluated education institutions did not satisfy the requirement for libraries (meaning they had an insufficient number of Vietnamese and foreign books, textbooks, references; no electronic library with Internet/no electronic library with effective support of teaching, learning, and scientific research). 55% of educational institutions did not fulfill the required area of used land, in which the overall area of the ground did not reached the minimum level, as required in TCVN3981-85.

Comparison of the percentage of criteria met by state-owned higher educational institutions and privately owned higher educational institutions show that 17/17 (100%) of privately owned higher educational institutions that their education quality accredited have not met the requirement "to ensure that the revenue from scientific research and technology transfer is not less than the funding of universities for this activity" (criterion 7.5). Regarding criteria relating to the area (criterion 9.7), the testing and assessment (criterion 4.4), objectives and standard outcomes of the programmes (criterion 3.2), faculty qualification levels (criterion 5.6), financial allocation (criterion 10.3), strategic development plan (criterion 2.6), and survey of learner feedback (criterion 6.9), many privately owned educational institutions have a higher underachievement rate than the overall level and than that of the state-owned educational institutions. The results are shown in Fig. 9.2.

Analysis of the Results of Quality Accreditation of Programmes

As mentioned above, 8 higher education programmes have been accredited, all of which have been recognized as satisfying the quality assessment standards for higher education programmes set by MoET (promulgated in Circular No. 04/2016/TT-BGDDT dated March 14, 2016) (MoET,

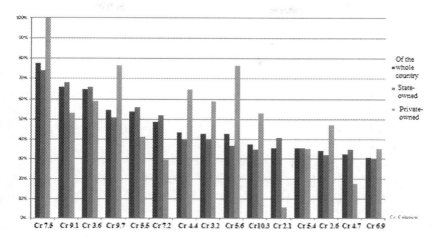

Fig. 9.2 Comparison of the percentage (%) of underachieved criteria (*Note* Criterion = Cr)

2016). The accreditation results of the 8 education programmes are summarized in Table 9.4.

A summary of the main results shows that there is substantial room for quality improvement in the management of programmes in Vietnam's higher educational institutions as follows:

Table 9.4 The consolidated quality accreditation results of 8 programmes under the set of quality assessment standards

Standards	Average score
Standard 1: Objectives and learning outcomes of the training programme	4.03
Standard 2: Programme specifications	4.23
Standard 3: Structure and content of the curriculum	4.00
Standard 4: Teaching and learning approach	4.43
Standard 5: Assessment of student's learning outcomes	4.20
Standard 6: Lecturers and researchers	4.33
Standard 7: Support staff	4.12
Standard 8: Students and activities supporting the students	4.28
Standard 9: Facilities and equipment	3.82
Standard 10: Quality improvement	4.22
Standard 11: Output	4.24

i. The standard outcomes of the programme do not present a clear connection with each subject. These outcomes are not specifically designed to be measurable and do not focus on the practical and soft skills of the learners.
ii. Each programme does not have a detailed and clear roadmap and implementation strategy and has not been notified to the parties concerned. Each programme lacks a proper distribution between general knowledge, skills, and specialized knowledge.
iii. There is no full and regular involvement of the parties concerned, including students, former students, employers, national and international experts in the design, and adjustment of the programme. No thorough research into the demands of the domestic and foreign labor markets has been conducted when designing and adjusting the programme.
iv. The teaching and learning strategies do not receive full attention during programme execution. They are not designed and assessed regularly, objectively, and effectively, thus failing to ensure that the strategy is being properly employed.
v. No specific criteria have been established to assess student entry level, progress, and learning outcomes. A variety of assessment methods have not been used to help assess student competency. The assessment tools for teaching, administrative, and supporting staff are not standardized. No encouragement has been given to improve and develop the faculty in terms of quantity and quality. No detailed job description or schedule for teaching and publishing research works is provided to the faculty. No master plan has been developed to enhance teaching staff quality.
vi. No proper landscape and psychosocial learning environment have been created for learners. No updates and expansions have been done of infrastructure, equipment for learning. There are no regular updates of books, reference materials, no digitalization of teaching materials, and no expansion of e-learning resources.
vii. The system for collecting feedback from stakeholders has not been enhanced, and there is no sufficient database of assessment, feedback, and data from students and former students.

Achievements, Existing Problems, and Solutions

Achievements

From the overall results as summarized in the aforementioned section, it can be seen that, over the past 15 years of establishment and development, the system of higher education quality assurance and education quality accreditation in Vietnam has achieved following results:

i. The policies on quality assurance and education quality accreditation of higher education are being applied in line with the general development trends of global higher education. The strategies and policies of the Party and State, and the legal framework for education quality accreditation have been created, facilitating the implementation of higher education quality assurance and education quality accreditation. The operation of a system of higher education quality assurance and education quality accreditation has gained practical experience in system operations step-by-step.
ii. The system of quality assurance centers operates inside educational institutions, and the higher education quality accreditation organizations have been established and put into operation. The human resources for operating higher education quality assurance and education quality accreditation activities have basically fulfilled the requirements for operating such activities (Nguyen, 2018).
iii. There have been marked changes in societal and higher education institution awareness of the quality assurance and education quality accreditation, which has worked to build trust with the society in the quality of higher education.

Remaining Problems

However, in addition to positive results, several problems remain, as follows:

i. Policies on quality assurance and education quality accreditation have not been implemented synchronously, and there is no sanction strong enough for education quality accreditation to be implemented by all educational institutions. The results of education quality accreditation have not been effectively used by educational institutions to increase the effectiveness of education quality management. Several legal documents have not been drawn up and promptly adjusted, leading to some difficulties in the performance of these activities. The results of education quality accreditation have not been analyzed and evaluated to supplement or formulate more effective policies on education quality accreditation (Nguyen et al., 2017).
ii. The model for education quality accreditation organizations is not stable. Some organizations are under the administrative management of educational institutions, leading to public suspicion of the objectivity of education quality accreditation activities. The connection between quality assurance inside and outside educational institutions is not clear and the management role of the state over internal quality assurance activity is not absolutely effective.
iii. The team of accreditors have limited experience and professional qualification and are not allocated properly and sufficiently based on their specialization and level of education (Nguyen, 2018).
iv. Among 106 programmes that were accredited by regional and international education quality accreditation organizations, several programmes that need to be accredited in the 2nd phase have not applied for re-accreditation, and the mechanisms/methods for improving quality are unclear or even reduced in number compared with the first phase of accreditation.
v. Communication of the results of higher education quality accreditation, as well as priority policies on state management of educational institutions and accredited programmes has not been given enough attention, leading to public suspicion of the effectiveness of higher education quality accreditation.
vi. International partnership in terms of quality assurance and education quality accreditation of higher education has not been encouraged and systematically implemented.

vii. The financial resources for quality assurance and education quality accreditation activities are unclear, resulting in many difficulties for the activities of educational institutions and education quality accreditation organizations.

Solutions and Proposals

To address the above problems, state management authorities, higher education institutions, and education quality accreditation organizations should consider implementing the following basic solutions:

i. Review and evaluate previously implemented quality assurance and education quality accreditation policies; summarize, evaluate and draw lessons from the implementation experience in order to create stability.
ii. Consider both international experience and practical experience in Vietnam in the gradual development of an independent system of education quality accreditation; build a clear model of quality assurance with regulations designed to enhance both internal and external quality assurance for higher education institutions; increase the capacity of education quality accreditation agencies to set out strategies for the development, organization, administration, and management of education quality accreditation organizational activities (Nguyen et al., 2017).
iii. Study the plan for establishing a National Council on Education Quality Accreditation in order to direct accreditation organizational operations and organize professional activities independent of MoET on behalf of the government (Nguyen et al., 2017). Carry out further examination, inspection, and assessment of accreditation organizations' operations on the condition that the independence of said organizations is respected; periodically grant operating licenses to education quality accreditation organizations.

iv. Enhance the capacity of managers and officers in charge of quality assurance and education quality accreditation; promulgate mechanisms developed to promote the quality assurance system inside educational institutions and prepare for quality improvements to meet the requirements of new higher education quality assessment standards issued in the Circular No. 12/TT-BGDDT dated May 19, 2017; maximize the resources for the professional training of the education quality accreditation organizational staff; strengthen the capacity of the educational administrative staff in terms of quality assurance; and increase the abilities of quality accreditors.
v. Promote society's and the higher education system's awareness of the significance of quality assurance and education quality accreditation; communicate with and encourage societal trust in the results of quality assessment and quality accreditation in order to create a consensus and support accreditation activity.
vi. A government mechanism should aim to increase worthwhile investment in education quality accreditation (via the state budget or other sponsors and projects); this will strongly motivate educational institutions to self-assess and apply for the education quality accreditation of educational institutions and programmes.
vii. Regarding educational institution/programmes of national, regional, or international accreditation, MoET continues to review its policies, mechanisms to make appropriate investment and issue specific warnings to institutions that fail to implement quality assessment or meet requisite quality standards. Regarding financial mechanism, the state should establish a fund for the education quality accreditation to provide financial assistance to both education quality accreditation organizations and educational institutions.
viii. Strengthen the role of state management authorities in the creation of a mechanism to both promote and supervise the quality accreditation applications of regional and international education quality accreditation organizations, as well as enhance education quality following accreditation. Extend international cooperation on quality assurance and education quality accreditation; the operation of international education quality accreditation organizations within Vietnam may well enhance competitiveness, but suitable supervisions mechanisms are recommended.

References

Central Committee of the Communist Party (CCCP). (2013). *Resolution No. 29/NQ-TW on fundamental and comprehensive renovation of education and training, meeting the requirement of industrialization, modernization in the condition of socialist-oriented market economy and international integration*. Hanoi: Central Committee of the Communist Party.

Do, Q. T. N., Pham, H. T., & Nguyen, K. D. (2017). Quality assurance in Vietnamese higher education: A top-down approach and compliance-driven QA. In M. Shah & Q. T. N. Do (Eds.), *The rise of quality assurance in Asian higher education* (pp. 51–66). Cambridge: Chandos Publishing.

General Department of Education Testing and Accreditation (GDETA). (2011). *List of universities, colleges and professional secondary schools completing self-assessment reports (updated on November 30, 2011)*. Hanoi: GDETA.

Government. (2005). *Resolution No. 14/2005/NQ-CP on fundamental and comprehensive renovation of Vietnamese higher education over the period of 2006–2020*. Hanoi: The Government.

Ministry of Education and Training (MoET). (2007a). *Decision No. 65/2007/QD-BGDDT promulgating regulations on standards for accreditation of universities*. Hanoi: MoET.

Ministry of Education and Training (MoET). (2007b). *Decision No. 72/2007/QD-BGDDT promulgating regulations on standards for accreditation of primary school teacher training programmes*. Hanoi: MoET.

Ministry of Education and Training (MoET). (2008). *Directive No. 46/2008/CT-BGDDT on strengthening educational assessment and accreditation exercises*. Hanoi: MoET.

Ministry of Education and Training (MoET). (2010). *Decision No. 4138/QD-BGDDT on approval of the project on the development of the higher education accreditation system in the period of 2010–2020*. Hanoi: MoET.

Ministry of Education and Training (MoET). (2011). *Circular No. 23/2011/QD-BGDDT promulgating regulations on standards for accreditation of vocational teacher training programmes*. Hanoi: MoET.

Ministry of Education and Training (MoET). (2012). *Circular No. 49/2012/TT-BGDDT promulgating regulations on standards for accreditation of high school teacher training programmes*. Hanoi: MoET.

Ministry of Education and Training (MoET). (2014). *Circular No. 33/2014/TT-BGDDT promulgating regulations on standards for accreditation of nursing programmes.* Hanoi: MoET.

Ministry of Education and Training (MoET). (2016). *Circular No. 04/2016/TT-BGDDT promulgating regulations on assessment standards for higher education programmes.* Hanoi: MoET.

Ministry of Education and Training (MoET). (2017). *Circular No. 12/2017/TT-BGDDT promulgating regulations on accreditation of higher education institutions.* Hanoi: MoET.

Ministry of Education and Training (MoET). (2018). *Statistics on education and training in 2018.* Hanoi: MoET.

National Assembly. (2005). *Education law.* Hanoi: National Assembly.

National Assembly. (2009). *Law on amending, supplementing a number of articles of the education law.* Hanoi: National Assembly.

National Assembly. (2012). *Higher education law.* Hanoi: National Assembly.

Nguyen, H. C. (2017). Impact of international accreditation on the emerging quality assurance system: The Vietnamese experience. *Change Management: An International Journal, 17*(3), 1–9.

Nguyen, H. C. (2018). How to fulfil Vietnam's higher education accreditation strategic plan 2017–2020? *International Journal of Educational Organization and Leadership, 24*(3/4), 17–25.

Nguyen, H. C., Evers, C., & Marshall, S. (2017). Accreditation of Vietnam's higher education: Achievements and challenges after a dozen years of development. *Quality Assurance in Education, 25*(4), 475–488. Retrieved from https://doi.org/10.1108/QAE-11-2016-0075.

Prime Minister. (2001). *Decision No. 201/2001/QD-TTg on the approval of the education development strategy 2001–2010.* Hanoi: The Prime Minister.

Vietnam Education Quality Management Agency. (2018a). *List of higher education institutions, teacher training colleges and teacher training schools completing self-evaluation reports, being accredited (until June 30, 2018).* Hanoi: VQA.

Vietnam Education Quality Management Agency. (2018b). *List of programmes that were evaluated/recognized (until June 30, 2018).* Hanoi: VQA.

10

Digital Innovation and Impact on Quality Assurance

Tuan Van Pham, Hien Thu Thi Ta and Huong Thu Thi Nguyen

A Potential Approach for Vietnam Higher Education to Meet the Requirements of the Workforce for the Industrial Revolution 4.0

Legal Framework for Changes in Vietnamese Higher Education in the Digital Era

The 4th Industrial Revolution (Industry 4.0) showcased a development trend based on the integration of high-level digital-physical-biological

T. Van Pham (✉)
University of Science and Technology,
The University of Danang, Danang, Vietnam
e-mail: pvtuan@dut.udn.vn

H. T. T. Ta · H. T. T. Nguyen
University of Education,
Vietnam National University, Hanoi, Vietnam

© The Author(s) 2019
C. H. Nguyen and M. Shah (eds.), *Quality Assurance in Vietnamese Higher Education*, https://doi.org/10.1007/978-3-030-26859-6_10

connection systems. Vietnam's higher education (HE) currently has several potential approaches for development, particularly to meet the needs of the Industry 4.0 workforce, from Information Communication Technology (ICT) applications in HE administration and governance to the management of teaching, learning, research, and community service. According to a study by Chui, Manyika, and Miremadi (2016), 60% of all jobs could see 30% or more of their constituent activities automated. Due to this, it is important to consider how higher education institutions (HEIs) in Vietnam can successfully ensure that their graduates are prepared for future jobs. The Global Education and Skills Forum reports on some of the most important skills every worker will need by 2030, including digital literacy—underlying training in computational and logical thinking (World Economic Forum [WEF], 2017); the four Cs—critical thinking, communication, collaboration, and creativity (US National Education Association [NEA], 2010); and multi-skilled (David, 2017). According to the "Future of Jobs" Report (WEF, 2018), four specific technological advances—ubiquitous high-speed mobile Internet; artificial intelligence; widespread adoption of big data analytics; and cloud technology—are set to dominate the 2018–2022 period as drivers that positively affect business growth.

To proactively seize opportunities and offer practical solutions to maximize advantages while minimizing the negative impacts of Industry 4.0, the Vietnam government has set up policies and issued legal documents to orient and implement various solutions for different aspects of economy and society. In 2014, the Prime Minister approved the project "Application of IT in managing vocational training and learning activities until 2020" through Decision No. 1982/QD-TTg dated October 31, 2014 (Prime Minister, 2014). Then, in 2017, the Prime Minister issued Directive No. 16/CT-TTg on strengthening the accessibility to modern ICT of Industry 4.0. One strategic goal was to drastically change the policies, content, and educational and vocational methods to create human resources capable of adopting new production technology trends. Two important solutions were identified as: "Creating a real breakthrough in infrastructure, application and human resources of ICT; Developing digital connection infrastructure and ensuring network safety and security" and "Vigorously changing educational, vocational resources and methods to create human resources capable of receiving new production technology trends" (Prime Minister, 2017).

Document No. 1891/BGDDT-GDDH was issued on May 5, 2017, by Ministry of Education and Training (MoET) on the task of training human resources capable of adapting to the Industry 4.0, requesting that universities implement many key tasks, such as: (i) review, adjust, and update training programs, innovate content and teaching methods to enhance simulation practices, digitize learning and teaching materials, adapt e-learning to personalize to learners, and enable learners to develop parts of lifelong learning capabilities; (ii) promote scientific research and cooperation of domestic and foreign enterprises and organizations in order to update technologies applied to teaching; explore the needs of the labor market to equip students with skills and knowledge to meet the requirements of the labor market immediately; create a real working environment in schools; and build education ecosystems where students have the opportunity to both practice and experience; and (iii) enhance the exchange and sharing of information and learning materials as well as the use of open resources (OER—Open Education Resources; OCW—Open Course Ware) for universities around the world to help students and lecturers access and update global information and knowledge (Ministry of Education and Training [MoET], 2017).

Future Changes and Challenges for Higher Education in Vietnam

Education has been heavily impacted by Industry 4.0 because it lends to the creation of future Industry Revolutions. For HEIs to remain relevant during Industry 4.0, they must transform their educational management system and governance structure into an innovation-producing ecosystem by exploiting disruptive technologies. The evolution of the education system which is named as Education 4.0 should be studied and exploited for Vietnam HEIs, "Education as ubiquitous where people, things and machines are connected to produce personalized learning. This new ecosystem transforms education institutions into an innovation-producing ecosystem" (Bin & Nguyen, 2017).

The development of information technology, digital tools, networking systems, and big data will alter the teaching and learning methods and organization of HEIs. Traditional classes, which suffer from disadvantages such as high organization costs, limited-service space, and unfavorable conditions for some subjects, will be replaced by online and virtual classes. Big data will become an endless data source from which to learn, analyze data, identify trends, and forecast business. Digital learning resources in the context of real and virtual space connections will continue to develop. The library space is no longer a specific place, but can be accessed anywhere with a simple operation. Curriculums will also be re-designed to better meet the needs of learners, becoming more diverse and specific. Trans-disciplinary curricula that promote innovation and breakthroughs in which new disciplines can flourish are therefore extremely needed. Ideas of smart education, universities, learning environments, and campuses (e.g., see Tikhomirov, 2015) should be strategically studied, developed, and implemented for Vietnam HE.

Vietnam HE will face many challenges in responding to Industry 4.0: to educate learners on the skills and abilities needed to respond to changes; to facilitate learners to have creative and innovative lifelong learning competences; and to assist learners in seeking learning outcomes with regard to learning management by the teacher.

The mission of universities in the coming period, therefore, is to train and support learners in acquiring adequate information technology knowledge and skills and actively equip graduates with relevant digital knowledge and skills to meet social needs in Industry 4.0. However, current training programs are inflexible and inconsistent with the needs and trends of the labor market of Industry 4.0. This places greater pressure on universities when the training programs should meet the requirements of high professionalism in certain and interdisciplinary fields (information technology, digital, networking, specialized knowledge, etc.) and other indispensable skills, such as systematic thinking, synthesizing, ability to link real and virtual worlds, creativity, teamwork, and ability to match interdisciplinary work. These kinds of T-Shape model have been recently developed in order to update HE programs (Saviano, Polese, Caputo, & Walletzký, 2016).

Development Trends in Higher Education in Asia

Development Trends of Higher Education and Some Advanced University Models in Asia

Asia, as a continent, has fairly diverse educational divisions. Thailand has established two open universities, many regional universities, and four prestigious national universities. Korea, Indonesia, Japan, and the Philippines rely heavily on private systems for education. Specifically, Korean education consists of 87% private schools, with 78% of students in Korea studying at these universities. Respectively, the statistics in Japan are 86 and 77%, in the Philippines—75 and 81%, and in Indonesia—71 and 96%.

China has impressively contributed huge financial resources toward schools identified as the most successful, created both high-quality and economic-efficient schools, and made efforts to create a highly productive learning environment (Altbach, 2013). China's world-class university (WCU) development campaign is a good example, as the country seeks to create the top 100 universities, of China's socioeconomic development in the twenty-first century and efforts to reach international levels. The Ministry of Education and Finance in China initiated Program 211 (1995), investing heavily in more than 100 universities with a total of US$5.44 billion over 10 years. Recently, some universities, such as Peking University, Tsinghua University, Shanghai Jiaotong University, Fudan University, Zhejiang University, and Nanjing University, have made significant progress in world-class rankings (Altbach, 2013).

Recognizing the role of the HE as a superior force and with the aim of increasing enrollment by 5% by 2012, the Indian government advocated the establishment of 14 WCUs by investing significant resources in the Indian Institute of Technology. Japanese HE is also famous for the "Twenty-First Century Centre of Excellence Programme" and the "World Premier International Research Centre Initiative," as they have focused on investing in elite universities. Korea has made efforts to build a world-class HE system by implementing policies such as investing $3.4 billion in the national program "Brain Korea 21" (1999–2012) and the WCUs program (2008), which promote postgraduate training and research activities.

In Singapore, with the "Manpower 21" program (1998) was outlined to develop globally competitive human resources and attract 10 WCUs within 10 years through training links, independent campuses, and campus settings. The policy was complemented by the government's "Global Schoolhouse" initiative (in 2002), which sought to attract 150,000 international students by 2015, raising the contribution of education to GDP from 1.9 to 5% in this period, on a par with the leading international education centers such as the UK and Australia, by providing initial loans and financial support to schools through 5–7 year contracts. Singapore has focused on investing in developing the National University of Singapore and Nanyang Technological University so that these two schools could earn positions in the top 100 leading universities in the world.

Singapore's neighboring governments in Malaysia and Hong Kong have also focused investment resources on top universities. For example, Malaysia initiated their "Accelerated Programme for Excellence," aiming to have one university ranking in the top 100 universities of the world. The Hong Kong University of Science and Technology was established with an investment of nearly US$500 million. This funding was higher than that of any other university in Hong Kong. In addition, the university has been highly autonomous in personnel decisions, faculty recruitment, and finances. After more than 10 years, the Hong Kong University of Science and Technology has become one of 10 leading research universities in Asia and is regarded as a symbol and pride of Hong Kong's HE (Marginson, 2011).

Development of Higher Education Systems in Vietnam

Vietnam's HE system has also rapidly changed and increased in scale, diversified with complex structures, and produced excellent universities. There are national universities, regional universities, key universities, academies and research institutes, and colleges including local colleges, pedagogical colleges, community colleges, and vocational colleges. This system structure is complex in terms of ownership, overlaps in management, and does not guarantee common quality ground among HEIs (Nguyen, 2015).

Therefore, to facilitate HEI reforming in Vietnam, many strategies have been developed and implemented. The Resolution No. 14/2005/NQ-CP was passed by the government to promote the fundamental and comprehensive innovation of Vietnamese HE from 2006 to 2020, with the goal that "by 2020, Vietnamese HE must reach an advanced regional level and prepare the approaches to world-class levels while adapting to the socialist-oriented market mechanism" (Government, 2005). In 2013, the Resolution No. 29-NQ/TW issued by the Central Committee of the Communist Party—the 11th Term gave direction to: "Renovate the education system towards open, flexible models and increasing connection among levels and modes of education and training. Standardize and modernize education and training" and "Be proactive, actively integrate into the world to develop education and training, at the same time, education and training must meet the requirements of international integration to develop the country" (Central Committee of the Communist Party [CCCP], 2013).

The government established Hanoi Open University in 1993 and Ho Chi Minh City Open University in 2006. Although these two public HEIs directly under MoET, they are autonomous in expenditure. In addition, some Vietnamese HEIs have joined the Asian Association of Open Universities, which is a non-profit organization for educational institutions interested in open and remote education.

The approval of Vietnam's National Framework of Qualifications (Decision No. 1982/2016/QD-TTg dated December 28, 2016) by the Prime Minister was an important milestone that referred Vietnam's qualifications to ASEAN through the ASEAN Qualifications Framework (AQRF) and international qualification framework, enhancing integration in training human resources. The National Qualification Framework (NQF) of Vietnam has identified 8 levels in the Vietnamese national education system (Prime Minister, 2016). Each level of qualification is clearly described, showing connection and development, and standardized with specific learning outcomes in terms of knowledge, skills, degrees of autonomy, and learner responsibilities for future careers at each level. This is an essential tool, not only for state management agencies, training institutions, professional associations, labor recruitment units, but also for learners and learners' families.

In addition, Vietnamese education is also experiencing a dramatic change in university administration. In 2018, the National Assembly passed a Law (Law No. 34/2018/QH14 dated November 19, 2018) with amendments and supplements to a number of articles in the higher education Law, emphasizing four main issues: expansion and improvement of the efficiency of university autonomy; innovation of university management; innovation of university administration; and state management reform in the context that universities exercise their autonomy. University autonomy is emphasized, especially academic autonomy when a university has fully met the conditions of quality accreditation and other quality assurance requirements (National Assembly, 2018). The re-planning of the HE network is also a task required to reform the education administration in Vietnam. According to the evaluation of MoET, the network of HEIs does not have the proper quality classification needed to establish investment priority policies that prioritize development. The system of open and distance education institutions has not developed in response to demand yet. Implementing the Government's Planning Law promulgated under Resolution No. 11/NQ-CP dated February 5, 2018, MoET resulted in the review of the strategy to re-plan the network of HEIs and teacher training in the period 2021–2030 and the vision to 2035, as well as developed the overall strategy for HE development in the period 2021–2030 and the vision to 2035 (MoET, 2018).

MoET has also promoted the application of information technology in teaching and educational management as one of nine key tasks being actively implemented by the education sector. MoET has issued a document guiding specific training mechanisms for university-level information technology domains from 2017 to 2020. These mechanisms aim to increase the quantity and quality of human resources in IT and meet the requirements of Industry 4.0. MoET has continued to build and update their e-learning lecture repository to be shared at elearning.edu.vn, which has been continuously updated and now holds over 5000 quality lectures; deployed the construction of a digital learning repository for the whole sector to aid in the renewal of contents, teaching methods, testing, and assessment in schools; and connected with the digitalized knowledge system. Within HE, schools have demonstrated increasing interest in building and upgrading electronic libraries and electronic learning materials. Higher education has implemented an e-learning system with a total of 4,252,702 electronic books and documents, including 2,548,247 e-books and materials purchased abroad. The percentage of units applying e-learning within specific subjects accounted for 35% of online coursework, reaching 11,269 courses (MoET, 2018).

The Rise of International Higher Education in Vietnam

Models of Vietnam's International Higher Education Institutions

To quickly integrate regional and international HE, MoET has issued an "overall strategy of international integration up to 2020 with the vision until 2030." This vision outlines cooperation in scientific research, training cooperation, credit recognition, inter-program coordination, and degree-granting among universities certified by prestigious accrediting organizations. In addition, the strategy has fostered international cooperation on student and faculty exchange among countries within the ASEAN region and around the world; Vietnamese overseas and foreign lecturers have participated in teaching and conducted research at HEIs in Vietnam.

Decree No. 86/2018/ND-CP (dated June 6, 2018 of the Government) provides clear regulation of education and training cooperation with foreign countries, foreign-invested educational establishments, foreign education representative offices opening in Vietnam, international organizations and foreign individuals engaged in HE cooperation and investment activities, and joint education and training programs with foreign countries in Vietnam (including those granting graduate, master, doctoral degrees, and foreign language competency certification examinations) (Government, 2018). The amended Law on higher education prescribed two types of educational institutions in Vietnam: (a) state-invested HEIs ensure working conditions and be the owner's representative and (b) private HE establishments sponsored by domestic or foreign investors to ensure operation conditions (National Assembly, 2018).

Cross-Border Higher Education and Vietnam's System of International Education Providers and Markets

The 9th Party Congress proposed a policy of "proactive international economic integration." Resolution No. 07-NQ/TW on "international economic integration" was later issued in 2001. The 10th Party Congress affirmed a policy of "proactive and active international economic integration, while expanding international cooperation in other fields." Resolution No. 22-NQ/TW (dated April 10, 2013) stated "Promoting bilateral and multilateral cooperation on culture, society, science—technology and education—training." First of all, it is necessary to build ASEAN cultural and social community and focus on developing human resources, especially high-quality human resources. In order to implement international integration in the education sector in Vietnam, the direct expression of globalization in HE is the participation in the "transboundary HE" market. Collaborations include research programs, training programs, and training services (including distance education) in which learners hail from different countries. Cross-border education is often conducted for commercial purposes through educational services (RMIT model) or sponsorship via non-profit support (e.g., Vietnamese–Japanese, Vietnamese–French university model).

As of February 2018, Vietnam holds 236 universities, including 5 foreign-invested educational institutions. The foreign-invested educational establishments rely on foreign investment capital and are operated by foreign-invested economic organizations; they may use their own seals and accounts according to Vietnamese Law provisions. The MoET agency organizes the examination, inspection, supervision, and evaluation of the operation results, addresses complaints and denunciation, and handles violations of foreign cooperation and investment activities in the field of education. MoET reports progress to the Prime Minister.

Vietnam starts to join and implement the mutual recognition arrangements (MRAs) for eight specific types of services under the ASEAN framework agreement on mutual recognition arrangements (ASEAN, 1998). Though there are challenges in implementing MRAs, Vietnam HEIs will benefit from such arrangements once they go beyond the borders of each country, find common ground, and make use of jointly trained resources across regions and continents. In addition, Vietnam has also recently allowed transnational education for certain study programs. A joint UNESCO/Council of Europe *Code of practice in the provision of transnational education* defined transnational education as follows: "All types of HE study programmes, sets of courses of study, or educational services (including those of distance education) in which the learners are located in a country different from the one where the awarding institution is based."

The introduction of educational services discussions within the framework of the General Agreement on Trade in Services (GATS) is now underway in the World Trade Organization (WTO). These discussions have placed HE as a potential commercial service. GATS distinguishes four modes of international education service: (1) cross-border service (distance education, virtual education institutions, enterprise education, and training software through the distribution of communications and information technology); (2) overseas student training (international students); (3) cooperation in bilateral education services (franchising or cooperation with partner or satellite campuses, private companies) or educational programs or exchanges; and (4) faculty exchange (professors, teachers, and researchers working abroad). All collaborations pose quality assurance challenges for host countries (Lane, Owens, & Kinser, 2015).

University-Enterprise Linkage Model

The Triple Helix model concept clearly defines the relationship between universities, businesses, and government. This paradigm shift from a business-state relationship dominating industrial society to a tripartite relationship between universities, business, and government aims to innovate and enhance economics within a knowledge society (Leydesdorff & Meyer, 2003). All parties of the Triple Helix model play a leading role in creating new social formats for production, transference, and the application of knowledge. The Triple Helix model begins when universities, businesses, and the state enter into a mutual relationship wherein each party (helix) attempts to improve the performance of the remaining parties (helixes). Most such initiatives occur at the regional/local level, where the specific context of industrial clusters (businesses), the development of science (schools), and the presence or expenditure of power (state) affects the development of all three parties.

In Vietnam, the Law on amendments and supplements to a number of articles of the higher education Law has supplemented a number of state policies on HE development. Specifically, the Law requires the association of training with labor market demands. The shift to customer demands for education market transparency increasingly requires quality educational service providers. New forms of government management have been created to better evaluate the credibility of market mechanisms. Quality requirements and EQA mechanisms must be culturally adaptive and focus more on input controls than outcomes.

In the context of market economy and international integration within the world's HE, the connection between HEIs and enterprises in training is crucial. Vietnam must foster such a link to develop high-quality and highly qualified human resources. The university-business linkage model will gradually eliminate the gap between university education and enterprises' actual human resource needs. This model requires HEIs alter the objectives, curriculums, structures, and quality of training to meet employer needs. In order to successfully implement this model, a university transformation roadmap is required to meet the needs of enterprises, including training integration and technology transfer and deployment. This roadmap requires three groups of basic elements that are coherently and closely coordinated: the benefit factors group, group of process elements, and group of condition factors.

Vietnam National University (VNU) has proven a pioneer in connecting university and business. Since 2009, VNU has recognized cooperation between universities, institutes, and businesses as characteristic of the research university model. This cooperative model attracts and enables scientists and businesses outside VNU to participate in training and facilitate student research and practices associated with real life (http://www.vnu.edu.vn). In recent years, Vietnamese HEIs have actively adhered to the requirements of the labor market through closer business connections. Private universities receive "training orders" from businesses. The design of "business semesters" and the establishment of independent company enterprises within education institutions are also no longer emerging practices. And in the last 5 years, business participation in university education has increased. FPT Corporation, Nguyen Hoang, Pheenika, and others have made substantial investments in university education institutions with the goal of developing HEIs into highly ranked universities. Another impact of the university-business linkage model is Vietnam HEIs' adaptation to Industry 4.0 development and challenges. Characteristics of Education 4.0 require HEIs to work together with industries to determine a development roadmap, make necessary preparations, and reach solutions that attain educational goals.

Investment Activities in Joint Ventures; Domestic and Foreign Cooperation in Education and Research

Those entities targeted by Vietnam's educational cooperation initiatives include "Vietnam's private preschool educational institutions, private general education establishments and educational establishments lawfully operating overseas are organized by agencies and organizations accredited or recognised by accreditation agencies or foreign authorities for educational quality." Objects and forms of training cooperation include (a) university education establishments which have been established, accredited, and operated lawfully in Vietnam and (b) HEIs which have been established and operated lawfully in foreign countries or accredited by accreditation agencies and recognized by competent Vietnamese agencies and organizations. In addition, partners may also organize examinations for foreign language competency certifications, including regular education, training organizations in the field of Vietnamese education, and agencies, organizations, and establishments evaluating foreign language competence that have been established and operated lawfully in foreign countries. Training cooperation in Vietnam is defined as (a) direct training cooperation; (b) online training cooperation (online); and (c) combined direct-online training cooperation.

The 2018 amendment to higher education Law stipulates investor regulations. Investors are defined as domestic or foreign organizations and individuals who invest in the establishment of private universities or private universities operating without profit by non-budget capital. University-established investors can invest through two methods: investing in the establishment of an economic organization that establishes a private university or directly establishing a private university. Investors possess the responsibility and authority to adopt strategies, plans for developing HEIs, university-university development plans, or merging with other universities as proposed by the councils, schools, and college councils. Investors make the decision on the total contributed capital of the investor, the investment project for the development of HEIs, and the mobilization of investment capital (if any). Investors plan to use the annual revenue-expenditure difference or handling losses of HE establishments, approving annual financial statements of HEIs (National Assembly, 2018).

As of December 2018, Vietnam hosted 526 international university joint training programs (MoET, 2018). However, the application of technologies, foreign education models, investment in education, and students enrolled in these government agreement scholarship programs remains focused on several big cities. The management and inspection of education programs at the secondary level have not yet received adequate attention. Thus, a number of violations which adversely affect investment cooperation activities with foreign countries have arisen.

Competition Within Vietnamese Higher Education

The 2018 amendment to higher education Law encourages the arranging and merging of large universities, as well as the development of private universities, directing policy of exemption, reduction of tax for donated assets, and support for HE, granting scholarships and participation in student credit transfer programs. The expansion of international cooperation in the field of education via cross-border HE services has provided both opportunities and challenges for HE systems. Private businesses can provide better HE services. In addition, foreign partners can introduce learners to creative educational activities and research opportunities. New training programs and advanced teaching technologies provided by foreign-based educational institutions also facilitate greater competition for local educational institutions.

Direct cooperation between national and international educational institutions can improve education quality by transferring knowledge and practice innovation. However, Vietnamese HE may face many challenges when joining the trans-boundary HE market due to various quality standards ensured by different suppliers of educational products which may provide inconsistent benefits for learners. This requires rigorous quality assurance systems that ensure customer trust by controlling and recognizing quality. The WTO is interested in educational services within the framework of the GATS. This interest has increased HE's perception as a global market benefit without the legal framework at the international level.

Vietnam's Development Perspectives on the Autonomy of Higher Education and Investor Opportunities

Vietnam's Development Perspectives on Educational Autonomy

The issue of university autonomy has been a central concern of the Government of Vietnam. The Charter of the University (Decision No. 153/2003/QD-TTg of the Prime Minister, Article 10) clearly states that "universities are entitled to autonomy and self-responsibility in accordance with the Law on planning, development plan, organization of training, science and technology, finance, international relations, organization and personnel." The Education Law (dated July 2005, Article 14) references assignment, decentralization, and strengthening of educational institutions' autonomy and self-responsibility. Similarly, the Prime Minister's Directive on the renovation of educational management between 2010 and 2012 (Directive No. 296/CT-TTg dated February 27, 2010) highlights the innovation of HE management, including state management of education and training institutions as a breakthrough to create comprehensive innovation of HE. The Prime Minister has assigned MoET with several urgent tasks, including the review, supplementation and adjustment of promulgated legal documents, as well as the development of new legal documents pertaining to university establishment, enrollment, training, financial and quality management, recruitment, lecturer's responsibilities and regimes in training and scientific research, relations between the Board of Rectors, the University Council, the Party Committee, and other belonged organizations (Prime Minister, 2010).

These MoET tasks enable universities and colleges to exercise autonomy and hold social responsibilities under the provisions of the Education Law. The Resolution No. 29-NQ/TW (dated November 4, 2013, of the 8th Conference of the 11th Central Committee of the Communist Party) addresses basic and comprehensive education and training innovation designed to meet the requirements of industrialization, modernization in country's socialist-oriented market economy, and international integration (CCCP, 2013). This resolution also affirms the importance of improving HE development policies that ensure autonomy and social responsibility of university education, the State's HE management, and the role of societal supervision and evaluation of HE. HEIs must, therefore, transform their management system to governance system and take responsible for training, research, organization, human resources, and finance. Meanwhile, the mechanisms of managing ministries should be abolished, and mechanisms of state ownership representation for public HEIs should be formulated. The Resolution No. 44/NQ-CP (dated June 9, 2014, of the Government) promulgates the Government's Action Program to implement the Resolution No. 29-NQ/TW.

On the basis of the pilot project innovating autonomous mechanism for 4 universities under MoET (the National Economics University, the Foreign Trade University, the University of Economics in Ho Chi Minh City, and Hanoi University), the Prime Minister approved Resolution No.

77/NQ-CP on implementing the innovation of operational mechanisms for public HEIs in the 2014–2017 period. In this pilot phase, the State and MoET paid great attention to autonomy and tried to create a legal platform for HEI autonomy; yet this autonomy proved ineffective due to the incompletion and inconsistency of the State's system of policies and guidelines, as well as a lack of HEI capacity and willingness.

In August 2017, the Prime Minister signed a decision approving the pilot scheme to innovate the operational mechanism for 23 HEIs, including public universities directly beneath ministries or central branches. Nine universities are administered by MoET (accounting for 47.4% of autonomous schools), 9 universities fall under the jurisdiction of ministries/organizations (including the Ministry of Industry and Trade, Ministry of Agriculture and Rural Development, Ministry of Finance, Ministry of Information and Communication, Ministry of Health, Vietnam General Confederation of Labor), and one university belongs to the People's Committee of Tra Vinh province. Though this university autonomy initiative is still in its pilot stage, many barriers exist. Policies and Laws on autonomy are not synchronous or adequate, and the management mechanisms of the regime of managing ministries remain inappropriate. Even so, some administrative and state management constraints have been adjusted to foster autonomy transformation. In response, universities are proactively opening new training programs, recruiting better-qualified lecturers, and connecting with international institutions to diversify their training products. MoET evaluated the practices of university autonomy in this pilot phase as follows (MoET, 2018):

– Academic autonomy: The universities have exercised autonomy in choosing enrollment methods, determining the content of the curriculum, selecting curriculum (except for compulsory subjects such as National Defense Education, Political Theory), and determining proposed research content. For HEIs that have been piloting to exercise autonomy under Resolution 77/NQ-CP, 3-year review results demonstrate that administrative procedures have been reduced; meanwhile, the process of opening domestic and international joint training programs has improved and opportunities to open training majors to meet societal needs have been seized.

- Financial autonomy: As part of this pilot-program autonomy, university financial activities have been effectively and transparently implemented. HEIs are proactive in making financial plans for short-term, medium-term, and long-term budgets; they have also adequately managed and used financial resources in service of teaching, learning activities, and other duties.
- Organizational and human resources autonomy: Most universities have tried to develop the organizational structure, especially university council activities. Autonomous pilot institutions have also reviewed the structure of lecturers and managers to ensure effective operation.

Finally, the Government issued a revised higher education Law in November 2018, which will take effect from July 1, 2019. This Law includes more allusions to university autonomy and accountability (Article 320 outlines specific issues of autonomy in academic expertise, enrollment, opening of training, scientific research, and international cooperation). This Law also clearly specifies personnel autonomy. According to Dang and Ta (2019), Vietnamese HEIs' responsibilities, as they pertain to autonomy, relate to accountability and responsibility in four main areas: (i) quality of teaching and learning; (ii) transparency of output; (iii) financial transparency; and (iv) financial support for students. In addition to improving HEI autonomy, the roles of information transparency and stakeholders in fostering accountability have also been emphasized, reflecting a clear change in the State's HE policy. Amended Articles 16 and 18 of the revised Law dictate the function of the University Council is to oversee the accountability of the Rector. Article 20 stipulates the Rector must exercise due diligence. Article 32, which details university accountability, stipulates that "HEIs implement autonomy and accountability in accordance with the Law"; "Autonomy in academia, professional activities including promulgation, implementation of quality standards, quality policies, enrollment, training, science and technology activities, domestic and international cooperation in accordance with the provisions of the Law." The Law clearly outlines a qualified management mechanism guaranteeing the accountability of HEIs through quality accreditation.

Vietnam's Views and Approaches to Economic Sectors' Investment in Higher Education

The Decree 73/1999/ND-CP (issued in 1999) crystallizes the Resolution of the Party Central Committee on the socialization of education by encouraging the development of additional non-public establishments and non-banking activities. This decree clarifies types of non-public universities as including private, people-founded, and semi-public schools. Based on this decree, a private university is a school established by an organization. In contrast, a semi-public university is established on the basis of cooperation between a state organization and a non-public organization. Finally, a private university is established by private or private companies. All three types of schools are operated without reliance on the state budget. Decree 43/2006/ND/CP regulates the autonomy and self-responsibility of non-business units, including public universities. As a result, universities are less likely to depend on the state budget and must operate under a financial autonomy mechanism which balances financial revenues and expenditures. According to Resolution 47/2014/NQ-CP, public institutions are given full financial autonomy and freely decide on the level of tuition fee according to the ceiling set by the State.

By 2018, the amended higher education Law 2018 had supplemented several of the State's HE development policies. The Law requires the integration of training with the labor market demands and encourages universities to merge into larger universities. Domestic investors or foreign organizations and individual investors can establish private universities and private universities operating without profit via non-budget capital (National Assembly, 2018). The former policies and legal regulation barriers have been gradually removed to enable better international and domestic HE integration opportunities within Vietnam. A trend of HE privatization via private enterprises and large corporations has emerged. Private universities operate primarily on private financial resources and must remain fully financially autonomous. In contrast, public schools receive a majority of their funding from the state's budget. As the privatization process accelerates, public universities with gradual autonomy mechanisms must compete to survive through further development. This requires both public and private schools to affirm their quality and take responsibility for the quality of their training products and activities, especially training and scientific research.

Implications of Digital Innovation in Higher Education Quality Assurance and Quality Accreditation

Impacts of Digital Innovation on the Quality of Higher Education

Quality assurance currently focuses on assuring the institutional integrity of HE provisions yet has paid less attention to learning outcomes and other performance indicators (Hazelkorn, Coates, & McCormick, 2018). Quality assurance has also not yet sufficiently identified standards for digital technologies used in teaching, learning, and recognition (Camilleri & Rampelt, 2018). Digital solutions offer new forms of learning and new modes of learning delivery. However, such technologies also present new challenges to existing quality assurance procedures. Ensuring and improving teaching and learning quality for all HE students are a central challenge for institutions and policymakers. These addressed issues of quality assurance will be significantly challenged.

To endow future generations with skills and knowledge relevant to the capacity requirements of the Industry 4.0, one must determine how HEIs will be affected by the Industry 4.0 and how education delivery will be transformed within an innovative quality assurance framework. In the context of disruptive technology, HE quality is a multi-dimensional concept that embodies not only quality assurance procedures, but also accessibility, employability, academic freedom, public responsibility, and HE mobility. Quality assurance processes serve multiple purposes; they enhance learning and teaching, build trust among stakeholders throughout the HE system, and increase regional and international harmonization and comparability. Digital innovation applies digital frameworks to internal and external quality assurance mechanisms as Industry 4.0 concepts are integrated to meet educational reform requirements.

Given the digital era, a new form of a university is emerging that teaches, researches, and provides services differently. This type of university educates via interdisciplinary majors with virtual classrooms, laboratories, libraries, and even teachers. However, this virtualization does not degrade educational experience, but augments it (Xing & Marwala, 2017). While HEIs are trusted by society and stakeholders and have longstanding accreditation experience, the primary issues facing massive open online course (MOOCs) relate to quality, trust, and accreditation in the associated credential, as reported by World Economic Forum (2018). Future education's mixing of MOOCs and traditional education can provide HEIs the opportunity to expand their services using their lecturers' experience. Data regarding student performance, behavior, development, and interaction inside classrooms and MOOC online platforms, as well as data from smart campuses, would create diversity and fast-changing of the HE system. The ability of HEIs to integrate this intelligent dataset would result in better decisions, customized education delivery, and personalized learning experiences for students.

The GAIHE project prepared for the European Commission in 2015–2016 concludes that innovations of the HE including but not limited to digital innovations. These innovations include changes in teaching methods, curricula, and programs that allow for a new student demographic. Recommendations highlight the following important issues:

i. HEIs must provide the right institutional support, organizational flexibility, financial incentives and evaluation, impact and quality assurance frameworks to support innovation and digital aspects;
ii. New technologies are not an end product—they must be included in a coherent pedagogical approach. HEIs should not only invest in technology, but also prioritize training staff and developing support structures that facilitate the inclusion of digital innovation in a coherent teaching and learning approach (McGrath et al., 2016).

When paired with disruptive technologies, Industry 4.0 can accelerate progress toward quality assurance within this new framework. In each step of the Plan-Do-Check-Act cycle, a framework of the university's IQA and data collection and analysis process for the purpose of quality improvement become extreme demand today. In addition, digital surveys are also frequently employed as a systematic assessment tool; these surveys can be administered as course evaluations, program evaluations, or institution-level evaluations. HEIs may embrace data mining to gain a better understanding of student performance and deliver personalized education tailored to meet job market demands and fulfill students' needs.

Challenges Facing Internal and External Quality Assurance Due to Implementation and Utilization of Innovation

As previously reported, the key challenges of opening up HE, improving teaching and learning quality, reforming assessment and recognition, and promoting internationalization and mobility have remained the same for all countries in the last 20 years (European Higher Education Area [EHEA]). With the Industry 4.0, digitalization may significantly contribute to overcoming the challenges. Though digitalization has not been ignored within the Bologna process, it is being viewed as an additional challenge rather than as a tool for meeting existing HE challenges. According to the Governance and Adaptation to Innovative Modes of Higher Education (GAIHE) project, one of the obstacles faced by HEIs when dealing with the utilization of innovation is "an obstacle in terms of innovation is teacher resistance to technology, new methods, modernisation. [...] Information transparency and accountability is needed in all quality processes to create a new and better perspective" (McGrath et al., 2016, p. 141).

Future education initiatives will focus on cyber universities and open universities where e-learning is a key component. According to the EUA's report on e-learning (Gaebel, Kupriyanova, Morais, & Colucci, 2014), 91% of institutions surveyed have integrated e-learning into their teaching (in the forms of distance learning, blended learning, problem-based learning, work-based learning, or simulation). In contrast, the quality assurance of such provisions has been given far less consideration. Namely, in the realm of external quality assurance, the authors suggest an apparent shortcoming and cite that only 23% of national quality assurance agencies give special consideration to e-learning. In summer 2016, the ENQA working group on quality assurance and e-learning aims to address the challenges associated with the alternative learning and teaching methods that ICT creates. The ENQA has set the standard for e-learning: "Institutions should have a policy for quality assurance that is made public and forms part of their strategic management. Internal stakeholders should develop and implement this policy through appropriate structures and processes, while involving external stakeholders" (Huertas et al., 2018). Due to the lack of an on-campus presence, involvement of stakeholders (e.g., students, academic staff, support staff, alumni, employers, etc.) in internal e-learning quality assurance can prove challenging. In response, HEIs may need to take actively engage all stakeholders in internal quality procedures.

External quality assurance should address the effectiveness of the internal quality assurance processes described above. External quality assurance considers the e-learning characteristics in terms of innovation in teaching and learning processes. Specific e-learning criteria for external quality assurance procedures must be, therefore, made publicly available. In addition, all relevant stakeholders should be involved in developing such e-learning criteria (via institutional or program evaluation).

The following challenges are addressed in Bologna digital, 2018: (i) simplifying and scaling recognition of learning at different and flexible locations of learning (both formal and non-formal) remains a challenge. Thus, procedures must be developed and published to assess and recognize prior (digital) learning achieved through different forms of (open) online education. Such efforts build upon the quality assurance of MOOC providers; and (ii) A student-centered approach fosters learner motivation and emphasizes relevance of learning to learners' own context. This approach reflects how learning occurs beyond the institutional setting, but it is difficult to offer on a large scale within an institutional setting. It requires the development of learning materials and teaching skills that surpass knowledge transition. HEIs should make use of digitally enhanced learning environments as an institutional strategy (Bologna, 2018).

As reported by Orr, van der Hijden, Rampelt, Röwert, and Suter (2018), if digital learning leads students to acquire knowledge across many different settings, a less institutionally focusing provision could also lead to a more learner-centered quality assurance framework. Therefore, existing criteria and measures for quality assurance must be renewed and supplemented to account for digitalization in teaching and learning and ensure security and transparency for all status groups. Additionally, quality standards for digital technologies used at HEIs must be discussed. Digital platforms may prove advantageous, since they can capture relevant data directly from a learning platform instead of indirectly through surveys.

Vietnam must implement changes and adjustments within HE to meet the demands of the 4th Industrial Revolution. Digital technology applications in training, research, and community service have been implemented. Smart education and smart university models are being researched and applied by universities with comprehensive technological integration and the ability to access and connect all things via the Internet. Universities are encouraged to open e-learning programs which capitalize on these new teaching technologies. Vietnam's higher education Law, amended in 2018, includes specific provisions on the value of regular training and continuing education in encouraging lifelong learning and regulating quality accreditation for all online training programs.

As training programs continue to adapt to the 4th industrial period, IQA and EQA systems in Vietnam HE will face challenges in ensuring education quality. In order to monitor and evaluate the quality of online training that includes digital technology applications, both IQA and EQA systems must adopt a technical framework that evaluates programs with internal and external quality assurance mechanisms. All stakeholders—the Government, the Ministry of Education and Training, HEIs, and quality accreditation agencies—will be required to work together to identify a set of quality criteria and indicators for online training programs (Nguyen, 2018; Nguyen, Evers, & Marshall, 2017). The state management agency should issue a set of standards for continuing training program quality assessments, as well as appropriate guidelines for testing training program quality. HEIs need to prepare the resources required to ensure training program quality and self-assessment mechanisms. In turn, quality accreditation agencies and accreditors must better understand online learning techniques and develop specific methods for the quality accreditation of online training programs and cyber-institutions (Nguyen & Le, 2019).

References

Altbach, P. G. (2013). The Asian higher education century? In *The international higher education* (pp. 143–147). Rotterdam: Sense Publishers.
ASEAN. (1998). *ASEAN framework agreement on mutual recognition arrangements.* https://asean.org/?static_post=asean-framework-agreement-on-mutual-recognition-arrangements-2.
Bin, J. O. C., & Nguyen, T. M. N. (2017). *The 4Cs framework to transform higher education institution into an innovation-producing ecosystem.* http://johnsonongcheebin.blogspot.com/2017/06/the-4cs-framework-to-transform-higher.html.
Camilleri, A., & Rampelt, F. (2018). *Assuring the quality of credentials to support learning innovation.* https://eua.eu/downloads/publications/p19_camilleri_rampelt.pdf.
Central Committee of the Communist Party (CCCP). (2013). *Resolution No. 29/NQ-TW on fundamental and comprehensive renovation of education and training, meeting the requirement of industrialization, modernization in the condition of socialist-oriented market economy and international integration.* Hanoi: Central Committee of the Communist Party.
Chui, M., Manyika, J., & Miremadi, M. (2016). Where machines could replace humans—And where they can't (yet). *McKinsey Quarterly, 2016*(3), 58–69.
Dang, U. V., & Ta, T. T. H. (2019). Higher education accreditation and university autonomy. *VNU Journal of Science: Education Research, 35*(1), 84–95.
David, J. D. (2017). The growing importance of social skills in the labor market. *Quarterly Journal of Economics, 132*(4), 1593–1640.
Gaebel, M., Kupriyanova, V., Morais, R., & Colucci, E. (2014). *E-learning in European higher education institutions.* Brussels: European University Association (EUA).
Government. (2005). *Resolution No. 14/2005/NQ-CP on fundamental and comprehensive renovation of Vietnamese higher education over the period of 2006–2020.* Hanoi: The Government.

Government. (2018). *Decree No. 86/2018/ND-CP on foreign cooperation and investment in education*. Hanoi: The Government.

Hazelkorn, E., Coates, H., & McCormick, A. C. (Eds.). (2018). *Research handbook on quality, performance and accountability in higher education*. Cheltenham: Edward Elgar.

Huertas, E., et al. (2018). *Considerations for quality assurance of e-learning provision*. Brussels: ENQA. https://enqa.eu/indirme/Considerations%20for%20QA%20of%20e-learning%20provision.pdf.

Lane, J., Owens, T., & Kinser, K. (2015). *Cross border higher education, international trade, and economic competitiveness: A review of policy dynamics when education crosses borders*. Toronto, Geneva, and Brighton: ILEAP, CUTS International Geneva and CARIS.

Leydesdorff, L., & Meyer, M. (2003). The Triple Helix of university-industry-government relations. *Scientometrics, 58*(2), 191–203.

Marginson, S. (2011). Global perspectives and strategies of Asia-Pacific research universities. In N. C. Liu, Q. Wang, & Y. Cheng (Eds.), *Paths to a world-class university: Global perspectives on higher education* (pp. 3–27). Rotterdam: Sense Publishers.

McGrath, C. H., Hofman, J., Bajziková, L., Harte, E., Lasakova, A., Pankowska, P., ... Krivogra, J. (2016). *Governance and adaptation to innovative modes of higher education provision (GAIHE)*. https://www.rand.org/content/dam/rand/pubs/research_reports/RR1500/RR1571/RAND_RR1571.pdf.

Ministry of Education and Training (MoET). (2017). *Document No. 1891/BGDDT-GDDH on the task of training human resources capable of adapting to the Industry 4.0*. Hanoi: MoET.

Ministry of Education and Training (MoET). (2018). *Final report of the 2017–2018 school year*. Hanoi: MoET.

National Assembly. (2018). *Law amending and supplementing a number of the higher education law*. Hanoi: National Assembly.

Nguyen, H. C. (2018). Advantages and disadvantages when implementing the higher education accreditation plan in the period of 2017–2020. *Journal of Science: Educational Sciences, 63*(2), 17–26.

Nguyen, H. C., Evers, C., & Marshall, S. (2017). Accreditation of Viet Nam's higher education: Achievements and challenges after a dozen years of development. *Quality Assurance in Education, 25*(4), 475–488.

Nguyen, H. C., & Le, M. P. (2019). Quality assurance and accreditation of distance education programs in Vietnam: Rationale and future directions. *VNU Journal of Science: Education Research, 35*(1), 1–10.

Nguyen, T. T. H. (2015, June 23–25). How to stratify Vietnam higher education institutions? *Proceedings of 2015 International Hokkaido Forum—Organizational Behavior, Psychology, and Education* (ISSN 2412-0189), Sapporo, Japan.

Orr, D., van der Hijden, P., Rampelt, F., Röwert, R., & Suter, R. (2018). *Position Paper Bologna Digital.* https://www.researchgate.net/publication/323759351_Position_Paper_Bologna_Digital_Version_10-March_9th_2018.

Prime Minister. (2010). *Directive No. 296/CT-TTg on renewal of tertiary education administration during 2010–2012.* Hanoi: The Prime Minister.

Prime Minister. (2014). *Decision No. 1982/QD-TTg on application of IT in managing vocational training and learning activities until 2020.* Hanoi: The Prime Minister.

Prime Minister. (2016). *Decision No. 1982/2016/QD-TTg on Vietnam's qualification framework.* Hanoi: The Prime Minister.

Prime Minister. (2017). *Directive No. 16/CT-TTg on strengthening the accessibility to modern ICT of Industry 4.0.* Hanoi: The Prime Minister.

Saviano, M., Polese, F., Caputo, F., & Walletzký, L. (2016). *A T-shaped model for rethinking higher education programs.* Conference: 19th Toulon-Verona International Conference "Excellence in Services". University of Huelva, Huelva, Spain.

Tikhomirov, V. (2015). *Development of strategy for smart university.* https://conference.oeconsortium.org/2015/wp-content/uploads/2015/02/oeglobal2015_submission_231.pdf.

US National Education Association (NEA). (2010). *Preparing 21st century students for a global society: An educator's guide to the "Four Cs".* http://www.nea.org/assets/docs/A-Guide-to-Four-Cs.pdf.

World Economic Forum (WEF). (2017). *Realizing human potential in the Fourth Industrial Revolution—An agenda for leaders to shape the future of education, gender and work.* A White Paper by the World Economic Forum. https://www.weforum.org/whitepapers/realizing-human-potential-in-the-fourth-industrial-revolution.

World Economic Forum (WEF). (2018). *The future of jobs report.* https://www.weforum.org/reports/the-future-of-jobs-report-2018.

Xing, B., & Marwala, T. (2017). *Implications of the fourth industrial age for higher education.* The Thinker, Issue 73, Third Quarter, 2017.

11

Building National Capacity for Quality Assurance

Cuong Huu Nguyen

Introduction

Human resource capital is considered the most valuable property of organizations in the twenty-first century (Drucker, 1999) because a well-prepared and motivated workforce is possibly the most important asset for creating value. Generally, human resource capital, along with other assets, underpins every agency or institution activity (Cribb, 2006; Khasawneh, 2011). Consequently, capacity building and development of human resources have become one of the most significant agendas for many nations and organizations (Oh, Ryu, & Choi, 2013). Many countries worldwide (both developed and developing) have recently placed more emphasis on human resource development and capacity building in their national development strategies.

As an emerging economy in the Asia-Pacific region, Vietnam has carried out significant human resource development and capacity building strategies as it "needs a knowledgeable and skilled workforce to help it progress to

---

C. H. Nguyen (✉)
University of Education, Vietnam National University, Hanoi, Vietnam
e-mail: nhcuong@moet.edu.vn

© The Author(s) 2019
C. H. Nguyen and M. Shah (eds.), *Quality Assurance in Vietnamese Higher Education*, https://doi.org/10.1007/978-3-030-26859-6_11

an industrialized country by 2020" (DFAT, 2015, p. 4). Human resource development and capacity building practices in Vietnam vary significantly depending on ownership, stage of technological development, and extent of internationalization. Many Vietnamese organizations are dramatically aware of the importance of human resource development and capacity building, but lack resources for implementation (Garavan & Akdere, 2016).

Considered to be a nascent area in Vietnam's higher education sector, quality assurance and accreditation has received attention from the central government, local governments, society, and institutions (Madden, 2014; Nguyen, Oliver, & Priddy, 2009). Human resource development and capacity building within this field alone have become a hot topic conversation, discussion, and study (Nguyen, Evers, & Marshall, 2017). This chapter investigates the development of Vietnam's higher education quality assurance and accreditation system with a focus on human resource development and capacity building policies and practices.

Vietnam's Higher Education

Higher education in Vietnam includes academic education at colleges and universities that award associate, bachelor's, master's, and doctoral degrees (Do & Do, 2014). The 5 year Socioeconomic Development Plan 2011–2015 approved by the National Assembly accords higher education an important role in improving the quality of the nation's human resources and facilitating economic growth (National Assembly, 2011). Additionally, the government adopted the Higher Education Reform Agenda (HERA) for 2006–2020 (Resolution 14/2005/NQ-CP), which establishes a substantial and comprehensive renewal of Vietnam's tertiary education during the period of 2006–2020 in order to modernize the higher education system by 2020 (Hayden & Lam, 2007). Most recently, the Vietnamese Prime Minister approved a project to enhance the quality of higher education during the period of 2019–2025 (Decision No. 69/QD-TTg dated January 15, 2019) (The Prime Minister, 2019). These macro-policies have contributed to the rapid expansion of the Vietnamese higher education sector during the past few years. Since the 1990s, the number of tertiary education institutions has increased significantly, from 110 in 1993 to 436 in 2015. At the same time, university and college enrollment has grown 15-fold, from 162,000 to 2.4 million in 2015 (MoET, 2015; World Bank, 2008). In the academic year 2017–2018, 236 universities had over 1.7 million students (Ministry of Education and Training [MoET], 2018).

Despite the fact that Vietnam's higher education sector has expanded rapidly, it can be argued that it has been "unable to meet market demand in terms of both quantity and quality" (DFAT, 2015, p. 9). While the number of students has increased by more than 1 million since 2005 (from 1.3 million in 2005 to 2.4 million in 2015), the number of academic staff has increased by only 48,000 (from 43,728 to 91,183) (MoET, 2015; World Bank, 2008). Moreover, most of Vietnam's universities and colleges, which are small when compared with regional and world standards, have less than 3000 enrolled students (DAFT, 2015; Dao, 2015). Consequently, the expansion in capacity of student places has not kept up with the demands of population growth (DAFT, 2015). Also, while there has been a significant increase in employment opportunities for higher education graduates, many of them "lack some of the skills needed for good performance in the workplace" (World Bank, 2008, p. xix).

Regarding management and governance, the Vietnamese government maintains tight control over management and academic affairs in higher education institutions (Do & Do, 2014). This is excepting the two national universities (Vietnam National University, Hanoi—VNU-HN and Vietnam National University, Ho Chi Minh City—VNU-HCM), which directly report to the Cabinet. All other public universities and colleges are under control of MoET, line ministries, or provincial people's committees (Dao, 2015; Do & Do, 2014; World Bank, 2008). Regardless of ownership, MoET, as a regulatory and overseer body, controls most important decisions for every public university, such as enrollment quotas, maximum tuition fees, and curriculum frameworks. MoET is also in charge of administering the national high school examinations for admission to higher education institutions, managing the new enrollment selection process, and supervising the higher education quality assurance system (Do & Do, 2014).

Quality Assurance for Vietnam's Higher Education

Vietnam's higher education quality assurance system has been developed largely based on the framework proposed by the Asia-Pacific Quality Network (APQN Chiba Principles). Additionally, Vietnam also used ideas from quality assurance models implemented in the United States, Australia, Europe, and other countries in the region (MoET, 2010; Ta, 2016). Currently, the model for Vietnam's higher education quality assurance consists of three components: internal quality assurance, external quality assurance, and external quality assurance agencies (Pham, 2013). By law, accreditation (as a quality assurance approach implemented in Vietnam) is mandatory for all higher education institutions and programs (National Assembly, 2005, 2012, 2018). The procedure for both institutional accreditation and program accreditation consists of four steps: self-evaluation by educational institutions; registration for external evaluation with an accrediting agency; external evaluation by accrediting agencies; and recognition of accreditation outcomes (MoET, 2012, 2013b; Nguyen et al., 2017).

The quality movement in Vietnam's higher education began in the 1990s. Initial quality assurance activities were observed through the establishment of two bodies specializing in assessment and evaluation within the two national universities in the 1990s. The Center for Education Quality Assurance and Research Development (now called Institute for Education Quality Assurance—INFEQA) was established in VNU-HN in 1995 and the Center for Educational Testing and Quality Assessment (CETQA) was established in VNU-HCM in 1999 (Do & Do, 2014; Ta, 2016). In 2000, the need to establish quality assurance systems at the national and institutional levels in Vietnam was first discussed among Vietnamese educators, scholars, and policy-makers at the Da Lat Conference (Nguyen et al., 2009). Two years later, the Division of Education Accreditation was established within the Department of Higher Education, MoET. Then, in 2003, this office was upgraded to a department of MoET called the General Department of Education Testing and Accreditation (GDETA) (Do, Pham, & Nguyen, 2017; MoET, 2010; World Bank, 2012). GDETA was renamed the Vietnam Education Quality Management Agency (VQA) in May 2017. GDETA/VQA acts as a national quality assurance agency in Vietnam and is responsible for the organization, management, and instruction of the implementation of quality assurance and accreditation for all educational institutions and programs nationwide (MoET, 2017b).

Since the establishment of GDETA, quality assurance of Vietnam's higher education has witnessed several achievements. Specifically, the legal framework has been developed and implemented (including laws approved by the National Assembly, decrees adopted by the government, circulars promulgated by MoET, and guidelines issued by GDETA). Five accrediting agencies were established with the primary purpose of undertaking external evaluation and recognizing institutions and programs that satisfy accreditation standards (Nguyen et al., 2017; VQA, 2019a). Furthermore, under the umbrella of GDETA, there is now a network of quality assurance units established in all higher education institutions throughout the country. In addition, quality cultures have, step-by-step, been created and developed in many universities (Nguyen, 2015; Ta, 2016). As of April 30, 2019, 218 universities had completed self-evaluation reports and 128 universities have undergone external evaluation by accrediting agencies, 121 of which were awarded accreditation certificates. Moreover, two universities have been assessed by ASEAN University Network-Quality Assurance (AUN-QA), and four other universities have been accredited by the High Council for Evaluation of Research and Higher Education, France (HCERES) (VQA, 2019a). For program accreditation, 16 programs have been accredited by the local standards and processed and 126 programs (the majority from VNU-HN and VNU-HCM) have been assessed or accredited by regional or international accreditation agencies, such as the Accreditation Board for Engineering and Technology (ABET), the Accreditation Council for Business Schools and Programs (ACBSP), AUN-QA, Engineering Accreditation Institution, France (CTI), and the Foundation for International Business Administration Accreditation (FIBAA) (VQA, 2019b).

Capacity Building for Vietnam's Higher Education Quality Assurance System

Capacity Building Policy

The development of human resources and capacity building in higher education quality assurance areas in Vietnam at both the national and institutional level have been a main topics of discussion. Aligned with the 5 year Socioeconomic Development Plan 2006–2010 (Resolution 56/2006/QH11), which identifies human resource development as a key breakthrough area to achieve the nation's development goals (National Assembly, 2006), in 2008, MoET promulgated Directive No. 46/2008/CT-BGDDT to strengthen educational assessment and accreditation exercises. This legal document emphasizes the need for professionally trained quality assurance staff in local and overseas institutions, who have been provided with knowledge and skills that allow them to implement quality assurance activities successfully (MoET, 2008).

In 2010, MoET proposed the Project for the Establishment and Development of Vietnam's Accreditation System for Higher Education and Professional Secondary Education for the period of 2010–2020 (Decision 4138/QD-BGDDT, dated September 20, 2010) (MoET, 2010). Two out of four main objectives of this project target human resource development in the field of quality assurance and accreditation. Specifically, at the national level, the project aims to build the capacity in accreditation policy-making for 20 officials annually. At the institutional level, it aims at training 350 external evaluators yearly in 2011 and 2012 and 200 external evaluators yearly from 2013 to 2020. In addition, the project also proposes the educational managers, lecturers, and staff be trained at higher education institutions (1100 people annually) (MoET, 2010).

Policies on capacity building and human resource development in higher education quality assurance and accreditation have been highlighted in a number of MoET documents as well as repeatedly mentioned in discussions among educational policy-makers, administrators, and leaders of MoET. For example, during a meeting on the plan to implement higher education accreditation, the Minister of MoET stressed the importance of developing human resources and capacity building for quality assurance staff at both the national and institutional level (MoET, 2016). Most recently, MoET issued the Higher Education Accreditation Strategic Plan 2017–2020 (Plan No. 118/KH-BGDDT dated February 23, 2017). One of this plan's three goals is to enhance the professional competencies of staff working at the national quality assurance organization, accrediting agencies, assessors/accreditors, and internal quality assurance units of higher education institutions, (MoET, 2017a).

Capacity Building Strategies

MoET, GDETA (VQA), accrediting agencies, and higher education institutions have conducted many strategies and activities associated with human resource development in accreditation, such as conferences, workshops, short courses, internships, study visits, postgraduate programs, and coaching. In this section, only the most popular ones, including workshops, short courses, and study visits, are discussed.

Regarding workshops, Huffman, Thomas, and Lawrenz (2008) state that a common approach used to help develop individuals' capacity is the use of workshops. In Vietnam, workshops are the primary methods for staff development in quality assurance, particularly in the early years of this system (Nguyen, 2016, 2017). At the national level, GDETA, with support from several projects, has organized dozens of training workshops since 2004. For example, in 2012 alone, six workshops focused on quality assurance capacity building (GDETA, 2012). These workshops aim to provide participants (staff, MoET officials, and managers of higher education institutions) with knowledge, skills, and techniques used for self and external evaluation (Nguyen, 2017; World Bank, 2012). It was reported by GDETA (2012) that at the end of 2012, about 1000 staff were participating in self-evaluation workshops and 800 were participating in external evaluation workshops.

Regarding short courses, many of them have been organized by GDETA, INFEQA, CETQA, and other institutions. These short courses normally last from 3 to 7 days and focus mostly on self—or external evaluation (CETQA, 2013; Nguyen, 2016). However, different from these shorter courses, accreditors also provide training courses offered by accrediting centers such as the Center for Education Accreditation—Vietnam National University, Hanoi (VNU-CEA), the Center for Education Accreditation—Vietnam National University, Ho Chi Minh City (VNU-HCM CEA), and Center for Education Accreditation—Da Nang University (DNU-CEA). These operate for one month with permission from MoET. Moreover, they combine online training with face-to-face training. The curriculum framework for these courses is promulgated by MoET (Circular No. 18/2013/TT-BGDDT, dated May 14, 2013). These courses establish several objectives in three groups: knowledge, skills, and attitudes. For example, in terms of knowledge, learners are provided with knowledge of quality assurance and accreditation; comprehension of the organizational structure and operation of quality assurance and accreditation in Vietnam, regionally and across the world; an understanding of Vietnam's accreditation standards and processes, as well as Vietnamese regulations for quality assurance and accreditation (MoET, 2013a). Earning certificates from these courses is a prerequisite to apply for accreditor's cards issued by MoET as well as for participating in external evaluation panels. By the end of 2018, accrediting centers had trained over 1000 accreditors, 346 of whom were issued accreditor's cards by MoET (Nguyen, 2018).

Study visits of other institutions have been used effectively by many Vietnamese tertiary institutions. Approaches in the form of written materials and workshops only provide theories on quality assurance and accreditation, and many Vietnamese universities have further sought to observe how quality assurance activities are conducted (Nguyen, 2016; Vo, 2013). Through this, they have found that study visits can be used to enhance their staff's capacity. Some institutions visited famous universities in Australia, the Netherlands, and the United States. Although a visit usually lasts for about a week, these universities have reported that they gained significant knowledge on how foreign institutions conduct quality assurance activities, particularly the processes, techniques, and evaluation tools used to undertake self-evaluation. By combining this experience with self-evaluation guidelines and workshop knowledge, they have successfully implemented several internal quality assurance activities in their institutional context (CETQA, 2013; Pham & Nguyen, 2013). The success of this approach has since been broadened. Many more universities have organized study visits to higher education institutions overseas.

Further, instead of going overseas, some universities visit local institutions that have good reputations for undertaking quality assurance programs (Phan, Dao, & Chau, 2013). Hence, study visits have been an effective approach for developing human resources in quality assurance in Vietnamese universities.

Involvement of Higher Education Institutions and Organizations

Vietnamese universities have played an important role in human resource development in quality assurance. Many universities have dedicated particular attention to developing lecturers and staff with knowledge and skills in this area. Almost every institution has established a unit specializing in quality assurance (Nguyen et al., 2017). Each of these units employs from three to seven full-time staff members, and in 2011 nearly 1000 quality assurance staff were working in Vietnam's higher education institutions (Ta, 2012). In addition to tertiary institutions, other ministries such as the Ministry of Health, Ministry of National Defence, and Ministry of Public Security have allocated human resources specializing in quality assurance. The human resource development activities organized by these institutions and organizations include workshops, conferences, study visits, and sending staff to attend short courses and postgraduate programs in educational assessment and evaluation (Pham & Nguyen, 2013; Phan et al., 2013).

Apart from building capacity in quality assurance for lecturers and staff, some institutions have also supported others. For example, INFEQA has collaborated with partners such as MoET, the Second Higher Education Project (HEP2), the Department of Schools, and the Ministry of National Defence to organize many workshops and short courses centered around external and self-evaluation (INFEQA, 2013). Furthermore, as mentioned above, accreditor training courses offered by accrediting agencies provide high-quality knowledge, skills, and attitudes related to higher education quality assurance and accreditation for quality assurance staff nationwide.

The master's and doctoral courses in educational measurement and evaluation run by VNU-HN are also said to have contributed to enhancing the quality of human resources in quality assurance among local higher education institutions (Hoang & Ta, 2013; Ta, 2016). Such courses provide in-depth, specialized knowledge and skills in assessment, evaluation, and quality assurance. Those who have completed these courses are believed to make up the core quality assurance human resources of quality assurance agencies, educational offices, and institutions. As a result, they contribute to the development of the country's quality assurance system (Hoang & Ta, 2013). As of the end of 2018, over 200 students had graduated from master's programs, and ten students had graduated from Ph.D. programs. VNU-HN is the sole institution in Vietnam to offer master's and doctoral courses in educational measurement and evaluation (Hoang & Ta, 2013).

Support from International Partners

Higher education quality assurance was introduced to Vietnam through participation and support from international experts and foreign projects (Madden, 2014; Nguyen, 2012; Niedermeier & Pohlenz, 2016). The First Higher Education Project (HEP1) and Second Higher Education Project (HEP2), which together spanned from 1998 to 2007, are said to have made great contributions to the development of Vietnam's higher education quality assurance system, specifically via capacity building for quality assurance staff. While HEP1 aimed to assist MoET in setting up a quality assurance office at the system level to undertake institutional quality assessment, HEP2 focused on providing technical assistance in setting minimum standards, establishing independent accreditation agencies and developing institutional quality culture. Arguably, training workshops in quality assurance facilitated by HEP1 and HEP2 have had a direct impact on human resource development in Vietnam's higher education quality assurance (Nguyen, 2012).

Another project directly involved in higher education quality assurance is ProfQim (acronym for Professionalizing Quality Improvement), one of the two sub-projects of the Vietnam-Netherlands Higher Education project. ProfQim had two objectives: (i) develop quality assurance centers at five selected universities (Thai Nguyen University, Vinh University, Hue University, Da Nang University, and Can Tho University);

and (ii) contribute to MoET via the development of Vietnam's higher education quality assurance system (Nguyen, 2012; Westerheijden, Cremonini, & Empel, 2010). During the three-year project (2005–2008), quality assurance experts from the Netherlands conducted several on-site missions designed to train university and MoET staff in evaluation, quality assurance, and accreditation (Westerheijden et al., 2010).

Apart from these major projects, several smaller projects or programs have been funded or organized by regional and international agencies, including the Asia-Pacific Quality Network (APQN), AUN-QA, Southeast Asian Ministers of Education Organization (SEAMEO), and the United Nations Educational, Scientific and Cultural Organization (UNESCO). Organizations from several developed countries, such as Australia, Germany, the Netherlands, and the United States, also contributed to building the capacity of Vietnamese quality assurance staff (Madden, 2014; Nguyen, 2015). Support from international partners has played a clear, important role in the development of Vietnam's higher education quality assurance system and human resources that facilitate it.

Challenges

Vietnam's higher education quality assurance system faces several challenges, particularly those related to human resources. First, some argue that a serious lack of quality assurance staff exists at the system level (Madden, 2014; Nguyen et al., 2017). MoET has encountered "challenges with a limited staff to manage the enormity of managing and building capacity for a new QA [quality assurance] system" (Madden, 2014, p. 100). In fact, as of February 2017, GDETA (within MoET) contained only six officials responsible for policy-making for Vietnam's entire higher education quality assurance and accreditation system. These officials must supervise and ensure the quality assurance management of four accrediting centers, over two hundred universities and a dozen teacher training colleges and professional secondary schools. Clearly, with such limited human resources, GDETA is overloaded with the scope of its responsibilities (Tran, 2014; Westerheijden et al., 2010), and it has proven difficult for this national quality assurance organization to supervise, monitor, and guide accreditation implementation (Nguyen, 2015).

The second challenge faced by Vietnam's higher education quality assurance system relates to accreditors. Only 30% of accreditors were able to participate in external evaluation teams. This means a large number of accreditors are incompetent, and accrediting centers have difficulty selecting qualified accreditors for site visits. It is calculated that 50 accreditors employed full-time by an accrediting agency can accredit only 50 institutions or 60 programs annually. Consequently, one accrediting agency is capable of accrediting, at most, 250 institutions or 300 programs during a 5 year accreditation cycle (Ta, 2016). As discussed above, Vietnam has only four accrediting centers, while the country hosts over 300 tertiary education institutions and more than 5000 programs. How accrediting centers can deal with such a large number of institutions and programs remains a big, unanswered question.

Thirdly, it is stated that both the quantity and quality of quality assurance staff at the institutional level are inadequate. On average, each higher education institution's quality assurance unit has just five quality assurance staff. However, in some cases, these staff members are in charge of not only quality assurance but also institutional testing and inspection. The inadequacy of institutional quality assurance staff is largely attributed to accreditation's infancy in Vietnam (Nguyen, 2012). Also, most of those involved in quality assurance have not been academically trained in the field. Similarly, changes in personnel working in quality assurance units are frequent and can result in further difficulties and ineffectiveness in institutional quality assurance activities (Ta, 2016).

Lastly, no formal professional development policy for quality assurance staff exists either the macro (national) or micro (institutional) levels (Nguyen et al., 2017). As discussed above, most professionals working in the field of quality assurance and accreditation in Vietnam are not trained professionally in quality assurance or assessment and evaluation. Therefore, professional development activities are the best way for them to gain the knowledge and skills necessary to their current work. However, the national quality assurance agency's professional development policy has not been documented (Nguyen, 2016). At the institutional level, many universities and colleges primarily rely on MoET for the capacity building for their staff. In this regard, Madden (2014, p. 100) states that a policy of "all things wait for MoET" is typical within Vietnam's higher education quality assurance system.

Lessons Learned

Through the investigation of achievements and challenges in Vietnam's higher education quality assurance and accreditation system, five lessons have been drawn for the benefit of future policy-making and practice in human resource development and capacity building in this area.

Lesson 1: Human resource development is particularly important for Vietnam's newly established higher education quality assurance system

Vietnam has dedicated attention to the development of human resources in quality assurance within tertiary education since the system was officially established in 2003. Human resource development activities have been witnessed at the macro-level (MoET, GDETA/VQA), meso-level (accrediting centers), and micro-level (universities and colleges). To this end, a diversity of strategies has been implemented in these organizations and institutions, including workshops and conferences, short courses, study visits, and postgraduate programs.

Lesson 2: Professional development and capacity building for quality assurance staff are crucial for sustainable development of the quality assurance system

Professional development and capacity building play an important part in the existence and enhancement of any educational institution or organization. It is one of the key aspects of human resource management that specifically deals with training and development of staff. In the context of Vietnam, higher education quality assurance and accreditation remain in a nascent stage. Those working in this new area require new knowledge and skills, which they can best gain through professional development or capacity building programs.

Lesson 3: The national quality assurance organization and two national universities play an essential role in human resource development within the quality assurance system

In addition to policy-making, GDETA/VQA, Vietnam's national quality assurance agency, has called for, developed and coordinated projects in quality assurance. GDETA/VQA and two national universities (VNU-HN and VNU-HCM) also provide quality assurance training for institutions. Additionally, accreditor training courses run by accrediting agencies, including VNU-CEA, VNU-HCM CEA, and DNU-CEA, contribute to improving the quality assurance staff members' knowledge and skills. Particularly, the master's and doctoral programs in educational measurement and evaluation offered by VNU-HN have provided key quality assurance staff to educational offices, agencies, and institutions.

Lesson 4: International support is necessary for the development of human resources in Vietnam's higher education quality assurance
International partners not only initially supported human resources development in quality assurance but also provided support during the development of Vietnam's higher education quality assurance system. Many Vietnamese organizations and institutions also benefited as members of regional and international networks such as the International Network for Quality Assurance Agencies in Higher Education (INQAAHE), APQN, ASEAN Quality Assurance Network (AQAN), and AUN-QA. These networks have helped build the quality assurance capacity of hundreds of Vietnam's educational leaders, staff, and lecturers.

Lesson 5: Local quality assurance experts are core human resources in developing the capacity for quality assurance staff nationwide
The first cohort of Vietnamese quality assurance experts, most of whom have been awarded graduate degrees in related areas by overseas universities, were trained through international projects such as HEP1 or international networks such as APQN. This set of around twenty professionals is sourced from different agencies and institutions (MoET, VNU-HN, VNU-HCM, and several other key universities). They actively participated in programs organized by HEP2 and other projects and also serve as core trainers at many workshops or capacity building programs in quality assurance at both national and institutional level.

Recommendations and Conclusion

In its last ten years of development, Vietnam's higher education quality assurance and accreditation system has witnessed several achievements. The most successful accomplishment may be the establishment of a quality assurance mechanism consisting of three levels (macro, meso and micro), which has been finalized with the increasing number of staff working in each level. However, many challenges still remain, particularly the inadequate quantity and quality of quality assurance staff at all levels. To ensure the sustainable development of the system, actions in human resource development should be seriously undertaken by many actors, including the central government, provincial governments, line ministries, national quality assurance organization, accrediting agencies, and higher education institutions.

First, VQA and higher education institutions should employ more human resources in quality assurance. Obviously, this recommendation is much easier said than done. The staff quota of VQA depends on MoET, which must in turn follow the personnel regulations of the government. At the institutional level, the number of staff is decided by the authorized agency (line ministry or provincial government) and must adhere to many central standard rules and processes. To enact this recommendation, the central government, line ministries, and provincial governments must be informed that quality assurance is a new field requiring the allocation of new staff. In conjunction, quality assurance organizations and educational institutions could hire part-time staff or transfer staff from other units to work in quality assurance.

Second, MoET, VQA, and tertiary education institutions should lay out strategic long-term human resource development plans regarding quality assurance and accreditation. They should encourage staff and teachers to undertake postgraduate programs in assessment and evaluation (at home or overseas) with thesis topics focusing on quality assurance. They should also develop policies designed to attract professionals who hold graduate degrees in quality assurance-related areas to positions in quality assurance. Quality assurance staff and lecturers should also be encouraged to conduct research and publish papers in quality assurance and accreditation.

Third, additional training for quality assurance staff should be conducted at both the national and institutional levels. Quality assurance officials, accreditors, educational managers, and lecturers at universities and colleges require periodic training and retraining. The content for these training courses could dedicate additional focus to higher education administration, leadership and management, global trends in quality assurance, and best practices in implementing quality assurance across the region and around the world. Ideally, some training would be conducted overseas or include international experts invited to Vietnam as trainers.

Fourth, VQA and universities should continue hosting international workshops and conferences in quality assurance, as they are among the most effective methods for staff development; moreover, workshops and conferences also benefit staff and lecturers within the higher education system. Notably, GDETA hosted the 2009 APQN Conference and Annual General Meeting and the 2013 AQAN Seminar and Roundtable Meeting, and the Foreign Trade University hosted the 2014 APQN Conference and Annual General Meeting.

Finally, quality assurance agencies and educational institutions should pay more attention to the professional development and capacity building of their quality assurance staff. Specifically, professional development policies should be developed and documented, and the resulting programs and processes should be carefully designed, thoroughly prepared and effectively implemented. When professional development and capacity building become an organizational/institutional policy commitment, it clearly signals that the organization/institution is willing to provide ongoing growth opportunities for staff.

References

Center for Educational Testing and Quality Assessment (CETQA). (2013). Internal quality assurance at Vietnam National University—Ho Chi Minh City (VNU-HCM). *Proceedings of the 2013 ASEAN Quality Assurance Network Seminar and Roundtable Meeting Building Quality Culture and National Qualifications Framework* (pp. 86–90). Ho Chi Minh City: Ton Duc Thang University.

Cribb, G. (2006). Human resource development: A strategic approach. *Access, 20*(3), 13–16, 20.

Dao, K. V. (2015). Key challenges in the reform of governance, quality assurance, and finance in Vietnamese higher education—A case study. *Studies in Higher Education, 40*(5), 745–760.

Department of Foreign Affairs and Trade, Australian Government (DFAT). (2015). *Australia-Vietnam human resource development strategy*. Retrieved from http://dfat.gov.au/about-us/publications/Pages/australia-vietnam-human-resource-development-strategy-2014-2020.aspx.

Do, H. M., & Do, Q. T. N. (2014). Higher and tertiary education in Vietnam. In L. Tran, S. Marginson, & H. Do (Eds.), *Higher education in Vietnam: Flexibility, mobility and practicality in the global knowledge economy* (pp. 29–53). New York: Palgrave Macmillan.

Do, Q. T. N., Pham, H. T., & Nguyen, K. D. (2017). Quality assurance in Vietnamese higher education: A top-down approach and compliance-driven QA. In M. Shah & Q. T. N. Do (Eds.), *The rise of quality assurance in Asian higher education* (pp. 51–66). Cambridge: Chandos Publishing.

Drucker, P. (1999). Knowledge-worker productivity: The biggest challenge. *California Management Review, 41*(2), 79–94.

Garavan, T., & Akdere, M. (2016). Human resource development in CIVETS. In T. Garavan, et al. (Eds.), *Global human resource development: Regional and country perspectives* (pp. 303–319). London: Routledge.

General Department of Education Testing and Accreditation (GDETA). (2012). *Report on the quality assurance and accreditation activities in the academic year 2011–2012*. Hanoi: GDETA.

Hayden, M., & Lam, Q. T. (2007). Institutional autonomy for higher education in Vietnam. *Higher Education Research & Development, 26*(1), 73–85.

Hoang, X. H. & Ta, T. T. H. (2013). Developing quality assurance system: Experience of Vietnam National University Hanoi. *Proceedings of the 2013 ASEAN Quality Assurance Network Seminar and Roundtable Meeting Building Quality Culture and National Qualifications Framework* (pp. 97–105). Ho Chi Minh City: Ton Duc Thang University.

Huffman, D., Thomas, K., & Lawrenz, F. (2008). A collaborative immersion approach to evaluation capacity building. *American Journal of Evaluation, 29*(3), 358–368.

Institute for Education Quality Assurance—Vietnam National University (INFEQA). (2013). *Report in competency and experiences of organising workshops and conferences*. Hanoi: INFEQA.

Khasawneh, S. (2011). Human capital planning in higher education institutions. *International Journal of Educational Management, 25*(6), 534–544.

Madden, M. (2014). Walking the line: Quality assurance policy development and implementation in Viet Nam. *Higher Education, 67*(1), 91–104.

Ministry of Education and Training (MoET). (2008). *Directive No. 46/2008/CT-BGDDT on strengthening educational assessment and accreditation exercises*. Hanoi: MoET.

Ministry of Education and Training (MoET). (2010). *Project on establishment and development of Vietnam's higher education and professional secondary education accreditation in the period 2010–2010*. Hanoi: MoET.

Ministry of Education and Training (MoET). (2012). *Circular No. 62/2012/TT-BGDDT promulgating regulations on procedures and cycles of university, college and professional secondary school accreditation*. Hanoi: MoET.

Ministry of Education and Training (MoET). (2013a). *Circular No. 18/2013/TT-BGDDT promulgating accreditor training programme for higher education and professional secondary education*. Hanoi: MoET.

Ministry of Education and Training (MoET). (2013b). *Circular No. 38/2013/TT-BGDDT promulgating regulations of procedures and cycles of programme accreditation for universities, colleges and professional secondary schools*. Hanoi: MoET.

Ministry of Education and Training (MoET). (2015). *Viet Nam education and training 2015*. Hanoi: MoET.

Ministry of Education and Training (MoET). (2016). *Announcement of the conclusion of MoET Minister Phung Xuan Nha at the meeting on the implementation of higher education accreditation*. Hanoi: MoET.

Ministry of Education and Training (MoET). (2017a). *Plan No. 118/KH-BGDDT on accreditation implementation for higher education institutions in the period from 2017 to 2020*. Hanoi: MoET.

Ministry of Education and Training (MoET). (2017b). *Decision No. 2077/QD-BGDDT promulgating regulations on functions, tasks, responsibilities and organisational structures of MoET units*. Hanoi: MoET.

Ministry of Education and Training (MoET). (2018). *Viet Nam education and training*. Hanoi: MoET.

National Assembly. (2005). *Education law*. Hanoi: National Assembly.

National Assembly. (2006). *The socio-economic development plan 5 years 2006–2010*. Hanoi: National Assembly.

National Assembly. (2011). *The socio-economic development plan 5 years 2011–2015*. Hanoi: National Assembly.

National Assembly. (2012). *Higher education law*. Hanoi: National Assembly.

National Assembly. (2018). Law amending and supplementing a number of the higher education law. Hanoi: National Assembly.

Nguyen, H. C. (2016, May). *Professional development for external quality assurance officials: An essential factor for the sustainable development of Vietnam's higher education accreditation system*. Paper presented at the 2016 Asia-Pacific Quality Network (APQN) Conference and Annual General Meeting, Natadola, Fiji.

Nguyen, H. C. (2017). Policy and practice of undertaking accreditation for higher education programmes in Viet Nam. *Journal of Education, 1–3*(401), 11–15, 32.

Nguyen, H. C. (2018). Advantages and disadvantages when implementing the higher education accreditation plan in the period of 2017–2020. *HNUE Journal of Science: Educational Sciences, 63*(2), 17–26.

Nguyen, H. C., Evers, C., & Marshall, S. (2017). Accreditation of Viet Nam's higher education: Achievements and challenges after a dozen years of development. *Quality Assurance in Education, 25*(4), 475–488.

Nguyen, K. D., Oliver, D. E., & Priddy, L. E. (2009). Criteria for accreditation in Vietnam's higher education: Focus on input or outcomes. *Quality in Higher Education, 15*(2), 123–134.

Nguyen, T. (2012). *Internal quality assurance in Vietnam's higher education: The influence by international projects* (Unpublished master thesis). University of Twente, Enschede, The Netherlands.

Nguyen, T. P. L. (2015). *Quality assurance and accreditation in upper secondary schools in Hatinh province in Vietnam* (Unpublished doctoral dissertation). The University of Newcastle, Newcastle, Australia.

Niedermeier, F. & Pohlenz, P. (2016). *State of play and development needs: Higher education quality assurance in the ASEAN region*. Jakarta, Indonesia: German Academic Exchange Service (DAAD).

Oh, H., Ryu, H., & Choi, M. (2013). How can we assess and evaluate the competitive advantage of a country's human resource development system? *Asia Pacific Education Review, 14*(2), 151–169.

Pham, V. H. & Nguyen, T. T. H. (2013). Development of the internal quality assurance system in Thai Nguyen University. *Proceedings of the 2013 ASEAN Quality Assurance Network Seminar and Roundtable Meeting Building Quality Culture and National Qualifications Framework* (pp. 116–121). Ho Chi Minh City: Ton Duc Thang University.

Pham, X. T. (2013). *Higher education quality assurance in Vietnam and improvement for better collaboration*. Retrieved from https://www.britishcouncil.vn/sites/default/files/ged_2013_day_1_group_2_dr_pham_xuan_thanh.pdf.

Phan, H. H., Dao, L. P., & Chau, T. T. (2013). Building an internal quality assurance system and shaping quality culture in higher education institutions: From the reality of Can Tho University. *Proceedings of the 2013 ASEAN Quality Assurance Network seminar and roundtable meeting building quality culture and national qualifications framework* (pp. 106–110). Ho Chi Minh City: Ton Duc Thang University.

The Prime Minister. (2019). *Decision No. 69/2019/QD-TTg on approval of the project on higher education enhancement in the 2019–2025 period.* Hanoi: The Prime Minister.

Ta, T. T. H. (2012). *Report from the survey of Vietnam's higher education quality assurance.* Hanoi: The Second Higher Education Project (HEP2).

Ta, T. T. H. (2016). *Impacts of accreditation policy on training management of two national universities* (Unpublished doctoral dissertation). Vietnam National University, Hanoi, Vietnam.

Tran, T. T. (2014). Governance in higher education in Vietnam—A move towards decentralization and its practical problems. *Journal of Asian Public Policy, 7*(1), 71–82.

Vietnam Education Quality Management Agency. (2019a). *List of higher education institutions, teacher training colleges and teacher training schools completing self-evaluation reports, being accredited (until 30 April 2019).* Hanoi: VQA.

Vietnam Education Quality Management Agency. (2019b). *List of programmes that were evaluated/recognized (until 30 April 2019).* Hanoi: VQA.

Vo, S. M. (2013). A setting up an internal quality assurance system in the institution of higher education: Some recommendations. *Proceedings of the 2013 ASEAN Quality Assurance Network Seminar and Roundtable Meeting Building Quality Culture and National Qualifications Framework* (pp. 122–129). Ho Chi Minh City: Ton Duc Thang University.

Westerheijden, D. F., Cremonini, L., & Empel, R. V. (2010). Accreditation in Vietnam's higher education system. In G. Harman, M. Hayden, & P. T. Nghi (Eds.), *Reforming higher education in Vietnam* (pp. 183–194). London: Springer.

World Bank. (2008). *Vietnam: Higher education and skills for growth.* Retrieved from http://siteresources.worldbank.org/INTEASTASIAPACIFIC/Resources/Vietnam-HEandSkillsforGrowth.pdf.

World Bank. (2012). *Vietnam—Second higher education project.* Retrieved from http://documents.worldbank.org/curated/en/548761468315847205/Vietnam-Second-Higher-Education-Project.

12

The Future of Quality Assurance in Vietnamese Higher Education

Cuong Huu Nguyen and Kim Dzung Nguyen

Introduction

The previous eleven chapters provide an overall picture of quality assurance and accreditation in Vietnamese higher education during the last two decades. Details on the development of Vietnam's higher education quality assurance system were discussed. In addition, the system's achievements and challenges were described and analysed. As the legal framework for quality assurance has been developed and implemented, major achievements have been observed. Five domestic accreditation agencies have been established, quality assurance units have been set up in most

---

C. H. Nguyen (✉)
University of Education, Vietnam National University, Hanoi, Vietnam
e-mail: nhcuong@moet.edu.vn

K. D. Nguyen
Ho Chi Minh City University of Education, Ho Chi Minh City, Vietnam

© The Author(s) 2019
C. H. Nguyen and M. Shah (eds.), *Quality Assurance in Vietnamese Higher Education*, https://doi.org/10.1007/978-3-030-26859-6_12

higher education institutions as focal points for their internal quality assurance activities, almost every university has completed self-assessment evaluation reports, and dozens of institutions and programmes have undertaken an external evaluation exercise and been awarded accreditation certificates (Nguyen, 2018; Nguyen, Evers, & Marshall, 2017). However, the Vietnamese higher education quality assurance system is facing many challenges. These include lack of necessary legal documents regulating quality assurance activities, limited human and material resources for quality assurance, problems with accreditation standards and criteria, inadequate awareness of quality assurance and accreditation among higher education institutions, and unclear independence of the quality assurance system (Nguyen, 2018; Nguyen et al., 2017).

To solve current challenges with Vietnamese higher education quality assurance, time is needed as well as further efforts from the government, accrediting agencies and universities. However, it is important to foresee the development of this system in future. Researchers argue that the quality assurance programmes of Vietnam's higher education should follow both regional and international trends. Specifically, together with institutional accreditation, Vietnam must promote programme accreditation. Next, quality assurance and accreditation of distance or online education should be considered. In addition to accreditation, Vietnam should also implement other quality assurance approaches including auditing, benchmarking and ranking. Furthermore, those working in quality assurance should regularly update their knowledge and skills through professional development or capacity building programmes. For higher education institutions, building and developing a quality culture is crucial tasks for enhancing the quality of teaching, learning and research. Additionally, in the era of globalisation, Vietnamese higher education should consider quality assurance of internationalisation and the internationalisation of quality assurance. Finally, securing the independence of quality assurance systems and the autonomy of accreditation agencies is vital for the sustainable development of Vietnamese higher education quality assurance and accreditation.

Regional and Global Trends in Higher Education Quality Assurance

Quality assurance is now commonly used in higher education across the world with a focus on the need to maintain and enhance quality. The quality assurance movement in the field of higher education has been developed through three primary phases (Woodhouse, 2012). The first occurred over one hundred years ago in the USA, where quality assurance was approached through accreditation. The first external quality assurance agencies, called accreditors, were founded in the USA at the behest of institutions and professional associations, and they were independent of the government. The second phase occurred in the 1960s, when external quality assurance agencies were created by governments, such as those in the UK and Ireland. These agencies were established not to address perceived problems but to actively guide and direct growing and diverse higher education sectors. The third phase then started in the 1990s and witnessed an explosion of external quality assurance agencies worldwide. The International Network for Quality Assurance Agencies in Higher Education (INQAAHE) was formed in 1991 with 8 members—quality assurance agencies and institutions implementing quality assurance. Then, 25 years later, there are over 200 members in most countries and territories across the world.

Quality assurance mechanisms in higher education across the world are diverse. There are three main approaches to quality assurance: accreditation, assessment and audit. Each quality assurance system adopts one or more of these approaches according to their higher education systems and traditions (Woodhouse, 1999). In practice, many higher education systems follow a combination of these models (SEAMEO RIHED, 2012). Accreditation is the most common method of external quality assurance, with accreditation of both institutions and programmes being the primary quality assurance method used in the USA (Eaton, 2015). In Europe, the most common quality assurance approaches are accreditation and assessment, followed by audit; others such as benchmarking and ranking are also in use. Approximately two-thirds of external quality assurance agencies use programme-level procedures (accreditation or assessment of programmes), whereas institutional-level procedures (accreditation, assessment or audit of institutions) are only implemented by only about 40% of agencies. The use of programme audits is not common in European quality assurance (ENQA, 2008). Interestingly, most European countries apply more than one approach in quality assurance. For example, the Netherlands uses programme accreditation and institutional audits, Norway uses accreditation for both institutions and programmes and audits for institutions, and Slovenia uses programme accreditation and institutional evaluation. Only a few countries use one type of quality assurance procedures; for example, Finland uses institutional audits, and the UK uses institutional reviews (EQAR, 2018). Of the 11 countries in Southeast Asia, every country, except Myanmar and Timor-Leste, has developed quality assurance systems. Most of these countries have implemented accreditation of both institutions and programmes, while only two countries (Singapore and Thailand) use the assessment model. The audit approach has been implemented in three countries (the Philippines, Singapore and Thailand) in combination with accreditation or assessment (SEMEO RIHED, 2012). In 2000, the ASEAN University Network-Quality Assurance (AUN-QA) established both institutional and programme assessments for its university members in the ASEAN region (AUN-QA, 2018).

Application of quality assurance procedures to open and distance learning (including online learning) has received attention from many countries across the world in recent years. This phenomenon has been driven by the growing demand for accountability and cost-effectiveness in open and distance education types, particularly due to the need to show that the quality and learning outcomes of open and distance institutions and programme is comparable to more traditional systems (Latchem & Jung, 2011). Quality assurance practices for distance institutions and programmes also vary. Many countries use the same procedures and criteria for distance learning and conventional institutions and programmes. This approach has been implemented in 72.2% of quality assurance agencies in Europe (EADTU, 2017) and many countries in Asia, such as China, Japan and Singapore. Several agencies have also added a couple of criteria to the conventional evaluation standard sets to assess online and distance institutions and programmes. This method of quality assurance is used by many professional accreditors in the USA, such as the Association to Advance Collegiate

Schools of Business (AACSB), the Accrediting Bureau of Health Education Schools (ABHES) and the Montessori Council for Teacher Education (MACTE). Other countries and agencies have developed specific standards and procedures to assess the quality of distance learning institutions and programmes. Founded in 1926 in the USA, the Distance Education Accrediting Commission (DEAC) is the oldest external quality assurance agency that specialises in accrediting postsecondary distance education institutions both in the USA and all over the world. Several countries in Asia and Europe have applied specific guidelines for evaluating distance education quality, including India, Malaysia, Sri Lanka and the UK.

Recently, attention has been given towards improving the competencies of the personnel involved in quality assurance processes. At the global level, INQAAHE, with a grant from the World Bank and support from UNESCO, developed materials for a comprehensive programme for the training and professional development of quality assurance professionals. This programme consists of four different modules: (i) higher education in a global world: the context of quality assurance; (ii) external quality assurance: What is quality and how it has been implemented in different countries; (iii) operating an external quality agency: practical training in the structure and management of quality assurance agencies around the world; and (iv) maintaining quality within the institution: assessing learning, conducting self-study and using data (INQAAHE, 2017). In an attempt to standardise and support external quality assurance practitioners, regional quality assurance networks have developed quality assurance professional competency frameworks. In the European setting, European Association for Quality Assurance in Higher Education (ENQA) has introduced the ENQA quality assurance professional competencies framework, identifying common core competencies of quality assurance and quality enhancement professionals in ENQA member agencies. ENQA's external quality assurance agencies are expected to use this competency framework in job design, recruitment and staff development activities. The core competencies of this framework are categorised into three groups: knowledge, systematic/technical and interpersonal competencies (ENQA, 2016). In the Asian context, AUN-QA has developed the AUN-QA professional development competency model, considering elements such as outcome, skills, knowledge and attitude at four levels: practitioner, assessor, lead assessor and expert (AUN-QA, 2013).

Along with the mushrooming of external quality assurance agencies, a variety of internal quality assurance mechanisms have been introduced to higher education providers. One of the most widely implemented approaches involves building cultures of quality within campuses. This is a new trend in higher education because a quality culture helps establish an on-going process of improvement, in which it holds all of the organisational community accountable for sustaining a favourable work environment, leading to organisational excellence (Trewin, 2003, cited in Ali & Musah, 2012). The Quality Culture Project conducted by the European Universities Association (EUA) between 2002 and 2006 found that quality culture has a significant influence on the institutional settings where it is being implemented (EUA, 2006). A later project "Examining Quality Culture in European Higher Education Institutions" launched from October 2009 to Fall 2011 concluded that quality culture is important in higher education because "it is the most effective and meaningful way that quality assurance mechanisms can ensure and improve quality levels and support a dynamic of change in universities" (Sursock, 2011, p. 6). In an Asian context, Ali and Musah (2012) examined the relationship between quality culture and workforce performance in the Malaysian higher education sector, arguing that a quality culture results in higher job satisfaction and work performance among the academic staff, and also enriches instructional effectiveness.

Globalisation and internationalisation have resulted in the appearance of two new concepts in the area of higher education quality assurance: the internationalisation of quality assurance and quality assurance of internationalisation. The internationalisation of quality assurance integrates quality assurance procedures into the broader context of international activities in the field of quality assurance. In contrast, quality assurance of internationalisation relates to quality assurance as a method for improving internationalisation activities, strategies or policies (Komotar, 2018). The internationalisation of quality assurance in higher education has been developed and strengthened in many countries worldwide in recent decades. The most easily-recognised trend is the establishment of international and regional quality assurance networks such as INQAAHE (1991), ENQA (2000), the Asia-Pacific Quality Network (APQN) (2003), the Caribbean Area Network for Quality Assurance in Tertiary Education (CANQATE) (2004), the ASEAN Quality Assurance Network (AQAN) (2008) and AUN-QA (2000). Members of these networks have also increased rapidly. For example, APQN, from 2003 to 2018, grew from 52 to 194 members, and AUN-QA, from 2012 to 2018, grew from 2 to 57 members. Additionally, international accreditation and evaluation have become increasingly popular. Higher education institutions can register for and apply for accreditation from overseas agencies, while accreditation agencies can apply for review and recognition by quality assurance networks. Another new trend in quality assurance is that two or more external quality assurance agencies can cooperate to jointly assess and accredit institutions or programmes. Along with the internationalisation of quality assurance, quality assurance of internationalisation has also considered. In the 1990s, several Western European countries (e.g. Germany, the Netherlands) began developing and implementing tools for assuring and measuring the quality of internationalisation in higher education. These tools normally focus on institutional level and quantitative input and output indicators (e.g. the number of international students, staff or joint programmes; financial resources; and adequate facilities) (Komotar, 2018).

A Proposal for Vietnamese Future Higher Education Quality Assurance

Quality assurance has attracted the attention of Vietnamese academics and authorities since 2000. Conferences and workshops have since been held to introduce concepts and models. In 2003, quality assurance in Vietnamese higher education was formally established and has since achieved good results (see Chapters 5 and 9). Nevertheless, this system is facing a number of challenges. To better address, these current challenges, upcoming higher education quality assurance in Vietnam should follow international and regional trends.

Focusing More on Programme Accreditation

By law, all universities in Vietnam are required to implement institutional accreditation and programme accreditation. However, the achievements of institutional accreditation far outnumber those of programme accreditation. While most universities have completed their institutional self-evaluation reports and more than 50% of higher education institutions have been accredited, only about 0.2% of higher education programmes (10 out of 5000) have undergone an external evaluation and been awarded accreditation certificates by Vietnamese accreditation agencies. Moreover, only 106 programmes were evaluated or accredited by overseas agencies (VQA, 2018a, 2018b). Thus, the implementation of programme accreditation among Vietnamese higher education institutions should be encouraged in future.

At present, MoET has only promulgated 5 sets of standards for programme accreditation. Specifically, 1 set of standards has been implemented for all higher education programmes (adapted from AUN-QA) and the other 4 sets are for specific programmes, including: primary school teacher training, high school teacher training, vocational teacher training and nursing programmes. It is important to note that only a standard set for all programmes has been selected by universities to conduct self-evaluation and apply for accreditation, while the 4 standard sets for specific programmes have only been piloted by MoET. Programme accreditation is undertaken by five MoET-established accrediting agencies that also carry out institutional accreditation.

To promote programme accreditation, Vietnam should follow the US accreditation model. Specifically, programmatic or specialised accrediting agencies need to be founded. The first agencies should specialise in engineering, business, finance, nursing or teacher training. In addition, accreditation standard sets for these programmes should be developed by specialised accrediting agencies. These specialised or programmatic accreditation agencies, once established, will enhance the quality of higher education programmes and contribute to fulfilling the objective of accrediting approximate 10% of programmes by 2020, which is one requirement of the Higher Education Accreditation Strategic Plan 2017–2020 (MoET, 2017a).

Implementing Quality Assurance of Distance Education

Open and distance learning started in Vietnam in the early 1990s when the first distance bachelor programmes were offered at the Hanoi Open University and Ho Chi Minh City Open University. In 2017, there were 97 distance education programmes run by 17 Vietnamese universities. However, none of these programmes have undergone an external evaluation or been accredited. The Vietnamese government has issued several distance education regulations since 2003. Most recently, MoET promulgated a legal document regarding regulation of distance education programmes at a higher education level (Circular No. 10/2017/TT-BGDDT dated on 28 April 2017). This document sets minimum requirements for distance education programmes, requiring them to follow quality assurance processes in which institutions have to carry out self-evaluation for distance education programmes and register these programmes for accreditation with accrediting agencies (MoET, 2017b). The Vietnamese government has also paid special attention to the quality of distance education programmes and requires all of them to be accredited. MoET was assigned responsibility for developing an accreditation standard set for distance education programmes (The Prime Minister, 2015).

To accredit all distance education programmes, actions should be taken consistently at all levels of Vietnam's quality assurance system. First, MoET (at the macro-level) must develop accreditation standards and guidelines for distance education programmes. These standards should focus on specific requirements for distance education, including: IT facilities, learning resources for distance learning, competencies of lecturers and student support staff, interaction between distance student, lecturers and student support staff, and assessment methods appropriate for distance education. Assessment standards for distance education published by US accrediting agencies, the UK Quality Assurance Agency for Higher Education (QAA), Malaysian Qualifications Agency (MQA) and the APEC Quality Assurance of Online Learning Toolkit (prepared by TEQSA) are good references for MoET to develop its own accreditation standards. Second, accrediting agencies (at the meso-level) must open specific training workshops for accreditors that will assess distance learning programmes. These accreditors should be experienced in distance education and must understand specific techniques and methods in order to evaluate distance learning programmes. Third, higher education institutions (at the micro-level) need to conduct self-evaluation of any distance education programmes that they offer. Educational managers/administrators, lecturers, student support staff and even students involved in distance education need to be aware of the importance of quality assurance. Self-evaluation reports need to be well-prepared and ready for external evaluation (Nguyen & Le, 2019).

In addition, it is advisable that a new accreditation agency for distance education be established. This agency will specialise in accrediting distance education programmes, which will include training accreditors, conducting external evaluations and awarding accreditation certificates to programmes that satisfy quality standards.

Diversifying Higher Education Quality Assurance Arrangements

The associated literature indicates that many approaches for quality assurance and quality enhancement have been developed and implemented in higher education systems across the world. Major models include accreditation, assessment, auditing, benchmarking, ranking and reviewing, along with other methods such as certification, licensing, student surveys and public provision of verified data. However, in the Vietnamese higher education system, accreditation is the key quality assurance instrument. Other methods, including licensing, student surveys and public provision of verified data, are also available but they have been marginally employed as the effectiveness of these instruments is still questioned (Do, Pham, & Nguyen, 2017). The authors of this study argue that, besides accreditation, other quality assurance approaches, including audit, benchmarking and ranking, should be implemented in Vietnamese higher education.

Auditing in higher education is "the process of reviewing an institution or a programme that is primarily focused on its accountability, and determining if the stated aims and objectives (in terms of curriculum, staff, infrastructure, etc.) are met" (Vlăsceanu, Grünberg, & Pârlea, 2007, p. 31). An audit reviews the processes used by a higher education institution to monitor its academic standards and provides quality education within departments (SEMEO RIHED, 2012). Vietnamese higher education institutions can use audits (internal or management audits) to assess whether their internal quality assurance processes are appropriate and whether they are actually being implemented. Audits can also be implemented to strengthen the processes and techniques universities have in place to enhance the quality of their work.

Furthermore, benchmarking has been established as one of the most successful processes of assessment and improvement. Benchmarking can be defined as "the process of self-evaluation and self-improvement through the systematic and collaborative comparison of practice and performance with similar organisations in order to identify strengths and weaknesses, to learn to adapt and to set new targets to improve performance" (Burquel, 2012, p. 8). Using benchmarking as a tool of improvement, Vietnamese universities can compare themselves with other universities (particularly higher-ranking universities in the region and across the world) regarding aspects of performance and identify ways to improve their current performance. To do this, they can follow Achtemeier and Simpson's (2005) process of benchmarking, including identifying the problem area within one's own institution, identifying another institution with exemplary performance in the same area and sending a team of experts in the area to the exemplar institution in order to learn how it achieves its outstanding results. The team then adapts these best practices to improve the home institution.

University rankings are an established technique for displaying comparative positions of higher education institutions in terms of their performance. Rankings are quite popular and considered a useful instrument for public information. They also provide an additional incentive for quality improvement (Vlăsceanu et al., 2007). Around the world, academic rankings are published by the media and by a wide range of both public and private agencies and organisations. Among many higher education ranking systems in the world today, the most influential global rankings are the Academic Ranking of World Universities (ARWU), Times Higher Education (THE) World University Rankings and Quacquarelli Symonds

(QS) World University Rankings. Rankings are either regional (e.g. QS Asian University Rankings and QS Latin American University Rankings) or national. Vietnamese universities currently rank low globally. In 2017, only 5 universities were listed among the region's 400 leading higher education institutions in QS Asia University Rankings. The, in 2018, for the first time, two Vietnamese universities (Vietnam National University, Ho Chi Minh City and Vietnam National University, Hanoi) appeared in the top 1000 global universities in QS World University Rankings. Although the Vietnamese government issued a legal document regarding the stratification and ranking of Vietnamese universities in 2015 (Decree No. 73/2015/ND-CP) (see The Government, 2015), no higher education ranking system has been officially established. In September 2017, an independent panel of Vietnamese academics announced the country's first national ranking of 49 universities. This ranking was based on three criteria: scientific research (40% weighting), education and training (40% weighting) and institutional facilities (20% weighting). Most of the data used was collected from university websites. However, this ranking provoked considerable controversy as several universities received high scores for education quality despite having relatively low admission standards. On the other hand, some institutions had low ranking even though they had previously been recognised for their research reputation and advanced facilities. University ranking in Vietnam should be established by either public or private agencies; however, it should to follow The Berlin Principles on Ranking Higher Education Institutions (see: https://www.che.de/downloads/Berlin_Principles_IREG_534.pdf). Additionally, ranking has been linked to benchmarking and the acceptance of being compared to others in the sector. In this way, ranking contributes to the improvement of institutions and programmes because universities are able to improve through a process of assessment and evaluation to obtain higher positions in regional or global rankings (Tasopoulou & Tsiotras, 2017).

Strengthening Capacity Building for Quality Assurance Practitioners

An effective quality assurance system relies largely on the competent professional and technical staff members of the national quality assurance organisation, accreditation agencies and higher education institutions. The INQAAHE Guidelines of Good Practice suggests that an external quality assurance agency needs to have well-trained and qualified staff members in order to effectively and efficiently carry out external evaluation (INQAAHE, 2016). Similarly, ENQA states that quality assurance agencies should have adequate and appropriate human resources (ESG, 2015).

In the context of Vietnam, the higher education quality assurance and accreditation system seriously lack staff and experts at all levels. Furthermore, most of the current staff have not been trained professionally and academically in quality assurance. In order to perform their tasks effectively, these quality assurance staff need to be provided with updated professional knowledge and skills through professional development and capacity building programmes (Nguyen et al., 2017).

First, Vietnam must develop a competency framework for higher education quality assurance practitioners. This framework should highlight core competencies in knowledge, skills and attitude. Specifically, core knowledge skills should cover higher education administration and government, the national quality assurance system and regional and global trends in quality assurance. Core skill competencies should include organisational, planning, analytical, problem-solving, communication and interpersonal skills. Core attitude skills should be responsibility, honesty, transparency and commitment. The ENQA quality assurance professional competencies framework, the AUN-QA professional development competency model and the competency framework for external quality assurance practitioners in higher education (CFEQAP) proposed by Cheung (2015) are good reference sources for the development of a Vietnamese quality assurance competency framework. All organisations and institutions involved in higher education quality assurance in Vietnam should then use this competency framework to build the capacity of their staff members.

Second, the national quality assurance organisation, accrediting centres and higher education institutions should develop their professional development or capacity building policies for staff involved in quality assurance and accreditation. These policies should focus on (1) the importance of capacity building, (2) responsibilities of key stakeholders, (3) main methods for capacity building, (4) procedures for planning and undertaking capacity building programmes and (5) a budget for capacity building.

Third, capacity building methods for quality assurance staff should be diverse. Activities for capacity building can be formal and/or informal and can include short courses, workshops, conferences, coaching, staff exchange, study visits, internships, etc. It is important to note that all capacity building programmes must be consistently designed and implemented with the Vietnamese quality assurance competency framework.

Developing Quality Cultures Within Higher Education Institutions

As discussed previously, a quality culture has been introduced and promoted in a number of higher education institutions worldwide. Currently, the most cited definition of a quality culture is that proposed by EUA, which states:

> [Q]uality culture refers to an organisational culture that intends to enhance quality permanently and is characterised by two distinct elements: on the one hand, a cultural/psychological element of shared values, beliefs, expectations and commitment towards quality and, on the other hand, a structural/managerial element with defined processes that enhance quality and aim at coordinating individual efforts. (EUA, 2006, p. 10)

This definition states that the first elements of a quality culture are reflected through tools and processes to define, measure, evaluate and enhance quality. The second elements are reflected through personal commitment to strive for quality at the individual level, and individual attitudes and awareness then add up to a culture at the collective level. However, these two elements are not to be considered separately. Instead, they

Fig. 12.1 Elements of quality culture (*Source* Adapted from Loukkola & Zhang, 2010)

must be linked through good communication, discussion and participatory processes at the institutional level (EUA, 2006). Figure 12.1 highlights elements of quality culture.

Building a quality culture reflects a shift from control, accountability and regulation, to autonomy, credibility and educational enhancement based on an institution's experiences, expertise and values (Bendermacher, oude Egbrink, Wolfhagen, & Dolmans, 2017). The process of establishing a quality culture within a higher education institution contains three dimensions, including (1) strategy, policy and planning (to provide an internally coherent definition of quality and ensure its consistency with the institutional mission), (2) structures (such as establishing Quality Assurance Units or Centres of Teaching and Learning to facilitate and maintain quality commitment of its members) and (3) internal evaluations of programmes and activities (EUA, 2006). Additionally, several essential factors facilitate or impede the enhancement of quality cultures at the individual and institutional level. Important factors for establishing quality cultures at the individual level include (a) perceptions, values and beliefs, (b) motivations, (c) participation in professional development and (d) leadership. Important factors for establishing quality cultures at the institutional/organisational level are: support from institutional leadership, communication, data-driven reflection of enhancement activities, enhancement instrument designs, decision structures and provision of sufficient resources/staff development (Kottmann, Huisman, Brockerhoff, Cremonini, & Mampaey, 2016).

In Vietnamese higher education, the term "quality culture" has only been introduced in recent years through workshops and conferences organised by MoET and several universities. Vietnamese universities, therefore, need to build quality cultures on their campuses to improve the quality of teaching, learning and research. Institutions should consider the following: (1) the establishment of a quality culture requires both the top-down responsibility of management and a bottom-up involvement of academic and administrative staff and students (Kottmann et al., 2016); (2) continuous monitoring and evaluation of the process of developing a quality culture; and (3) continuous investment in financial and human resources (EUA, 2006). To make quality culture part of a school, Vietnamese higher education institutions need to make a stronger commitment to their internal quality assurance activities.

Strengthening Internationalisation of Quality Assurance and Quality Assurance of Internationalisation

Internationalisation of quality assurance has been observed in Vietnamese higher education. Vietnam received support from several international organisations (such as the World Bank and UNESCO) and foreign countries (such as Australia, Germany and the Netherlands) to develop a national quality assurance system. Moreover, many Vietnamese educational organisations and higher education institutions have participated in regional and international quality assurance networks. Specifically, five organisations are members (three full members and three associate members) of INQAAHE, six organisations/institutions are members (one full member, one intermediate member and four institutional members) of APQN, two organisations are members (one full member and one associate member) of AQAN, and 26 universities are members (three full members and 23 associate members) of AUN-QA. In addition, as of August 2018, six universities and 106 programmes were assessed or accredited

12 The Future of Quality Assurance in Vietnamese Higher Education

by overseas accreditation agencies, including the Accreditation Board for Engineering and Technology (ABET), the Accreditation Council for Business Schools and Programs (ACBSP), AUN-QA and the High Council for Evaluation of Research and Higher Education (HCERES). These above activities are only a small part of the big picture titled "internationalisation of quality assurance". Vietnamese higher education quality assurance and accreditation must more actively engage in global quality assurance movements, specifically:

1. The national quality assurance organisation along with accrediting agencies and universities should frequently host or organise international workshops or conferences on quality assurance.
2. More research on Vietnamese quality assurance should be undertaken by Vietnamese scholars and published in international peer-reviewed journals.
3. As members of regional and international quality assurance networks, Vietnamese agencies and institutions should have more papers presented at the workshops and conferences organised by these networks.
4. Capacity building programmes for quality assurance practitioners should be conducted in collaboration with overseas partners.
5. Universities should have more programmes accredited by USA and European accreditation agencies (as at present 77 out of 106 programmes have been assessed by AUN-QA).
6. Vietnamese accreditation agencies should invite international assessors to participate in site visit panels to carry out external evaluations of Vietnam's higher education institutions and programmes.
7. Vietnamese accreditation agencies should cooperate with overseas partners to jointly assess or accredit institutions and programmes in Vietnam and other countries.
8. Vietnam should more actively support the development of quality assurance systems in other countries in the region. (Vietnam already helped build capacity for the quality assurance officials of Laos PDR from 2015 to 2016.)

In addition to internationalisation of quality assurance, Vietnam has also developed instruments for the quality assurance of internationalisation. Specifically, a legal document regulating overseas collaboration and investment in the education sector (Decree No. 73/2012/ND-CP) requires that all foreign-funded education institutions and joint programmes between Vietnamese universities and overseas partners must be accredited by local or overseas accrediting agencies that are recognised by MoET (The Government, 2012). Most recently, Decree No. 46/2017/ND-CP dated 21 April 2017 on regulatory requirements for investment and operation in education requires all overseas accreditation agencies to register with MoET in order to legally provide services and for the accreditation outcomes to be recognised in Vietnam (The Government, 2017). However, this has had limited results. Only a few programmes among over 500 joint programmes were accredited and only four out of nine overseas accreditation agencies registered with MoET to provide their accreditation services in Vietnam. Clearly, Vietnam must take additional action to ensure the quality of internationalisation of higher education. Below are recommendations for a three-level Vietnamese higher education accreditation system:

At the macro-level (national level), MoET should set specific accreditation plans for foreign-funded universities and joint programmes. For example, they must be accredited by 31 December 2020; otherwise, they will not be allowed to recruit new enrolments.

At the meso-level, accrediting agencies should provide more training for their accreditors to be able to evaluate joint programmes. Accrediting agencies should also focus on assessing joint programmes.

At the micro-level (institutional), universities should carry out self-evaluations and apply for accreditation for all of their joint programmes. If they have plans to have their institution and/or programmes accredited by overseas agencies, they need to ask such agencies to register with MoET.

Securing the Independence of the Vietnamese Higher Education Quality Assurance System

Independence is a vital condition to secure the credibility and reliability of quality assurance agencies. One standard for quality assurance in the European Higher Education Area requires that quality assurance agencies "should be independent and act autonomously. They should have full responsibility for their operations and the outcomes of those operations without third party influence" (ESG, 2015, p. 22). Specifically, assurance agencies should have organisational independence (independence of the agency's work from third parties such as the government, higher education institutions and other organisations regulated by legal documentation), operational independence (agency operations, including the nomination and appointment of external experts, are carried out independently from third parties such as the government, higher education institutions and other stakeholders) and independence of formal outcomes (the final outcomes of the quality assurance processes remain the responsibility of the agency, though experts from other institutions may participate in quality assurance procedures). Across the world, while external quality assurance agencies (accreditors) in the USA are private, independent and non-profit, those in many other countries are public independent organisations. For example, the Tertiary Education Quality and Standards Agency (TEQSA) is Australia's independent national quality assurance agency, the HCERES is an independent administrative authority in France that evaluates higher education institutions and groupings, research bodies, scientific cooperation foundations, the French National Research Agency and research units, and the Office for National Education Standards and Quality Assessment (ONESQA) in Thailand is a government independent body responsible for developing the criteria and methods for external assessment and assessment of educational institutions at all levels of education.

In Vietnam, at the macro-level, the national quality assurance organisation is VQA, which is a department of MoET. Consequently, VQA depends on MoET for all of its human and financial resource allocation, including staff quota and recruitment, staff salaries, budget and appointment of the director general, deputy directors general, division heads and deputy division heads. In addition, all quality assurance policies and guidelines developed by VQA must be approved by the MoET Minister. At the meso-level, four out of the five accrediting centres were established by universities while their directors were appointed by the Minister of MoET. The staff members of these accrediting centres are recruited and paid for by their mother universities. Thus, the Vietnamese higher education quality assurance system does not act based on an independence mechanism. In fact, recommendations for the system's independence have been proposed by several scholars (e.g. Dao, 2015; Nguyen et al., 2017; Nguyen, Oliver, & Priddy, 2009; Nhan & Nguyen, 2018). Most of these have suggested that the national quality assurance agency should be beyond the control of MoET in order to ensure accreditation objectivity. We support this view and propose a future model of Vietnamese higher education quality assurance as outlined below:

The national quality assurance agency (the name VQA can still be used) will be directly under the umbrella of the government, and the leaders of this organisation (director general and deputy directors general) will be appointed by the government. The VQA will work independently and autonomously. It will not be subject to direction from anyone or any stakeholder in relation to the performance of its functions or the exercise of its powers. This new quality assurance agency will have the power to accredit all higher education institutions and programmes in Vietnam. It will be allocated a budget directly from the government for its operations and accreditation performance. In relation to MoET, the VQA will advise and make recommendations to the MoET Minister on matters relating to the quality of institutions and programmes. For the organisational structure, three regional accrediting agencies will be established in the north, middle and south to accredit institutions, while programmatic accrediting agencies will be established (with their head offices located in major cities) to accredit programmes. These regional and programmatic accrediting agencies will be under the umbrella of the VQA and be accredited/recognised by the VQA. Figure 12.2 presents this new model of Vietnamese higher education quality assurance.

Many things will need to be prepared and planned for the operation of this new Vietnamese quality assurance model. Below are some suggestions:

12 The Future of Quality Assurance in Vietnamese Higher Education

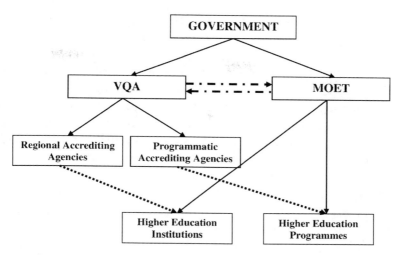

Fig. 12.2 A proposed new model for Vietnam's higher education quality assurance

- A proposal should be written to restructure the VQA Vietnamese system, focusing on the independence of the national quality assurance agency and getting the government's approval.
- Organisation leaders should be appointed by the government.
- Staff must be employed and recruited for all necessary positions of the organisation.
- A law on higher education quality assurance should be developed and approved by the National Assembly.
- Accreditation standards and guidelines for institutions and programmes should be developed and promulgated.
- Regional and programmatic accrediting agencies should be established.
- Training of accreditors/assessors should continue.
- All higher education institutions and programmes should be accredited.

Conclusion

After developing among Vietnamese higher education for more than 15 years, quality assurance and accreditation have gained certain attention and awareness from the government, MoET, universities and other stakeholder organisations. However, the development of this quality assurance system has not been consistent with regional and global trends. We argue that, for the sustainable development of Vietnamese higher education quality assurance in future, the independence mechanism of the national quality assurance organisation and accrediting agencies needs to be established. In the context of Vietnam, this means that the national agency in charge of quality assurance should belong directly to the government and be fully independent of MoET. All accrediting centres should also be independent from higher education institutions and be accredited by and directly under the umbrella of this national agency. By restructuring the quality assurance system in this way, evaluation and accreditation can be objective, trustworthy and reliable.

In addition, a variety of actions should be considered, including: further developing programme accreditation, undertaking quality assurance for distance education, diversifying quality assurance strategies at both the national and the institutional levels, focusing on professional development and capacity building for quality assurance officials, introducing and establishing a quality culture on university campuses, and promoting the relationship between internationalisation and quality assurance.

References

Achtemeier, S. D., & Simpson, R. D. (2005). Practical considerations when using benchmarking for accountability in higher education. *Innovative Higher Education, 30*(2), 117–128.

Ali, H. M., & Musah, M. B. (2012). Investigation of Malaysian higher education quality culture and workforce performance. *Quality Assurance in Education, 20*(3), 289–309.

ASEAN University Network Quality Assurance (AUN-QA). (2013, December 12–14). *AUN-QA assessors training workshop materials at VNU Hanoi.* Bangkok: AUN-QA.

ASEAN University Network Quality Assurance (AUN-QA). (2018). *AUN-QA Factbook 2018.* Retrieved from http://www.aun-qa.org/publication/AUN-QAFactbook2018.pdf.

Bendermacher, G. W. G., oude Egbrink, M. G. A., Wolfhagen, I. H. A. P., & Dolmans, D. H. J. M. (2017). Unravelling quality culture in higher education: A realist review. *Higher Education, 73*(1), 39–60.

Burquel, N. (2012). Benchmarking in European higher education. In D. Blackstock, N. Burquel, N. Comet, M. Kajaste, S. M. dos Santos, S. Marcos, & L. C. V. Sixto (Eds.), *Internal quality assurance benchmarking, Workshop Report No. 20* (pp. 6–12). Brussels: European Association for Quality Assurance in Higher Education (ENQA).

Cheung, J. C. M. (2015). Professionalism, profession and quality assurance practitioners in external quality assurance agencies in higher education. *Quality in Higher Education, 21*(2), 151–170.

Dao, K. V. (2015). Key challenges in the reform of governance, quality assurance, and finance in Vietnamese higher education—A case study. *Studies in Higher Education, 40*(5), 745–760.

Do, Q. T. N., Pham, H. T., & Nguyen, K. D. (2017). Quality assurance in Vietnamese higher education: A top-down approach and compliance-driven QA. In M. Shah & Q. T. N. Do (Eds.), *The rise of quality assurance in Asian higher education* (pp. 51–66). Cambridge: Chandos Publishing.

EADTU. (2017). *Quality assurance and accreditation of online and distance higher education*. Retrieved from https://www.slideshare.net/EADTU/quality-assurance-and-accreditation-of-online-and-distance-higher-education-eadtueu-summit-2017-75427865.

Eaton, J. (2015). *An overview of U.S. accreditation*. Washington, DC: Council for Higher Education Accreditation (CHEA).

ESG. (2015). *Standards and guidelines for quality assurance in the European higher education area*. Brussels: Belgium.

European Association for Quality Assurance in Higher Education (ENQA). (2008). *Quality procedures in the European Higher Education Area and beyond* (Second ENQA Survey Occasions Paper 14). Retrieved from https://enqa.eu/indirme/papers-and-reports/occasional-papers/ENQA%20Occasional%20papers%2014.pdf.

European Association of Quality Assurance Agencies (ENQA). (2016). *ENQA quality assurance professional competencies framework*. Retrieved from http://www.enqa.eu/indirme/papers-and-reports/occasional-papers/ENQA%20Competencies%20Framework.pdf.

European Quality Assurance Register for Higher Education (EQAR). (2018). *Country information*. Retrieved from https://www.eqar.eu/kb/country-information/.

European University Association (EUA). (2006). *Quality culture in European universities: A bottom-up approach* (Report on the Three Rounds of the Quality Culture Project 2002–2006). Brussels: EUA. Retrieved from http://www.eua.be/publications.

The Government. (2012). *Decree No. 73/2012/ND-CP on the foreign cooperation and investment in education*. Hanoi: The Government.

The Government. (2015). *Decree No. 73/2015/ND-CP on standards for stratification, framework and standards for ranking higher education institutions*. Hanoi: The Government.

The Government. (2017). *Decree No. 46/2017/ND-CP prescribing regulatory requirements for educational investment and operation*. Hanoi: The Government.

International Network for Quality Assurance Agencies in Higher Education (INQAAHE). (2016). *INQAAHE guidelines of good practice*. Retrieved from http://www.inqaahe.org/sites/default/files/INQAAHE_GGP2016.pdf.

International Network for Quality Assurance Agencies in Higher Education (INQAAHE). (2017). *QA graduate program*. Retrieved from http://www.inqaahe.org/qa-graduate-program.

Komotar, M. H. (2018). Quality assurance of internationalisation and internationalisation of quality assurance in Slovenian and Dutch higher education. *European Journal of Higher Education, 8*(4), 415–434.

Kottmann, A., Huisman, J., Brockerhoff, L., Cremonini, L., & Mampaey, J. (2016). *How can one create a culture of quality enhancement?* Center for Higher Education Policy Studies (CHEPS), University of Twente, The Netherlands.

Latchem, C., & Jung, I. (2011). Quality assurance and accreditation in open and distance learning. In I. Jung & C. Latchem (Eds.), *Quality assurance and accreditation in distance education and e-learning: Models, policies and research* (pp. 13–22). London: Routledge.

Loukkola, T., & Zhang, T. (2010). *Examining quality culture: Part 1—Quality assurance processes in higher education institutions*. Brussels: EUA.

Ministry of Education and Training (MoET). (2017a). *Plan No. 118/KH-BGDDT on accreditation implementation for higher education institutions in the period from 2017 to 2020*. Hanoi: MoET.

Ministry of Education and Training (MoET). (2017b). *Circular No. 10/2017/TT-BGDDT on regulations for distance higher education*. Hanoi: MoET.

Nguyen, H. C. (2018). How to fulfil Vietnam's higher education accreditation strategic plan 2017–2020? *International Journal of Educational Organization and Leadership, 24*(3/4), 17–25.

Nguyen, H. C., Evers, C., & Marshall, S. (2017). Accreditation of Viet Nam's higher education: Achievements and challenges after a dozen years of development. *Quality Assurance in Education, 25*(4), 475–488.

Nguyen, H. C., & Le, M. P. (2019). Quality assurance and accreditation of distance education programs in Vietnam: Rationale and future directions. *VNU Journal of Science: Education Research, 35*(1), 1–10.

Nguyen, K. D., Oliver, D. E., & Priddy, L. E. (2009). Criteria for accreditation in Vietnam's higher education: Focus on input or outcomes. *Quality in Higher Education, 15*(2), 123–134.

Nhan, T. T., & Nguyen, H. C. (2018). Quality challenges in transnational higher education under profit-driven motives: The Vietnamese experience. *Issues in Educational Research, 28*(1), 138–152.

The Prime Minister. (2015). *Decision No. 1559/QD-TTg on approval of the project "Development of distance education in the 2015–2020 period"*. Hanoi: The Prime Minister.

Southeast Asian Ministers of Education Organization Regional Centre for Higher Education and Development (SEAMEO RIHED). (2012). *A study on quality assurance models in Southeast Asian countries: Towards a Southeast Asian quality assurance framework*. Bangkok: SEAMEO RIHED.

Sursock, A. (2011). *Examining quality culture Part II: Processes and tools—Participation, ownership and bureaucracy*. Brussels: EUA.

Tasopoulou, K., & Tsiotras, G. (2017). Benchmarking towards excellence in higher education. *Benchmarking: An International Journal, 24*(3), 617–634.

Vietnam Education Quality Management Agency. (2018a). *List of higher education institutions, teacher training colleges and teacher training schools completing self-evaluation reports, being accredited (until 30 November 2018)*. Hanoi: VQA.

Vietnam Education Quality Management Agency. (2018b). *List of programmes that were evaluated/recognized (until 30 November 2018)*. Hanoi: VQA.

Vlăsceanu, L., Grünberg, L., & Pârlea, D. (2007). *Quality assurance and accreditation: A glossary of basic terms and definitions*. Bucharest: UNESCO.

Woodhouse, D. (1999). Quality and quality assurance. In Organisation for Economic Co-operation and Development (OECD) (Ed.), *Quality and internationalisation in higher education* (pp. 29–43). Paris: OECD.

Woodhouse, D. (2012). *A short history of quality*. Abu Dhabi, UAE: Commission for Academic Accreditation, Ministry of Higher Education and Scientific Research.

Index

Academic council 155, 156
Accountability 26, 60, 63, 82, 83, 99, 113, 115, 128, 142, 143, 153, 158, 187, 230, 234, 264, 270, 275
Accreditation agency 46, 62, 69, 70, 74, 114, 132–134, 188, 193, 209, 225, 236, 237, 245, 261, 262, 267, 268, 270, 273, 277
Accreditation Council 111, 133
Accreditation framework 65, 101, 105
Accreditation model 61, 98, 99, 116, 268
Accreditation outcomes 104, 244, 278
Accreditation procedure 62, 82, 92, 105, 151, 152
Accreditation standards 65, 66, 68, 82, 86, 93, 126, 130, 134, 154, 155, 157, 190, 195, 245, 248, 262, 268, 269, 281
Accreditation system 62, 69, 71, 75, 82, 83, 93, 94, 98, 100–103, 105–107, 109, 112–114, 116, 117, 124–126, 184, 185, 193, 197, 242, 246, 251, 253, 254, 273, 278
Accreditor 65, 91, 92, 105–109, 112, 114, 117, 127, 156, 194, 208, 210, 237, 247–249, 252, 253, 255, 263, 264, 270, 278, 279, 281
Advanced programmes 41, 42
ASEAN Quality Assurance Network (AQAN) 46, 85, 111, 199, 254, 256, 267, 276

Index

ASEAN University Network (AUN) 38, 72, 73, 127, 199
ASEAN University Network Quality Assurance (AUN-QA) 68, 71–73, 77, 86, 87, 91, 109, 111, 126, 129, 130, 133, 192, 195, 196, 199–201, 245, 251, 254, 264, 265, 267, 268, 273, 276, 277
Asia-Pacific Quality Network (APQN) 46, 110, 111, 127–129, 133, 137, 244, 251, 254, 256, 266, 267, 276
Assessment standards 189, 195–197, 204, 205, 210, 269
Assessors 153, 194, 247, 277, 281
Association of Southeast Asian Nations (ASEAN) 6, 9, 11, 26, 30, 32, 36, 47, 72, 75, 84, 93, 95, 110, 111, 219, 221–223, 264
Audit 83, 124, 144, 147, 263, 264, 270, 271
Autonomy 5–7, 9, 37, 38, 60, 63, 82, 83, 93, 115, 116, 125, 128, 130, 134, 143, 153, 155, 189, 219, 220, 227–231, 262, 275

B

Benchmarking 124, 262, 263, 270–272
Bologna Process 127, 150, 234
British Council 27–29, 32, 35, 36
British University Vietnam 33

C

Capacity building 109, 241, 242, 246, 247, 250, 252–254, 256, 262, 273, 274, 277, 282
Centralized mechanisms and regulations 81
Chiba Principles 137, 244
Circular 5, 13, 15, 64, 68, 70, 82–84, 86, 88, 89, 93, 104, 112, 188, 189, 192, 194, 196, 197, 204, 210, 245
Communist Party 38, 166, 184, 219, 228
Curriculum 8, 40–43, 60, 69, 91, 101, 125, 131, 132, 150, 202, 205, 216, 224, 229, 243, 248, 270

D

Decentralised system 69
Decision 5–10, 13, 14, 62, 65–67, 69, 74, 75, 82, 84, 88, 112, 113, 116, 129, 143, 146, 154, 155, 184, 193, 218, 226, 229, 233, 243, 276
Decree 3, 5, 64, 82–84, 88, 89, 93, 112, 231, 245
Diversity 40, 105, 233, 253
Doi moi 25, 59, 60, 153, 157, 166

E

Education Law 5, 13, 62, 63, 100, 102, 106, 126, 184, 186–188, 193, 227, 228
Education market 183, 224
Education reform 37, 60
Emerging economy 241

Employability 28, 41, 149, 150, 232
Evaluation standards 82, 86, 196, 264
Evaluator 116, 246
Examination 48, 121, 146, 156, 209, 222, 225, 243
External assessment 65, 70, 72, 74, 75, 95, 104–107, 189, 190, 193, 196, 279
External assessment experts 193
External evaluation 69, 101, 105–108, 112, 133, 151, 184, 244, 245, 247, 248, 252, 262, 268–270, 273, 277
External evaluation reports 115
External quality assurance (EQA) 76, 81, 113, 137, 143, 144, 146, 149, 151–153, 155, 156, 209, 224, 234–236, 244, 263, 265–267, 273, 279

Foreign accrediting agencies 108, 117
Foreign providers 38, 39, 41, 46–49

General Department of Education Testing and Accreditation (GDETA) 62, 69, 82, 98, 101–103, 105, 106, 109–112, 114, 116, 129, 191, 197, 199, 244, 245, 247, 251, 256
General Statistics Office of Vietnam (GSO) 27, 28, 165, 170
Globalisation 153, 262, 266
Graduate attributes 27

Higher education (HE) 2–6, 8, 10, 12, 13, 15–18, 25–31, 35–37, 42, 43, 45, 46, 48, 49, 60–64, 68, 69, 74–77, 82, 83, 85, 90–95, 97–101, 103, 104, 106–115, 117, 121–125, 127–131, 133, 134, 137, 138, 140–144, 151–155, 157–159, 163–168, 170–173, 175–180, 183–187, 189, 190, 193–197, 203, 204, 207, 208, 210, 214, 216–224, 226–228, 231–234, 236, 242–244, 246, 249–251, 253, 255, 256, 263, 265–273
Higher education Law 5–7, 9, 13, 60, 64, 100, 102, 122, 127, 129, 132, 154, 156, 220, 224, 226, 230, 231, 236
Human resource development 6, 40, 241, 242, 246, 247, 249, 250, 253–255
Human resources 5, 67, 77, 92, 103, 106, 107, 112, 128, 133, 202, 203, 207, 214, 215, 218–220, 222, 224, 228, 230, 241, 242, 246, 249–251, 253, 255, 273, 276

Independent accreditation 69, 108, 116, 250
Industrialisation 3, 5
Institutional accreditation 62, 64, 68, 72, 86, 92, 104, 105, 108, 109, 111, 113, 124, 126, 130, 156, 262, 268

Internal quality assurance (IQA) 81, 109, 113, 115, 126, 129, 137, 145, 146, 151, 152, 156, 192, 193, 208, 233, 235, 236, 244, 247, 248, 262, 271, 276
International cooperation 66, 89, 99, 101, 117, 123, 127, 193, 210, 221, 222, 226, 230
Internationalisation of higher education 35, 278
Internationalisation of quality assurance 262, 266, 267, 276–278
International Network for Quality Assurance Agencies in Higher Education (INQAAHE) 46, 116, 127, 129, 133, 199, 254, 263, 265, 266, 273, 276
ISO quality management system 129

K
Key stakeholders 274
Knowledge economy 128, 163

L
Labour market 28, 175, 176, 206
Law on education. *See* Education Law
Law on higher education. *See* Higher education Law
Legal documents 65, 82, 93, 100–104, 109, 112, 184, 185, 194, 208, 214, 228, 262
Legal framework 6, 39, 64, 99, 100, 103, 158, 187, 193, 207, 227, 245, 261
Line ministries 39, 85, 243, 255
Lower secondary certificates 172, 175

Lower secondary schooling 172, 175

M
Macro level 103, 253, 269, 279
Meso level 253, 269, 278, 280
Micro level 108, 109, 253, 270
Ministry of Education and Training (MOET) 2, 7, 8, 10, 15, 28–31, 34, 36, 37, 39–41, 46–48, 60–66, 68–72, 75, 85–90, 92, 93, 99–109, 111, 113, 114, 116, 117, 124, 129, 153, 156, 165, 167, 168, 177, 178, 185, 186, 189–199, 202, 204, 209, 210, 215, 219–223, 226, 228, 229, 236, 243–252, 254, 255, 268, 269, 276, 278–280, 282

N
Nascent period 99
National Assembly (NA) 5, 8, 63, 100, 102, 111, 126, 184–188, 192, 220, 222, 226, 231, 242, 244–246, 281

O
Overseas accreditation agencies 277, 278

P
Peer review 70, 124, 148, 156
Performance indicators 133, 232
Policy borrowing 28, 125
Policy-making 109, 112, 114, 246, 251, 253

Postgraduate education 2, 12
Prime Minister 3, 8, 14, 37, 39–41, 43, 47, 60, 88, 184, 192, 214, 215, 219, 223, 227–229, 242, 269
Professional accreditation 261
Professional development 13, 42, 129, 252, 253, 256, 262, 265, 273–275, 282
Professional qualification 40, 208
Programme accreditation 39, 68, 71, 74, 149, 156, 186, 262, 264, 268, 282

Q

Quality assurance framework 85, 110, 177, 232, 233, 236
Quality assurance mechanisms 233, 236, 263, 266
Quality assurance models 98, 124, 244, 280
Quality assurance procedures 143, 232, 264, 266, 279
Quality assurance processes 48, 155, 232, 265, 269, 279
Quality assurance units 99, 102, 134, 245, 252, 261, 275
Quality control 47, 121, 123, 177
Quality culture 86, 99, 113, 116, 124, 151, 192, 245, 250, 262, 266, 274–276, 282

S

Self-assessment 65, 91, 104, 113, 126, 177, 188, 190, 193, 194, 196, 237, 262

Self-assessment report 49, 65, 105–107, 197
Self-evaluation 62, 65, 148, 244, 247–249, 268–271, 278
Self-evaluation report 65, 86, 93, 104, 108, 245, 268, 270
Site visit 91, 104, 145, 148, 156, 252, 277
Socio-economic development 27, 202, 217
Soft skills 122, 206
Staff quota 255, 279
Student learning outcomes 85
Student mobility 29, 30, 32

T

Teacher-student ratio 88
Top-down approach 81, 93, 108
Transnational education 128, 223
Transparency 82, 88, 99, 100, 113–116, 128, 158, 224, 230, 234, 236, 273
Tuition fees 4, 6, 9, 48, 145, 166, 167, 171, 243

U

Undergraduate programmes 2
Upper secondary 168, 169, 171, 172, 174, 176

V

Vietnamese higher education institutions 33, 35, 97, 106, 108–111, 115, 122, 164, 199, 205, 249, 268, 270, 271, 276, 277

W

World Bank 1, 2, 9, 27, 28, 43, 45, 63, 103, 107, 110, 125, 129, 130, 132, 133, 243, 244, 247, 265, 276

Printed in the United States
By Bookmasters